LITERARY JOURNEYS

LITERARY JOURNEYS

Mapping Fictional Travels
across the World of Literature

John McMurtrie
General Editor

Princeton University Press
Princeton and Oxford

CONTENTS

INTRODUCTION   10

1   up to 1897   Quests & Explorations   14

HOMER   16
The Odyssey, ca. 725–675 BCE

RUSTICHELLO DA PISA   18
The Travels of Marco Polo, ca. 1300

GEOFFREY CHAUCER   24
The Canterbury Tales, ca. 1387–1400

THOMAS NASHE   28
The Unfortunate Traveller, 1594

MIGUEL DE CERVANTES   30
Don Quixote, 1605/1615

JOHN BUNYAN   35
The Pilgrim's Progress, 1678

MATSUO BASHO   40
Narrow Road to the Interior, 1702

DANIEL DEFOE   43
Robinson Crusoe, 1719

LAURENCE STERNE   46
A Sentimental Journey Through France and Italy, 1768

MARY SHELLEY   48
Frankenstein, 1818

SIR WALTER SCOTT   53
The Heart of Midlothian, 1818

STENDHAL   55
Charterhouse of Parma, 1839

NIKOLAI GOGOL   58
Dead Souls, 1842

WILLIAM WORDSWORTH   60
The Prelude, 1850

HERMAN MELVILLE   63
Moby-Dick; or, the Whale, 1851

HARRIET BEECHER STOWE   66
Uncle Tom's Cabin, 1852

JULES VERNE   68
Around the World in Eighty Days, 1872

MARK TWAIN   71
Adventures of Huckleberry Finn, 1884

JEROME K. JEROME   74
Three Men in a Boat, 1889

H.G. WELLS   76
The Wheels of Chance, 1896

BRAM STOKER   78
Dracula, 1897

Previous:
Chair Car by Edward Hopper.
Oil on canvas, 1965.

2 THE AGE OF TRAVEL   84

1898–1953

JOSEPH CONRAD   86
Heart of Darkness, 1899

PÍO BAROJA   91
Road to Perfection, 1902

JACK LONDON   94
The Call of the Wild, 1903

VIRGINIA WOOLF   96
The Voyage Out, 1915

KATHERINE MANSFIELD   99
The Voyage, 1921

JAMES JOYCE   102
Ulysses, 1922

JOSEPH ROTH   106
Flight Without End, 1927

HALLDÓR LAXNESS   108
The Great Weaver from Kashmir, 1927

WILLIAM FAULKNER   111
As I Lay Dying, 1930

ANTAL SZERB   114
Journey by Moonlight, 1937

JOHN STEINBECK   116
The Grapes of Wrath, 1939

ANNA SEGHERS   122
Transit, 1944

PAUL BOWLES   125
The Sheltering Sky, 1949

VILHELM MOBERG   127
The Emigrants, 1949

ALEJO CARPENTIER   130
The Lost Steps, 1953

3 POSTMODERN MOVEMENTS 132

1954–1999

VLADIMIR NABOKOV 134
Lolita, 1955

JACK KEROUAC 138
On the Road, 1957

PATRICK WHITE 142
Voss, 1957

BORIS PASTERNAK 144
Doctor Zhivago, 1957

JOHN UPDIKE 146
Rabbit, Run, 1960

CHARLES PORTIS 148
True Grit, 1968

VENEDIKT YEROFEEV 150
Moscow to the End of the Line, 1970

J.M. COETZEE 152
Life & Times of Michael K., 1983

LARRY MCMURTRY 154
Lonesome Dove, 1985

JEANETTE WINTERSON 157
The Passion, 1987

PAULO COELHO 160
The Alchemist, 1988

GAO XINGJIAN 162
Soul Mountain, 1990

VIKRAM SETH 164
A Suitable Boy, 1993

SHUSAKU ENDO 168
Deep River, 1993

W.G. SEBALD 170
The Rings of Saturn, 1995

ALESSANDRO BARICCO 172
Silk, 1996

ROBERTO BOLAÑO 176
The Savage Detectives, 1998

BARBARA KINGSOLVER 178
The Poisonwood Bible, 1998

Following:
Wanderer Above the Sea of Fog by Caspar
David Friedrich. Oil on canvas, 1818.

4 CONTEMPORARY CROSSINGS 180

2000–present

CÉSAR AIRA 182
An Episode in the Life of a Landscape Painter, 2000

TIM WINTON 186
Dirt Music, 2001

YANN MARTEL 188
Life of Pi, 2001

JOSEPH O'CONNOR 190
Star of the Sea, 2002

AUÐUR AVA ÓLAFSDÓTTIR 194
Butterflies in November, 2004

CORMAC MCCARTHY 196
The Road, 2006

OLGA TOKARCZUK 198
Flights, 2007

DACIA MARAINI 200
Train to Budapest, 2008

JANG EUN-JIN 202
No One Writes Back, 2009

KIM THÚY 205
Ru, 2009

YURI HERRERA 208
Signs Preceding the End of the World, 2009

WOLFGANG HERRNDORF 210
Why We Took the Car, 2010

RAHUL BHATTACHARYA 212
The Sly Company of People Who Care, 2011

TOMMY WIERINGA 214
These Are the Names, 2012

RACHEL JOYCE 218
The Unlikely Pilgrimage of Harold Fry, 2013

ARIKAWA HIRO 221
The Traveling Cat Chronicles, 2012

CHIMAMANDA NGOZI ADICHIE 224
Americanah, 2013

WU MING-YI 226
The Stolen Bicycle, 2015

COLSON WHITEHEAD 229
The Underground Railroad, 2016

MOHSIN HAMAD 233
Exit West, 2017

AZAREEN VAN DER VLIET OLOOMI 236
Call Me Zebra, 2018

PETINA GAPPAH 238
Out of Darkness, Shining Light, 2019

VALERIA LUISELLI 240
Lost Children Archive, 2019

AMOR TOWLES 242
The Lincoln Highway, 2021

Further Reading; About the Contributors; Index & Credits 244

INTRODUCTION

Two roads diverged in a wood, and I—I took the one less
traveled by, And that has made all the difference.

Robert Frost

We can't sit still. It's in our nature. For tens of thousands of years, human beings have roamed the earth like no other species, uniquely powered by a pair of legs that keep us upright. We have migrated for so long, out of necessity, that it's in our bones—we yearn to travel. There is something else that distinguishes us as a species: we are storytellers. We are known as Homo sapiens—"wise man"—thanks in no small part to our use of language to construct narratives. We love storytelling; in fact, we crave it. Not surprisingly, then, we have, for millennia, been drawn to stories that tell of our most fundamental desire to venture far from home.

Extending to the ends of the earth and spanning from the Middle Ages to the present day, the book you hold in your hands is an enthralling compendium of the most beloved works of international fiction to feature a journey. No collection such as this can hope to be wholly comprehensive, although it can aspire to as wide a coverage as possible. This volume's discriminating selection was driven by three main criteria: firstly, the work had to be a literary work of fiction, so explicit nonfiction travel writing was excluded; second, each book should contain a journey that is evidentially based on real, rather than imaginary, locations even if those places are not explicitly mentioned. For this reason, *The Pilgrim's Progress* is included whereas *Dante's Inferno* is not. Third, the aim was for the book to act both as a travel companion to different corners of the globe, and additionally as a time machine with the entries running chronologically. The book showcases more than seventy-five international works of fiction, which start as far back as *The Odyssey* (ca. 725-675 BCE) and end with *The Lincoln Highway* (2021). Other additional works are mentioned in a further reading section. The entries are written by more than fifty contributors and critics, who share with the reader insights about their chosen novel that have enriched their reading.

There are plenty of searchers in *Literary Journeys*—free spirits eager to bond with strangers and revel in new experiences. Among them is Laurence

Sterne's Yorick, the country parson at the heart of *A Sentimental Journey Through France and Italy*. Priest though he may be, Yorick at times seems as wanton as a pub-crawling man on the prowl. In some stories, the heroes are more guileless, like the wide-eyed wanderers in Mark Twain's celebrated picaresque novel *Adventures of Huckleberry Finn*. But as they drift down the Mississippi, the river growing ever wider, Huck and Jim's awareness also expands, their innocence fading as Twain exposes the evils of slavery in America. Not all journeys have such dark undercurrents. Jules Verne's global bestseller, *Around the World in Eighty Days*, epitomizes the fast-paced and breezy yarn that doesn't concern itself much with the inner workings of its characters' minds; the focus rests on the race to win a wager. Contrast this with Joseph Conrad's decidedly more sinister *Heart of Darkness*, which famously used the jungles of Central Africa to explore thorny psychological terrain—to say nothing of having us think about how "civilized" colonizers were so often the true savages.

The chronicles in *Literary Journeys* take place in a great variety of settings. There are arid lands: the North African desert of Paul Bowles's *The Sheltering Sky* and the Australian Outback of Patrick White's *Voss*. And there are frigid ones: the Iceland of Halldór Laxness's *The Great Weaver from Kashmir* and the Russia of Boris Pasternak's *Doctor Zhivago*. Not all the stories are on dry land: No volume such as this would be complete without Herman Melville's maritime masterpiece *Moby-Dick*, which is joined by Joseph O'Connor's historical novel *Star of the Sea*. And let's not forget about a somewhat less mighty vessel: the rowboat that transports a trio of friends—and a dog—between London and Oxford in Jerome K. Jerome's *Three Men in a Boat*. In Larry McMurtry's *Lonesome Dove*, it is horses that do the work of moving men around the American West, one destination as perilous as the next. Trains also figure prominently in a few of these stories, characters crossing India on them in Vikram Seth's *A Suitable Boy*, and young American dreamers riding the rails in Amor Towles's *The Lincoln Highway*. Even bicycles make an appearance, in H.G. Wells's *The Wheels of Chance*, and Wu Ming-Yi's *The Stolen Bicycle*. But it is the car that undoubtedly stands as the ultimate symbol of escape, of individual freedom, and few novels have captured its allure as much as Jack Kerouac's *On the Road*.

The world of travel, of course, is open not only to men, although women have long suffered from prejudices that have prevented them from enjoying the same opportunities available to men, of seeing the world on their own and having the privilege of sharing what they encountered. Thankfully, that's changing. And so in addition to writings from past generations—among

> You can cover a great deal of country in books.
>
> *Andrew Lang*

them Virginia Woolf's *The Voyage Out* and Katherine Mansfield's *The Voyage* —we are now seeing an emergence of more female authors in the field. These include Jeanette Winterson's Napoleonic era novel *The Passion*, Barbara Kingsolver's Belgian Congo odyssey *The Poisonwood Bible*, and Nobel Prize winner Olga Tokarczuk's experimental meditation *Flights*.

There's another promising development: We are hearing from more global voices, writers who aren't from the West. These voices are especially welcome as various crises fuel increased migration and displacement. In the tradition of empathic works that address flight and hardship—such as John Steinbeck's *The Grapes of Wrath*—we now have Kim Thúy's *Ru*, Mohsin Hamid's *Exit West*, and Valeria Luiselli's *Lost Children Archive*.

The world is getting smaller; we are all more connected and we are able to explore our planet in ways undreamed of by our ancestors. And yet we see divisions everywhere. There is distrust of others, and untruths are propagated. Travel can only help counter these trends—as can reading about others' experiences in other lands and other lifetimes. The contention of *Literary Journeys* is that we can cultivate our understanding of the planet and our fellow inhabitants through the resource of great literature as well as going out "on the road." There's a world out there to get to know, and getting lost in it, led by our curiosity, just might lead to inner journeys that can change us for the better.

Now, it is time to buckle up and enjoy the ride.

1 QUESTS & EXPLORATIONS

Early travelers were inspired by a quest for spiritual enlightenment, knowledge, a sense of adventure, and the hunger for discovery.

View of the bay of Naples, by Pieter Breugel, oil on panel ca.1563.

HOMER

THE ODYSSEY (ODÝSSEIA)
(ca.725–675 BCE)

Homer's epic poem charts Odysseus's long and perilous voyage home from Troy, besieged by monsters and foes from worlds unknown.

Homer, described in ancient Greek sources as "The Poet" (*poetes*, "maker"), is believed to have recorded the poem some time in the late eighth century BCE. It is approximately 2,700 years old.

James Joyce saw Ulysses–Odysseus as the most complete character in western literature: Leopold Bloom's misadventures in the 1922 novel *Ulysses* are based on those of Odysseus. Ulysses is the Romanized name for Odysseus.

Odysseus's wanderings have inspired many to identify his ports of call. The 1954 film *Ulysses*, starring Kirk Douglas, boasted: "Actually filmed along the route he traveled 3,000 years ago."

For all the fantastical monsters and locations, Homer sets much of *The Odyssey* in a recognizably human world of rawhide sandals, pitchers of shining wine, and dripping oar-blades. (Homer had an "ear for the sea-surge," said Ezra Pound.) The journey begins as Odysseus sets sail from the sacked city of Troy, his ships homeward bound for Ithaca and loaded with booty. The booty is not enough for Odysseus, who attacks the first settlement he comes to, the town of Ismarus on the Thracian coast opposite Troy.

In the course of his journey, Odysseus lands on the island of the one-eyed giant (Cyclops) Polyphemus. Attacked and blinded by Odysseus, Polyphemus prays to his father, Poseidon, that Odysseus may lose all his men and find only trouble at home in Ithaca. The prayer becomes the plot line of *The Odyssey* as it goes on to tell of storms, temptations, and other dangers. Odysseus has to pass with his fleet between the rock inhabited by the six-headed sea monster Scylla and the deadly whirlpool of Charybdis ("For on one side lay Scylla and on the other divine Charybdis sucked down terrifyingly the salt water of the sea," we read in Book 12). *The Odyssey* shows an acute awareness of Hellenic dominance in Libya, southern France, along the Black Sea, and on the southern coast of Italy and Sicily—later known as Magna Graecia or "Great Greece."

Nothing is known about Homer for certain, not his birthplace, nor his dates. His place in ancient Greek culture is central. *The Odyssey* remains one of the key works of antiquity. In a highly wrought, poetic language, the poem tells the story of a heroic wandering and homecoming. In the twenty years of his homesick exile and pining for his faithful wife Penelope, the Greek warrior Odysseus is seen to survive the toughest of human trials and solitude. In Homer's telling, he endures ten years of war in Troy, and another ten years of vagabondage around the islands of the Mediterranean and Aegean Seas, before reaching the metaphorical dry land of Ithaca in present-day Greece. Homer used two Greek words to describe Odysseus, *pollà plantke* ("much erring," or "driven to wander far and wide"), which explain in part why his Hellenic hero feels so close to us today.

Comprised of twenty-four books, *The Odyssey* was originally meant to

be heard, not read. The famous opening lines suggest a grand or (in modern terms) "epic" oral poem. In more than 12,109 lines of hexameter verse, it unfolds as a mythological rather than a historical tale. Man-eating giants, witches, and hydra-headed goddess creatures conspire to thwart the hero's drifting homeward journey. Homer's picture of the underworld became the model for all later western geographies of hell, most notably in Dante's *Divine Comedy*. In Hades Odysseus conjures a swarm of ghosts, among them an unburied friend, his aged mother, and the blind clairvoyant Tiresias—the "old man with wrinkled female breasts" of T. S. Eliot's *The Waste Land*.

A section of Roman mosaic illustrating *The Odyssey*. This mosaic, found in Tunisia, depicts Odysseus resisting the lure of the sirens.

> Sing to me of the man, Muse, the man of twists and turns driven time and again off course, once he had plundered the hallowed heights of Troy.

The Odyssey is, manifestly, a story of *nostos* or "homecoming" (the word from which we get "nostalgia," a yearning to return home). After Odysseus does finally arrive at his home in Ithaca, the second half of the poem traces a series of journeys from the Ithacan palace to the port of Ithaca and back. Each of these proximate locations seems to offer a different version of home. Will Odysseus ever settle to peaceful old age in Ithaca? The reader is left to doubt it.

For centuries, scores of English-language translations have ensured that Homer's poem has passed down the generations changed and enriched. Alexander Pope's version, a marvel of epigrammatic smoothness, is redolent of eighteenth century decorum and dandyism. Emily Wilson's celebrated 2018 verse translation has echoes of Pope, as well of E.V. Rieu's great prose version of 1946, and manages to restore the poem to its Hellenic toughness and sense of an ancient tradition of poetry as song. *The Odyssey* is no endangered species from the groves of academe; it is a timeless masterwork.

RUSTICHELLO DA PISA

The Travels of Marco Polo
(IL MILIONE) (ca.1300)

Marco Polo's book blends imagination with travelogue, reflecting a world of burgeoning trade and expansion in which merchants and money flow in and out of cities as freely as the water they travel on.

In 1298, Marco Polo found himself in a prison cell in Genoa. His cellmate was a writer of romances called Rustichello of Pisa, who wrote the earliest known tale of King Arthur in Italian, the *Roman de Roi Artus*. The collaboration that followed gave us *The Travels of Marco Polo*, soon translated into many languages and shared around the world.

Even though the term "Silk Road" has become a popular term to describe the trade routes followed by Marco Polo and other merchants, the term (originally German *"Seidenstrasse"*) was actually invented during the nineteenth century.

The book we know as Marco Polo's "Travels" is a strange chimera, combining the oral testimony of a merchant who really did go to East Asia with a gripping—and sometimes inventive—romance narrative that has attracted generation after generation of readers. The story was first recorded, its writer tells us, in an Italian prison cell in Genoa, in the year 1298. Recounted from his own experiences by the traveler and merchant Marco Polo (1254–1324), the story was put down in written form by his cellmate, Rustichello of Pisa. Almost overnight, their book was translated and adapted into a wide range of versions—Old French, Tuscan Italian, Venetian Italian, Latin, German, Aragonese, Catalan, Castilian, Irish, Portuguese, and even Czech. We still don't know exactly what the lost original text looked like, but the language of the earliest surviving version of the Travels is a hybrid of medieval French and Italian, a vernacular tongue that made the story accessible to a wide range of readers, and invited translators to make Marco Polo's text their own.

Even though the title "Travels" is the one most familiar to modern readers, it only began to be attached to Marco Polo's work during the seventeenth century, as travel literature became an established genre. Before then, the book of Marco Polo was known under a variety of names, illustrating the qualities that different audiences found appealing. The earliest version, written in Franco-Italian, is titled in manuscripts *Le Devisement dou monde*, or "The Description of the World." This original (or almost original) title highlights the book's combination of two very different ways of encountering the world: it at once celebrates the complex diversity of the world and eagerly rushes to classify everything contained in it. Later Italian versions usually title the work *Il Milione*, a name that was once thought to mean "the liar," but now is believed to be an adaptation of the Polo family name. One medieval French version titles the work *Le Livre des merveilles du monde* ("The Book of the Marvels of the World"), while another titles it *Li Livres du Graunt Caam* ("The Book of the Great Khan").

The exuberant variety of versions of Marco Polo's book has continued into the modern age, as the work—now dubbed *The Travels of Marco Polo*—came to be rendered in a wide range of editions, scholarly and popular. Editions printed in the British colonies of Hong Kong and Shanghai are particularly intriguing,

> The Emperor himself is carried upon four elephants in a fine chamber made of timber, lined inside with plates of beaten gold, and outside with lions skins.

as the record of a medieval encounter of Europe and China is transmuted into luxurious artifacts of Victorian colonialism in the British outposts of East Asia. During the last century, film adaptations, ranging from children's cartoons to pornography, have recast Marco Polo's account into new forms to suit the tastes of very different audiences. It is appropriate that a book that filtered into so many vernaculars and genres, and whose text spans such a wide range of locations, should have been known under such a variety of names.

The story opens by describing how Marco's father Niccolò and uncle Maffeo had traveled as far as China along the Asian trade routes known as the "Silk Road." After their return to Italy in 1269, they set out again—this time joined by Marco. His extended journey throughout the Middle East and Asia would last almost three decades. We read how Niccolò, Maffeo, and the young Marco came to the royal palace of the "Great Khan" (Kublai Khan), ruler of China and its surrounding regions, and how Marco entered into the Khan's service. Marco learned a great deal about local customs and standard practices of the imperial administration as well as acquiring the local languages, and ultimately became a trusted envoy and diplomatic messenger. He remained, by his own account, seventeen years in the service of the Great Khan. Later on, Marco gives a survey of "Lesser Java" (Sumatra, Indonesia) that contains an account of exotic wonders that can be seen there, including wild elephants and the elusive unicorn. Alongside these wonders, however, is practical information that would be of interest to a merchant, such as a list of the spices and other trade-worthy goods that are plentiful in the region. Marco also supplies information useful to navigation, such as his note that the Pole Star—sailors' main reference point in the Northern Hemisphere—"is not visible here." It is easy to see why Christopher Columbus carried a heavily annotated copy of Marco Polo's *Travels* with him on his voyages.

In addition to describing areas of East Asia, Marco also describes parts of South Asia and, on his return journey, the Middle East. In India, Marco encounters the virtuous and devout Brahmins, who eat and drink in extreme moderation and so revere all living things that they refrain from killing even an insect. Some aspects of this account of the Brahmins are fanciful, in the tradition of the "Wonders of the East" literature that began with ancient Greek writings on the eastern voyages of Alexander the Great. Yet other passages contain factual, detailed ethnographic description and offer a practical guide to exploration.

carauana es partida del uncti
a panar malcatayo :

folur

The practical guide of the merchant and the fanciful wonders of the romance-writer are equally present in the descriptions of the watercourses that run through the lands of the Great Khan. Rivers and canals mediate the two-way transport of goods, serving the huge capital city that lies at the heart of the empire. For example, the city of "Singiu" is said to be situated on the river "Quian" (Kiang), which is "the greatest river in the world," up to ten miles in width and requiring one hundred days to navigate. It flows through more than sixteen provinces, and is banked by more than two hundred cities "which all have even more fleets upon the river than that." The wealth generated by the trade carried out on the river rewards the merchants of the cities, as well as the magnificent figure at the head of them all—the Great Khan, who receives a portion of all the revenues.

Elsewhere in Marco Polo's *Travels*, we find cities that flow with traders and their goods, eager to buy and sell. For example, the city of Toris (Tabriz, Iran) is said to be perfectly situated for the confluence of traders: "the city is in such a good location that merchants come here from India and Baghdad and Mosul and Kerman and from many other places, and many European merchants come here to obtain the merchandise that comes here from exotic places."

A little farther east, we find "Cormos" (Hormuz, Persian Gulf), an island placed at the center of a great confluence of sea and land routes, visited by traders who bring "every kind of spice and precious stones and pearls and cloth of silk and of gold and elephants' tusks and many other types of merchandise." In the Far East, the capital city of Cambaluc (Khanbaliq, on the site of modern Beijing) experiences a similar tidal flow of goods and travelers, "so great a multitude" of merchants and travelers, continually arriving and departing, "that there is no man who could count their number." The multitude of traders is matched by the multitude of goods brought to the market, as all manner of "precious stones and pearls and all other valuable things are carried to this town."

But the flow of wealth in the world of Marco Polo is not limited to commodities, gold, and precious stones: it also includes the paper money issued by the Great Khan. The money made from the bark of trees and trimmed into different sizes depending on its worth: "he has made a small one, that is worth half a denier tournois; and another that is worth a denier tournois; and another that is worth half a silver groat, and another that is worth a silver groat." The passage goes on to give multiple exchange rates, converting each measure of paper currency issued by the Great Khan to the equivalent value in various European monies—deniers, groats, and besants. The currency is carefully controlled, with the Great Khan's own royal seal affixed to each note, and is distributed widely throughout all the lands under the Khan's rule. Use of this paper money is not optional but obligatory: "no one dares to refuse it, on pain of losing his life." It is widely accepted, exchanged "for merchandise and for pearls and for precious stones and for gold and for silver. All things can be purchased with it." Everyone freely uses this money, not just because its use is the law of the land, but because it can be exchanged without difficulty for

gold or jewels—in short, used to purchase "all things." It is universal currency, at least within the Grand Khan's borders.

Illustrated map of Marco Polo's route across the eastern deserts by Giovan Battista Ramusio in 1540, improved by Francesco Grisellini in 1761.

This paper currency, like the flowing rivers and canals of the Great Khan's territory, flows not only outward from the mint but also inward, since damaged or over-used currency can be easily exchanged: "when one has used this currency so that it tears or gets thin, he takes it to the mint and the notes are changed for fresh, new ones."

On rare occasions, however, paper money passes only in one direction, and goes out of circulation: that is, when it is used by the dead. In the province of Tangut, Marco tells us, the people cremate their dead with great ceremony, and carry out a peculiar practice: the mourners burn "pieces of paper" etched with the figures of men and livestock, believing that "in the other world, the dead one will have as many slaves and beasts and sheep as they burned in the form of paper." These "pieces of paper" are images that take the place of the objects they depict, whether servants, clothing, or farm animals. The paper pieces of money, however, are different. Presumably they are copies or simulacra of "real" paper money, for who would want to burn hard currency? If so, they are simulacra of something that is, in a sense, itself a simulacrum, a representative or place-holder for that which has intrinsic value. The flow of currency is one way, for there is no possibility of goods or money returning from the land of the dead. Even Marco Polo's world of exuberant trade and exchange has its limits.

GEOFFREY CHAUCER

THE CANTERBURY TALES
(ca.1387–1400)

A group of pilgrims entertain each other with stories as they make their way from the Tabard Inn on London's South Bank to Canterbury.

The Canterbury Tales was the first book in the English language known to have been produced on a commercial printing press, by William Caxton in 1476.

The book is generally thought to have been unfinished at the time of Chaucer's death, but it soon became hugely popular. More manuscript copies of *The Canterbury Tales* exist than for almost any other poem of its era.

Following his death in the year 1400, Chaucer became the first writer to be buried in Poet's Corner in Westminster Abbey.

The Canterbury Tales is a big book in nearly every sense of the word. It is ambitious, it is complex, and it is long. It is also hugely influential. It is not just that Chaucer has inspired everyone from Shakespeare to Milton to Dickens to the Beatles (Paul McCartney said it was the dirty parts in "The Miller's Tale" that "turned me on to poetry"). It is also that he helped shape the English language itself. As William Caxton's first successful printing project in English at the end of the fifteenth century, the text of *The Canterbury Tales* helped stabilize and shape the very words we use.

So it is that Chaucer is often called "the first English poet" and "the father of English literature." He was born in the 1340s during the reign of King Edward III and his life is unusually well documented for the time, because he had a long career as a public servant, and was closely involved in the courts of Edward III and Richard II. He worked as a valet, civil servant, clerk of the King's Works, and customs comptroller for London, as well as carrying out numerous diplomatic missions throughout Europe. It was on these European missions—especially during a stay in Italy where he became familiar with the work of Petrarch and Boccaccio—that he picked up some of the poetic techniques that would make him so famous. He wrote several extended works of elaborate verse including the dream vision *The Legend of Good Women* and the epic retelling of a love story from the Trojan War in *Troilus and Criseyde*, before beginning on *The Canterbury Tales* in the 1380s.

The premise of this great masterpiece is that a group of pilgrims on the way from London to Canterbury are holding a competition among themselves to see who can provide the most entertaining narrative, in order to while away the hours on the road.

In his prologue, Chaucer introduces us to thirty different characters who are each going to tell four stories. In fact, the book we have contains only twenty-two tales and a handful of fragments, and is often presumed to have been left unfinished when Chaucer died in 1400. But even without the full complement of stories, *The Canterbury Tales* still contains over seventeen thousand lines of prose and rhyming decasyllabic verse, covering a huge variety of themes and ideas.

Yet while almost everything about the book is epic in scale, there's one aspect of Chaucer's story that isn't so large. The actual journey that his band of pilgrims undertake from the Tabard Inn in Southwark, London, to Canterbury Cathedral would have been less than seventy-five miles long.

Of course, the distance wasn't the point. In his prologue, Chaucer has fun describing the delights of spring "whan that Aprill with his shoures soote the droghte of March hath perced to the roote" (when in April the sweet showers fall that pierce March's drought to the root) and how it makes people long "to goon on pilgrimages." He carefully sets the scene as he brings his characters together at the Tabard, and sends them "Caunterburyward" under the direction of the landlord Harry Bailey.

But after that, the physical aspects of the trip don't much concern our poet. He barely mentions the distance traveled, or the nature of the landscape. He doesn't even show his pilgrims reaching Canterbury. (Whether by design or because he didn't finish the book has been a matter of debate for centuries.)

But there are other journeys to consider. After all, the main concern of a pilgrimage is not what happens in this world but the next one. The purpose of the medieval pilgrimage was to earn forgiveness from sins and an easier path through purgatory and the afterlife by performing acts of prayer at a holy shrine. By visiting Canterbury to pay homage to the remains of the sainted Thomas Becket (who had been murdered in the cathedral in 1170), Chaucer's characters would be hoping to ease their own procession into heaven.

On a broader scale, the book can be seen as a tour around the clerical

Reeve. Chaucer. Clerk of Oxenford. Cook. Miller. Wife of Bath. Merchant. Parson. Man of Law. Plowman. Physician. Franklin. 2 Citizens. Shipman. Sh

CHAUCERS CAN
Painted in Fresco by William Blake & by him Eng

and lay structures of late-fourteenth-century England. There are characters from many walks of life, from knight to physician to shipmen—alongside all manner of religious occupations. There's a friar, a monk, two nuns, a prioress and a parson, and the pardoner and summoner—two sellers of fake indulgences and phony religious relics. But the book is also steeped in religious observance and belief; the characters invoke "Goddes name" and "Goddes dignitee" at every opportunity. As does the poet himself. When he writes himself into the poem, setting one "Chaucer" among the pilgrims, he says he tells his stories "by goddes sweete pine" (by God's sweet suffering). And when Chaucer takes his leave at the end of the book, he also writes that if anyone has enjoyed anything in it, they should "thanken our lorde Jesu Christ," and asks his audience to "preye" for him. The very last lines we have are devoted to thanking Jesus for giving up the "blood of his herte," a request that he may be one of those saved "on day of doome" and an invocation to Jesus.

That is not to say that Chaucer's view on religion is straightforward. One of the interesting questions in *The Canterbury Tales* is what kind of judgment lies in store for the pilgrims when their souls reach their ultimate destination —and whether indeed, they are taking the right kind of steps to get there. Chaucer makes it clear that instead of a Moses leading them, they have a bibulous barkeep. There's endless potential for misdirection and it is never clear that they have chosen the right path. In Chaucer's time, Canterbury had a bad reputation. The church levied extortionate charges on people who wanted to view archbishop Becket's bones and sold them all manner of junk such as waters in which his remains had been supposedly steeped.

BURY PILGRIMS

Sompnour Maunciple Pardoner. Monk. Friar. a Citizen. Lady Abbess Nun. 3 Priests. Squires Yeoman. Knight. Squire

shed October 8 1810. Ye gon to Canterbury God mote you spede,

Pilgrimages were often so raucous and drunken that they would better be compared to a bachelor party than Jesus's journey down Via Dolorosa.

Nor do the travelers embody any ascetic ideals. It is notable that most of the clerical figures are accepting bribes. (The Parson is not, but the fact that he is a "shepherde" rather than a "mercenary" is presented as something highly unusual.) And while the travelers' tales are suffused with religion they are also often bawdy, irreverent, and downright rude. Some of the most famous lines in the poem come in "The Miller's Tale" when we are told a clerk called Nicholas lets "fly a fart as great as it had been a thunder dent" before his "erse" is "smote" with a red hot poker.

Chaucer is forever bouncing us from high to low: from soaring piety to earthy humor. In doing so, he leads us on a tour of the medieval mind and society. It feels like visiting a strange and wonderful land full of the wonder of strange new horizons. The book becomes a journey into humanity, better and worse, right and wrong, misguided and mischievous—which goes a long way toward explaining why it has remained so resonant for so long.

William Blake's engraving of Chaucer's Canterbury pilgrims (1810), capturing the moment they embark on their journey from the Tabard Inn, Southwark, London.

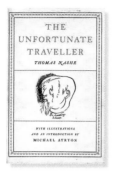

THOMAS NASHE

THE UNFORTUNATE TRAVELLER
(1594)

In this early example of prose fiction, Jack Wilton, Nashe's frolicking protagonist, travels by fits and starts from an English military encampment in France across Europe.

Thomas Nashe (1567–ca. 1601) was an Elizabethan poet, playwright, and noted hack writer, who bounced between London literary feuds and penury.

Nashe collaborated with several of his contemporaries and is rumored to have written much of the first act of Shakespeare's Henry VI Part 1. He also cowrote, with Ben Jonson, the play The Isle of Dogs, which was immediately suppressed for sedition and of which no copy survives.

The Unfortunate Traveller is thought to be the first English picaresque novel.

There's a moment toward the end of Thomas Nashe's 1594 picaresque novel, *The Unfortunate Traveller*, when his peripatetic hero, Jack Wilton, listens to an impassioned rant from an exiled English nobleman. In France, he says, all you learn is "falsehood in fellowship, perfect slovenry"; in Spain, the clothes are bizarre, and as for Italy—which is where we are at this point—he writes:

> From thence he brings the art of atheism, the art of epicurizing, the art of whoring, the art of poisoning, the art of sodomitry. The only probable good thing they have to keep us from utterly condemning it is that it maketh a man an excellent courtier, a curious carpet-knight, which is, by interpretation, a fine close lecher, a glorious hypocrite. It is now a privy note amongst the better sort of men, when they would set a singular mark or brand on a notorious villainy, to say, he hath been in Italy.

Some four hundred years after its publication, it is striking to read that the English had been having trouble with Europe even then; but Nashe here is making fun of the self-pitying expat rather than the Spaniard, Frenchman, or Italian—although it is clear that there is an element of his having his cake and eating it: the expression of xenophobia in the mouth of an unpleasant character is still the expression of xenophobia. And up until that point, Jack Wilton's travels through Europe had been anything but peaceful. The clue is in the title. Wilton himself is hardly the model tourist. "There are a number of other shrines and statues dedicated to the emperors," he says of Rome, "and withal some statues of idolatry reserved for detestation. I was at Pontius Pilate's house, and pissed against it."

Thomas Nashe was one of the first, if not the first, English writers to make a living by his pen. It wasn't much of a living—he was continually broke, and one of his personae was "Pierce Pennilesse"—but the work that survives is rich, boisterous, and quite sui generis. ("Why should I go gadding and fizgigging after firking flantado amphibologies?" Nashe asks.) He was able to write in any style, which made him an excellent and irrepressible parodist; this has always been a good way of getting into trouble with the authorities, which he duly did.

The Unfortunate Traveller, though, is a kind of escape from Nashe's domestic troubles; it is set during the reign of Henry VIII, and wholly on the continent. Europe here is a place of executions, rapes, religious hypocrisy, and endless (for want of a better word) shenanigans; the climax of the book has Wilton locked up, about to be dissected in an anatomy lesson.

But for all the high and low jinks, there is a moral core to the book, which is probably best shown when Wilton meets Erasmus and Thomas More, the great humanists, in Rotterdam, as they work on *The Praise of Folly* and *Utopia* respectively. Nashe summarizes the latter as a reaction against the fact that:

> . . . principalities were nothing but great piracies, which, gotten by violence and murder were maintained by private undermining and bloodshed, that in the chiefest flourishing kingdoms there was no equal or well-divided weal one with another, but a manifest conspiracy of rich men against poor men.

One bears in mind Nashe's own financial troubles, and concludes that these words, though ostensibly from More's mouth, come indeed from Nashe's heart. As so often, one goes abroad to learn home truths.

Painting of Wittenberg, Germany, by Lucas Cranach the Elder in 1536. Closely associated with Martin Luther, this town on the river Elbe is one of Jack Wilton's destinations in the novel.

MIGUEL DE CERVANTES

DON QUIXOTE
(EL INGENIOSO HIDALGO DON QUIJOTE DE LA MANCHA) (1605/1615)

Don Quixote, often said to be the first modern novel, is at once a quest narrative, a parody of the chivalric romance genre, and a sophisticated critique of contemporary literary culture.

Cervantes (1547–1616) lived a life of poverty and obscurity. In 1575, he was captured by Barbary pirates and spent five years as a slave in Algiers. Some believe he began to write *Don Quixote* in jail, after he was imprisoned for malfeasance.

Don Quixote has inspired works of art in every medium: an 1869 ballet by Russian choreographer Marius Petipa, the Broadway musical *Man of La Mancha*, Terry Gilliam's film *The Man Who Killed Don Quixote*, an orchestral piece by German composer Richard Strauss, a sketch by Pablo Picasso . . .

Don Quixote recounts the adventures of Alonso Quixano, an aging lesser nobleman from the Spanish region of La Mancha. It is one of the most widely read and translated works of Western literature and is often said to mark the birth of the modern novel. It tackles questions as diverse as the nature of political authority, idealism versus materialism, and the relationship between fiction and reality. But first and foremost, it is a journey, by fits and starts, through a hot, dry part of central Spain.

The book began as a parody of the chivalric romance, a previously popular literary genre that had fallen out of fashion. These were fantastic stories in which heroic knights with impeccable courtly manners set out on quests, encountering enchanted lakes, magic castles, benign wizards and so forth along the way. At the beginning of the novel, Quixano has read so many of them that he has lost the ability to distinguish between fiction and reality. Believing himself to be a knight-errant, he takes on the name Don Quixote de La Mancha, dons an old suit of armor, and sets out with his trusty steed (a battered old horse), vowing to revive the practice of chivalry and serve his nation in the name of his peerless lady love, Dulcinea del Toboso (a local peasant girl).

Don Quixote's journey, which is split into three "sallies" away from home, has no specific destination: the novel's loose, episodic structure is punctuated by his attempts to seek out and perform heroic deeds on Dulcinea's behalf. During his first sally, Quixote arrives at a castle (a local inn) populated by ladies (prostitutes) and demands that a lord (the innkeeper) dub him a knight, which the innkeeper dutifully does, if only to get rid of him. On the road again, Quixote attacks a trader who insults Dulcinea, but ends up out cold and is returned home by a neighboring peasant. As he lies unconscious in bed, his friends go through his library and burn all the books they believe contributed to his madness, thus allowing Cervantes a tongue-in-cheek comment on the contemporary literary scene and ongoing censorship by the Inquisition.

For his second sally, Quixote recruits a noble squire (a farmhand called Sancho Panza) to accompany him. Here the famous pair's adventures begin

Previous:
Don Quixote in the Mountains (ca.1850) by French artist Honore Daumier.

A ceramic mural from the Plaza de España, Seville, created in 1928, showing Don Quixote and Sancho Panza preparing to take on the windmills. The quote translates as "I am going to engage them in a fierce and unequal battle."

"QVE, YO VOY A ENTRAR CON ELLOS EN FIERA Y DESIGVAL BATALLA"

in earnest: they do battle with a field of windmills Quixote believes to be giants and later with a herd of sheep he mistakes for an army. Both he and Sancho are beaten up repeatedly: by a group of Galicians whose ponies are unsettled by Quixote's frisky horse; by a guest at another castle (inn) in defense of a princess (the servant girl); and by the lovestruck Cardenio, who Quixote attacks when he suggests Dulcinea might be unfaithful. At the end of Part I of the novel, Quixote is so battered and bruised that he is once again brought home.

Part I was so successful that in 1614 it spawned a spurious Part II, written by one Avellaneda and published by an admirer of Cervantes's rival, Lope de Vega. Cervantes's own Part II, written ten years after the publication of the original novel, is a response to criticisms of Part I and to the fraudulent sequel. As such, it takes a sophisticated metafictional turn: every character of consequence is aware both of their appearance in Part I and of the existence of Avellaneda's Part II. This knowledge allows certain characters to take advantage of the strange nature of Don Quixote's madness and, after he and Sancho set off once again on their adventures, to play elaborate tricks on him.

There are two key episodes in Quixote's third sally. First, his encounter with a Duke and Duchess (real this time) who stage a series of pranks designed to affirm his belief that Dulcinea has been enchanted. And second, his battle on the beach in Barcelona with a young man from his village posing as the Knight of the White Moon. Although *Don Quixote* was long understood to be a funny book, in recent years critics focusing on these episodes have argued that Quixote is a tragic figure and a helpless victim of his own madness. One well-known adherent to this reading is Nabokov, who famously called *Don Quixote* "one of the most bitter and barbarous books ever penned."

Where Part I is full of farcical, slapstick humor, Part II explores the inner life of its characters in sophisticated ways. Quixote and Sancho began their journey as stock characters: the tall, thin nobleman, with his highfalutin speech, and his short, fat, illiterate squire (whose last name literally means "belly") make the perfect comic duo, one that has become an enduring literary archetype. But as Part II goes on, Quixote transforms from a figure of ridicule into a paradoxical "wise fool." Sancho, too, becomes a more complex character, capable of manipulating his master and of judging wisely when given responsibility. This focus on character development is one reason why critics have described *Don Quixote* as the first modern novel, but it is not the only way in which the book is years ahead of its time. The novel's awareness of its own textuality and use of an unreliable narrator, for instance, also constitute a significant break with previous prose writing.

Quixote and Sancho's sporadic physical journey gives readers a bit of everything: humor, philosophy, politics, literary criticism, and a vision of contemporary Spain. It is also a fascinating journey through the mind of a character whose "madness" will make readers question everything they think they know about the distinction between fiction and reality.

JOHN BUNYAN

THE PILGRIM'S PROGRESS
(1678)

Regarded as one of the most significant works of theological fiction ever written, this two-part dream sequence follows Christian, the titular Pilgrim, on his journey of deliverance: from "this world" to "that which is to come."

In November 1660, shortly after the restoration of Charles II to the English throne, the non-conformist preacher John Bunyan, a tinker by trade, rode out to a farm in Lower Samsell, Bedfordshire, to preach before a congregation of dissenters. When, on arrival, Bunyan was advised that the local magistrate had issued a warrant for his arrest, he refused all entreaties to save himself with these defiant words: "I will not stir, neither will I have the meeting dismissed for this. Come, be of good cheer, let us not be daunted, our cause is good."

Bunyan was arrested and, having refused to stop preaching, would remain in prison for the next twelve years, the victim of a late-seventeenth-century religious purge. *The Pilgrim's Progress,* his great, redemptive allegory, opens with a ringing sentence inspired by this persecution:

As I walk'd through the wilderness of this world, I lighted on a certain place, where was a Den; And I laid me down in that place to sleep: And as I slept I dreamed a Dream.

A "Den" is a prison, and almost all of *The Pilgrim's Progress* was written in the shadow of Bunyan's incarceration, a torment he shares with Cervantes, the father of the Western novel. Like *Don Quixote, The Pilgrim's Progress* blends fact and fiction, a cornerstone of English fiction that begins as the self-expression of an outcast, whose writing had started with sermons.

Bunyan had a wonderful ear for the rhythms of colloquial speech and his allegorical characters come to life in dialogue that never fails to advance the narrative. An enthralling dream-story is one thing. The simple clarity and beauty of Bunyan's prose is something else. The fusion of style and content into a work of art makes it a timeless English classic, at once a quest and a flight:

The man (Christian) had not run far from his own door, but his wife and children perceiving it, began to cry after him to return; but the man put his fingers in his ears, and ran on crying, "Life, life, eternal life": so he looked not behind him, but fled toward the middle of the plain.

At the age of sixteen, during the first stages of the English Civil War, Bunyan enlisted to fight on the side of the Parliamentarians. After the war he joined a Puritan church, and later became a preacher.

Following the restoration of the monarchy in 1660, Bunyan was ordered to cease his preaching as a result of new religious laws. His refusal resulted in a twelve-year imprisonment in Bedford County Gaol.

Written during his imprisonment, *The Pilgrim's Progress* has been translated into more than 200 languages and has never been out of print since its first publication.

THE PILGRIMS PR[...]

Christian and Hopeful looking at the City through the Shepherds Glass.

Mount Clavton

Christian and Hopeful looking at the City

Mouth of Hill

Delectable MOUNTAINS

Ignorance

Country of Conceit

Christian and Hopeful

River of Water of Life

Doubting Castle

Shepherd directing the Pilgrims

The Arbor where Christian slept

Shepherd and his Flock

Palace of Beautiful

Giant Despair dr[...]

The Hill DIFFICULTY

The Lions

Christian fights

Christian climbs the Hill

Watchful the Porter

Porters Lodge

The Three Shining Ones

The three Sleepers

Sloth

The Three Shining Ones

C[hri]stian get rid of his Burden

Christian discovers the Sleepers

Simple

Pre-sumption

Village Morality

The CITY of DESTRUCTION

Christian leaves the City of Destruction.

Obstinate Pliable and Chr[...]

Evangelist directs Christian to the Wicket Gate

Or Christians journey from the City of Destruction in this evil WORLD to the CEL[...]

Published July 1 1813 by J. Pitts Nº 14 Great St A[...]

Holy Gate

CITY

Hopeful in the River

Country of Buls

By Ends

d Hopeful to his
Castle

Christian
going through
the Valley

Vanity Town

Enchanted
Ground

Fiends

Pope
and Pagan
CAVE

Christian
meets with
Faithful

Faithful burned   VANITY FAIR

Evangelist
Christian and
Faithful
meeting

The Valley of the Shadow of DEATH

Pilgrims bones

Interpreters House

Salvation Wall

Knock and it shall
be opened unto you

Salvation Wall

Mr Legality's
House

Beelzebub
Castle

Interpreter and Christian

Christian
at the Wicket
Gate

comes
the Hill

Evangelist
reproves Christian

Mr Worldly-wiseman

Christian
in the Slough

Help
comes to assist
Christian

The
Steps

Slough of Despond

CITY in the WORLD that is to Come.

Dials.

A print of a hand-colored etching depicting Christian's winding route from the "City of Destruction" to the "Celestial City," encountering many dangers along the way. Published by John Pitts, 1813.

The haunting music of Bunyan's prose, braided with its compulsive storytelling, becomes the soundtrack of a text that marks the debut of the English novel. Many subsequent landmarks of our most admired fiction will come in the guise of a journey: *Robinson Crusoe, Moby-Dick, Treasure Island, Ulysses, Rites of Passage,* and *Remains of the Day.*

The farther we travel with Christian into the Valley of the Shadow of Death, via Vanity Fair, toward Doubting Castle, the more we immerse ourselves in a supremely English setting. The pilgrim's crossing of the lethal Enchanted Ground, through the Land of Beulah, and thence to the River of Death, before the footslog up Mount Zion into the Celestial City has an addictive dream-quality, but it is a journey grounded in a provincial English reality.

The plain that Christian first crosses seems to have been an exact rendering of the landscape around Bunyan's Bedford. The Slough of Despond corresponds with the clay-pits of the brickworks in Stewartby. Farther on, the Wall of Salvation is the red brick wall marking the Bedford family estate, running beside the road from Ridgmount to Woburn. Today's Bedford to Ampthill road also matches Bunyan's narrative.

Elsewhere, it's said that the Palace Beautiful is Houghton House; Vanity Fair was probably inspired by Stourbridge Fair and the Delectable Mountains are the Chiltern Hills. Other commentators have identified the Land of Beulah as north Middlesex. Such was the crucible of Bunyan's imagination.

As well as being the record of Bunyan's dream, a now-familiar trope, *The Pilgrim's Progress* is the archetypal tale of a traveler beset with danger. In Hollywood jargon, its narrative has a perfect "arc." It also contains an unforgettable cast of characters, from Mr. Standfast, Mr. and Mrs. Timorous, and Mr. Worldly Wiseman to Lord Hate-good, Giant Despair, and Mr. Valiant-for-Truth.

With his good companions, Faithful and Hopeful, Christian will vanquish many enemies before arriving at the Celestial City with lines that still reverberate through the English literary tradition: "And as he went down deeper, he said, Grave, where is thy Victory? So he passed over, and all the Trumpets sounded for him on the other side."

The Englishness of *The Pilgrim's Progress* is political as well as cultural. A potent allegory of state repression, it was described by one historian as a "foundation text" for the English working-class. Part of its uniquely English quality is a robust sense of humor that has cemented its appeal to generations of readers.

The Pilgrim's Progress thus remains a canonical English classic, continuously in print, from its first publication to the present day, in an extraordinary number of editions. There's probably no book in English, apart from the Bible, to equal Bunyan's masterpiece for the range of its readership, or its influence on writers as diverse as Mark Twain, William Thackeray, Charlotte Brontë, C.S. Lewis, John Steinbeck, and even Enid Blyton.

Christian Reading in His Book, plate 11, from *The Pilgrim's Progress* series. Watercolor by William Blake. Blake began this series in 1824, and it remained unfinished at the time of his death in 1827. Blake's illustrations would not feature in a published edition of the book until 1941.

MATSUO BASHO
NARROW ROAD TO THE INTERIOR (OKU NO HOSOMICHI) (1702)

Matsuo Basho travels on foot through Japan's remote northern provinces, composing seventeen-syllable haiku on what is not just a journey, but also a poetic pilgrimage.

Matsuo Basho (1644–1694), one of Japan's most important and beloved literary figures, is considered the master of the haiku form.

Basho's traveling companion Sora was also a budding poet; he kept a prosaic account of their journey. Unlike Basho's work, this was simply a record.

Part of Basho's purpose was to visit places associated with Yoshitsune, a real hero and near-contemporary of Richard the Lionheart. Yoshitsune and his retainer Benkei traveled north in 1189, 500 years before Basho, fleeing the wrath of Yoshitsune's brother, the then shogun.

In spring 1689, Matsuo Basho set off on a walking trip to the remote north of Japan. He was so sure he would not return that he sold his beloved house with the basho (banana) tree in the garden, from which he took his pen name. He took little more than the clothes on his back "plus a paper coat to protect me in the evening, yukata, rainwear, ink, and brushes."

Basho was a hugely celebrated poet with a coterie of disciples and admirers around the country. He had only recently returned from his previous travels and, at forty-five, felt like an old man; but he could not resist the call of the road. "The spring mist filled the sky," he wrote, "and in spite of myself the gods filled my heart with a yearning to cross the Shirakawa Barrier."

He started off from the capital, Edo, now Tokyo, with his traveling companion, a budding young poet called Sora. In those days, travel was on foot or on horseback and often perilous. It took them nearly a month to reach the Shirakawa Barrier, which marked the crossing between the civilized south and the untamed north. Basho composed a haiku: "Culture's beginning: / rice-planting song / of the far north."

This was not just a journey through time and space. Each stone, each place on the road was overlain with layer upon layer of history, legend, and poetry. As he traveled north, he passed places that had inspired poets of old, saw ruins that evoked the distant past and sat down with local poets to compose linked verse. He wrote of the flowers, trees, and landscapes he saw and the people he encountered, weaving his travels and experiences together in a poetic tapestry. In many haiku there are juxtapositions and leaps from one mood to another; a sublime passage often quickly becomes humorous; the haiku is a literary creation, not an accurate record.

Heading up the east coast, they stopped at the ruins of Maruyama Castle. The twelfth-century hero Yoshitsune and his retainer, Benkei, had passed through here five hundred years earlier. Basho was moved to see Yoshitsune's long sword, as celebrated as Excalibur, and Benkei's gigantic travelling chest, displayed in a temple there. That night they stayed at Iizuka, "a poor wretched place". Basho was heartened to see the twin-trunked Takukuma Pine, "shaped exactly as described by the ancient poets". At Sendai the irises were in full bloom and Basho's host, an artist called Kaemon, gave him a pair of straw sandals with iris-blue thongs. The two walked on up the coast to Matsushima, an inlet where pine-clad islands dot the bay, famous for its exquisite beauty.

But when they left Matsushima, they got completely lost and followed a rough track "fit only for hunters or woodcutters". They found themselves at Ishinomaki, a port where cargo ships jostled in the harbor and smoke poured from the chimneys of cramped little hovels. They stayed in a miserable inn there. Famously, this passage is written with considerable poetic license (according to Sora's account, Ishinomaki was on their itinerary all along and they found an excellent inn).

They traveled to the city of Hiraizumi, once the capital of the northern Fujiwara lords. There, the twelfth-century hero Yoshitsune and his retainer Benkei who had taken refuge in the castle with eight followers, found themselves surrounded by an army twenty thousand strong. In a battle immortalized in epic, Benkei held them off single-handedly, long enough for his master to commit honorable suicide. Five hundred years later, Basho found nothing but a hillside covered in grass. He sat on his bamboo hat and wept and wrote a famous haiku lamenting the passing of all earthly glory. They now turned inland into steep and rugged mountain country. Basho hired a guide, a strapping young man who carried a short, curved sword and oaken staff. They tramped through thick forest and thickets of bamboo grass, waded through streams, and stumbled across boulders. When they finally reached the other side, the guide said cheerfully, "On this road there is always some terrible incident. It was lucky that I was able to bring you through in safety!"

Summer grasses
All that remains of
Mighty warriors' dreams.

Deep in the back country, they spent a few days at the house of a wealthy merchant. Locals gathered, eager to meet the great poet, and Basho led sessions composing linked verse. From here the two took a flimsy rice boat down the fast-moving Mogami River, swollen after the summer rains. Their destination was the Three Sacred Mountains of Dewa, home to a sect of hermit priests and the spiritual heart of the north. They climbed the cedar-clad slopes of Mount Haguro, the first of the three mountains, and spent several days in South Valley, where hundreds of hermit priests carried out austerities and esoteric practices.

Then, having fasted for a day, they put on the white robes of pilgrims and followed a guide up the second mountain, Gassan, or Moon Mountain. It was an arduous journey "through cloud and mist, over ice and snow, until we thought we must have crossed thebarrier of the clouds and were treading the very path of the sun and moon."

They spent the night at the top and the next day scrambled down near-vertical cliffs to Mount Yudono, the last and holiest of the three. Pilgrims are forbidden to reveal what they see there. Basho wrote simply: "Yudono / of which I may not speak / wets my sleeve with tears."

Finally, they reached the Japan Sea, having crossed the country from one side to the other. For two and half months they made the grueling journey southwards along the west coast, through the heat of summer. The two coasts have different faces and different moods. Having seen sunny Matsushima with its pine islands, Basho was struck by the lonely, tormented beauty of Kisagata, its counterpart on the Japan Sea coast. The two had to cross "the most dangerous places of the north country", where cliffs plunged into the sea, and they clambered from boulder to boulder through crashing waves. Basho recorded the ominous place names: "Abandon Your Parents", "Abandon Your Children", "Dogs Turn Back", "Send Back Your Horses".

A screen-print of Basho by the artist Hokusai, dated ca.1808.

At the checkpoint at Ichiburi, they showed their papers to the guards and stumbled into a nearby inn. But their sleep was disturbed by whispers from the next room, and they realized that there were a couple of prostitutes there. Amused that he, a grizzled old poet priest, had spent the night next to prostitutes, Basho wrote: "In the same house / we slept with play women / bush clover and the moon."

The final part of the journey was difficult. Sora became ill and went on ahead. Left to himself, Basho was eager to get home. Finally, after six months on the road, he reached Ogaki in central Japan. Friends came to meet him, fussing over him as if he had just returned from the dead.

In all he had covered 1,500 miles in 156 days, a pace so fast that a persistent story in Japan has it that Basho was a ninja. (To bolster the legend, he was actually born in Iga Ueno, the home of the ninja). It had been an epic journey, a literary, poetic, and religious pilgrimage in which he had seen many little-visited places rich in history and legend, had perfected his craft, and had also paid homage at the north's most holy shrine, Mount Yudono. Four years later, in 1693, Basho finally completed Narrow Road to the Interior, his masterpiece. He died the following year.

ADVENTURE OVER THE OCEAN TO THE CARIBBEAN, AND BACK AGAIN

DANIEL DEFOE
ROBINSON CRUSOE (1719)

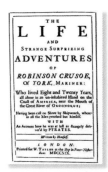

In this genre-defining epic, young Robinson Crusoe sets off to sea, unknowingly embarking upon a swashbuckling, decades-long journey–reckoning not only with pirates, cannibals, and inhospitable landscapes, but with his own moral and spiritual identity.

One may wonder what Robinson Crusoe (1719) is doing in a book of literary journeys, when, famously, its protagonist is shipwrecked and stays in the same place for twenty-seven years. Yet Crusoe's stay on the island is bookended by various adventures across the Atlantic and in Spain, France, and Portugal; and it is telling that people don't recall these details unless they've read it. But they add a layer of verisimilitude to the story; and it is remarkable how the author, Daniel Defoe, seems to know instinctively how to write a novel, even though the form was very much in its infancy (and there is a very plausible case for saying that this is, in fact, the very first novel in the English language).

The journey begins when the young Robinson sets off to sea, very much against his father's wishes. He becomes terrified on his first voyage and vows never to do it again; forgets his vows while drunk; is captured and enslaved by pirates; escapes after two years; becomes a prosperous landholder in Brazil; and then, on a journey to buy slaves from Africa, is marooned on a desert island approximately forty miles off the Venezuelan coast. After many years he encounters cannibals, who take vanquished prisoners to the island to be eaten; he rescues one, whom he names "Friday" after the day of the week Crusoe discovers him, and they eventually escape after gaining control of an English ship taken over by mutineers. His journey home is followed by a journey to Lisbon (via the Pyrenees, where he and Friday are attacked by wolves).

But even if we take out the physical adventures on either side of Crusoe's shipwreck there is very much a spiritual journey going on for Crusoe. He starts out as an impetuous youth, scornfully disregarding his father's advice to stay at home and seek nothing more than a modest, sensible existence, saying that "the calamities of life were shared among the upper and lower part of mankind, but that the middle station had the fewest disasters". As a result, Robinson's life is for long stretches of it one disaster after another – although there are also long periods of content, often occurring when he is delivered from one calamity and reflects on how much worse his life could be.

Daniel Defoe (ca.1660–1731), spent his early adulthood as a general merchant, but then turned his attention to politics and began writing essays and pamphlets. He was briefly imprisoned for his outspoken views.

The story is thought to be based on the life of Alexander Selkirk, a Scottish privateer who was cast away on a South Pacific island then called Más a Tierra and now renamed as Robinson Crusoe Island, Chile.

The Life and Strange Surprizing Adventures of Robinson Crusoe of York, Mariner, has seen hundreds of translations, adaptations, and spin-offs, and it even inspired a genre: "Robinsonade."

But Crusoe's real adventure is his journey from godlessness to religion: a religion not bound to any church, but a result of solitary contemplation of the Bible rescued from his shipwreck. (Crusoe calls his impulse to travel the world his "original sin.") Modern critics sometimes sidestep this aspect of the book, but it is crucial; Defoe himself was a Nonconformist, and found himself both pilloried (literally) and imprisoned for his beliefs. Resourceful, too, like his literary creation: Defoe was a businessman who made, and lost, and re-made astounding fortunes and one who, although a hugely prolific and tireless pamphleteer, did not start writing fiction until he wrote Crusoe– which was published in his fifty-ninth year (an age when most people in the early eighteenth century were contemplating the grave).

It happen'd one Day about Noon going towards my Boat, I was exceedingly surpriz'd with the Print of a Man's naked Foot on the Shore, which was very plain to be seen in the Sand: I stood like one Thunder-struck, or as if I had seen an Apparition…

Indeed, Robinson Crusoe may be read as an allegory of Nonconformism. There is a remarkable scene where Crusoe lies in ambush for the party of cannibals from whom he is later to rescue Friday; he is revolted to his very core by the idea of cannibalism, but then realizes that not only do the cannibals not think they are doing wrong, but also that he is not one to judge. Here is one of the book's great successes: not only in introducing the idea of moral relativism, but that we are made to appreciate his real horror of cannibalism, a genuine fear for travelers to the far side of the Atlantic in those days, and not the almost abstract memory it is now. He contemplates:

> Such a pitch of inhuman, hellish brutality, and the horror of the degeneracy of human nature, which, though I had heard of it often, yet I never had so near a view of before; in short, I turned away my face from the horrid spectacle; my stomach grew sick, and I was just at the point of fainting, when nature discharged the disorder from my stomach.

There is one last journey, and that is the book itself: the first steps of the English novel are here. How Defoe invents logical solutions to Crusoe's problems is nothing short of remarkable. It is an almost incredible feat of imagination, especially considering that all the well-thought-out practicalities have no fictional, or even substantial nonfictional, precedent. And it is also remarkable that a book written more than three hundred years ago should be as exciting to read now as it was then.

Left: Alexander Frank Lydon's illustration "Robinson Crusoe taking a survey of the Island" from the 1865 Groombridge and Sons edition of *Robinson Crusoe.*

LAURENCE STERNE

A SENTIMENTAL JOURNEY THROUGH FRANCE AND ITALY
(1768)

The continental travels of Yorick, an English clergyman, are perpetually interrupted by opportunities for philosophizing on the ways of humanity, and for flirting.

A European bestseller, *A Sentimental Journey* gave rise to a cult of "sentiment," whose members indulged in displays of emotion.

Three weeks after the book was published, Sterne died, at fifty-four. After the funeral, his body was stolen from his grave and sent to Cambridge to be dissected in anatomy lessons: reportedly the professor of anatomy recognized him and had the body returned for reburial.

Sterne's radical approach to novel-writing fell out of fashion in the nineteenth century, the age of the grand saga, but fans include Virginia Woolf, Italo Calvino, and Salman Rushdie.

A distinction is sometimes made between tourists, who want to visit places to see the sights and take selfies in front of them, and travelers, who want to immerse themselves in the locale, talk to the inhabitants, and try the cuisine. (It is travelers who make this distinction —perhaps tourists are too busy enjoying themselves to bother.) Yorick, the country parson who narrates Laurence Sterne's *A Sentimental Journey,* is definitely a traveler—more precisely, a "sentimental traveler." The label "sentimental" didn't have, in the eighteenth century, undertones of cheap or fake feeling: it meant sensitive, intuitive, thoughtful. Other Englishmen, finishing their education with the grand tour through France and Italy, talked about the great buildings they saw, the works of art, the picturesque landscapes. Yorick barely notices the country he passes through: his attention is drawn by the people, and sometimes the animals: a dead donkey on the road and a starling in a cage that has been taught to cry, "I can't get out! I can't get out!"

The sentimental journey begins in London, where Yorick, on the spur of the moment, packs a bag and rushes to Dover for the boat across the Channel to Calais. There, he falls briefly in love with a countess, who promises that she will one day tell him her sad story, and talks himself out of giving anything to a monk who is asking for alms (Yorick sometimes seems just as stingy or as interested in sex as coarse, unthinking tourists), before heading to Paris.

Sterne had spent a few months in the city a couple of years earlier. Until his mid-forties he was a priest in the Church of England, without much prospect of promotion. Then he began publishing *The Life and Opinions of Tristram Shandy* (1759–67), a huge, rambling novel that has been called the greatest shaggy-dog story in all literature, full of jokes, eccentric characters, spoof philosophy (and sometimes the real thing), and scarcely concealed smut. It was a hit throughout Europe: when Sterne visited France, it was as an international literary celebrity, invited to the finest houses, the most sparkling salons. Yorick—a minor character in *Tristram Shandy*—is Sterne's self-portrait. Yorick is a nobody, though, interested in other nobodies: he writes about peasants, shop girls, beggars. He does meet aristocrats: one rescues him from the threat of being thrown into the Bastille—having left

England in such a hurry, he doesn't have the right paperwork (and England and France are at war). This nobleman has heard of Yorick the court jester in *Hamlet* ("Alas, poor Yorick . . .") and assumes this Yorick is the same person. Life and literature are always getting muddled up.

For a priest, Yorick is oddly flirty: he holds hands and swaps innuendoes with the beautiful owner of a glove shop, and suffers terrible temptations while sitting on his bed next to a young maid who has brought him a message. When the book ends, on the road south toward Lyon, he is caught in mid-flirtation, forced to share a bedroom with a lady and her maid, and reaching out his hand in the dark to touch—! We know he makes it to Italy because he drops hints about what happens there; but with all the digressions—yarns, philosophizing, flashbacks, conversations with the reader—it is no surprise that the book doesn't get that far. It is a book that reminds you that neat beginnings and endings happen in stories, not in life. One of the most joyous travel books, it says that wherever you go, you will find things of interest and charm if you take the trouble to look. But it says, too, that wherever you go, you will never find anything that interests you half as much as yourself.

Yorick flirting with *The Beautiful Grisette* by English artist William Powell Frith (1853).

MARY SHELLEY
FRANKENSTEIN (1818)

Inspired by Shelley's own travels, Frankenstein *is a haunting tale of pursuit and escape from Ingolstadt to Geneva and across Europe.*

Mary Shelley (1797–1851) was born in London, the daughter of the leading radical philosopher of the day, William Godwin, and the pioneer feminist Mary Wollstonecraft Godwin, who died after childbirth.

Mary Godwin was first published at the age of twelve. She met Percy Bysshe Shelley in 1812 when she was barely sixteen. After secret love meetings by her mother's grave in St. Pancras churchyard, the pair eloped to Europe in July 1814.

The inspiration for *Frankenstein* came from a competition between Mary, Percy, and Lord Byron, who wished to see who could write the best horror story.

Frankenstein's narrative is criss-crossed with journeying. The novel opens with explorer Captain Walton on his ship, within tantalizing distance of the North Pole. Fascinated by electricity and its magnetic power, Walton aims to lay the first foot of man on this icy land, which he describes as the "navel of the world," and discover what pulls the compass needle—and the novel's characters—north.

In letters written home to his sister, Walton recounts how he witnesses a monstrous giant heading north at incredible speed in his sled over the ice, then shortly after, an exhausted pursuer, Victor Frankenstein, whom Walton rescues. Here begins the story within a story, as Walton gives up his own quest and returns home to pass on the extraordinary tale in Victor's own words.

Victor Frankenstein begins his history with his birth; he was born in 1769 in Naples but his family moved to Geneva when he was six: "I . . . as an infant accompanied them in their rambles." Victor's father holds a mayoral position in the Swiss city. At the age of fifteen, Victor witnesses the awesome power of lightning. What is it? "Electricity," his father says. It is a eureka moment for the boy, setting in motion a chain of events that will eventually lead to his monstrous creation.

The following year his father sends Victor to Ingolstadt University in Bavaria, where he studies for four years. Ingolstadt is where the secret society of the Illuminati, "the enlightened ones," is based. It encourages daring thought, though few of the university's scientists are as daring as Victor. Resolving to challenge God by creating life, he builds a new Adam, assembled from parts stolen at night from mortuaries and animal slaughterhouses. Electricity is the vital force.

When he sees what he has done, Victor is appalled by the ugliness of what he has created. The "newborn" eight-foot creature runs away, naked, into the deep Ingolstadt woods. Victor has a nervous collapse and, once recovered, is taken by his bosom friend Henry Clerval back to Geneva, his family, and his fiancée, Elizabeth.

But this is not the last he sees of his creation. Throughout Shelley's text, the two figures constantly overlap, crossing paths across Europe. As we discover

The frontispiece to the 1831 edition of *Frankenstein* by Theodor von Holst, one of the first two illustrations for the novel. The monster in this illustration is much closer to Shelley's description in the text than the various movie portrayals.

Previous:
A steel engraving of Villa Diodati (1833). Mary Shelley stayed in the villa, situated on the edge of Lake Geneva, over the summer of 1816. *Frankenstein* was conceived after her fellow guests —including Lord Byron and Percy Shelley—set themselves the challenge of writing a ghost story.

in the Creature's own story, he has learned language by eavesdropping on people living in the forest, and literacy from books he has come by. Since blundering out of Victor's laboratory, he has become an intelligent being and can read Victor's notes, picked up in his flight. He tracks Victor five hundred miles in the wild, from Ingolstadt to Geneva, living on roots and berries: "he had loitered in forest caves, or taken refuge in wide and desert heaths." Seven months after creation, Victor comes face to face with the Creature, living as a hermit in the icy mountains of Chamonix, on the Mer de Glace, in sight of Mont Blanc.

The journeys that both characters make are intertwining journeys of escape and pursuit. Victor resolves to remove himself from any chance of again encountering the Creature he now regards as a fiend from hell. He proposes a grand tour with Henry—leaving long-suffering Elizabeth in Geneva. The tour takes the young men through the Rhineland, Italy, and France (currently in violent Revolutionary upheaval) to England (currently at war with France) and, finally, Scotland. Unbeknown to the young travelers, the Creature has been following them. Passportless, he has, apparently, swum the English Channel. But the logistics of his pursuit are unimportant; what matters is his lingering presence, a shadowy reminder of the Pandora's box that Victor opened when he fused human ambition with natural phenomena.

> It is true, we shall be monsters, cut off from all the world; but on that account, we shall be more attached to one another.

The Creature confronts Victor and demands the scientist make him a mate. If he does so, the Creature promises that the monstrous couple will emigrate to South America, never to be heard of again in the civilized world. Desperate to be free of his creation, Victor initially agrees, but he is unable to fulfill the promise: the female Creature he makes is so appalling to him that he tears her to shreds. Doomed to species extinction, the Creature vows revenge: "I will be with you on your wedding night," he says. If he can have no mate, neither can his maker.

Victor's Creature stays true to his promise. On Victor's wedding night at Cologny (where Mary Shelley first conceived her novel), the Creature strangles Elizabeth. The pursued turns pursuer, and Victor chases the Creature across middle Europe, Turkey, Tartary, Russia, and Greenland to the Arctic. Ending where it began, the climax of the novel brings all three narrators together on Walton's vessel. Having carried the reader thousands of vividly evoked miles, the text ends abruptly.

SIR WALTER SCOTT

THE HEART OF MIDLOTHIAN
(1818)

When Effie Deans is sentenced to death for the murder of her child, her half-sister, Jeanie, determines to walk from Edinburgh, Scotland, to London, England, to seek a pardon from Queen Caroline.

The title of Walter Scott's seventh novel refers to the old jail—the Tolbooth —that in the eighteenth century lay at the heart of Edinburgh's noxious and teeming Old Town. It was described by one historian of the city as, "Antique in form, gloomy and haggard in aspect, its black stanchioned windows opening through its dingy walls like the apertures of a hearse." It was but a short walk from the Tolbooth to the Grassmarket where those condemned to death would be hanged before a vociferous and prurient mob.

This is the bleak backdrop to what has been called Scott's "happiest" novel, no irony intended. It purports to be related by one Jedidiah Cleishbotham, "parish-clerk and schoolmaster of Gandercleugh," who offers the story as part of a series known as "Tales of My Landlord." It opens, precisely, on September 8, 1736. A petty criminal called Andrew Wilson is to be executed, much to the dismay of the populace. It is their belief that the punishment is excessive for the robbery of a customs officer whom he felt was unjustly persecuting him. A few days later, by way of retribution, the mob seizes and hangs the officer responsible, Captain John Porteous.

It is in these early, historically accurate passages that Scott, who is often criticized for his verbosity and digressiveness, is in his element. Wilson's plight is entwined with that of a young woman called Effie Deans who is found guilty of murdering her illegitimate child. Her seducer, it transpires, was an accomplice of the charismatic Wilson—"a remarkable man in his station of life [. . .] gifted with a sort of rough eloquence"—whose power over his confederates is mesmeric. Jeanie, her half-sister, knows she is innocent but, having been brought up by her puritanically Presbyterian father, dares not tell even a white lie to save Effie's life. Consumed with guilt, Jeanie decides to travel from Edinburgh to London to appeal directly to Queen Caroline to save Effie from the scaffold.

It is a journey of around four hundred miles, which Jeanie makes partly on foot. In the eighteenth century, as Scott—a prodigious walker himself— acknowledges, this was not something to be undertaken lightly. The usual mode of traveling was by means of post-horses, the traveler occupying one and his guide another, in which manner, by relays of horses from stage to stage, the journey might be accompanied in a wonderfully short time by those who could

Walter Scott (1771–1832) was the most popular and admired writer of his era. Jane Austen, Lord Byron, and Honoré de Balzac were among those who revered him.

The Scott Monument in Edinburgh is the world's tallest memorial to an author. Waverley railroad station is named after his eponymous novel.

Heart of Midlothian football (soccer) club, formed in 1874, takes its name from Scott's novel. The club's heart-shaped crest is based on the mosaic that is situated where the Tolbooth once stood.

A lithograph based on Robert Scott Lauder's painting, *The Trial of Effie Deans*.

endure fatigue. At Newark, one hundred and twenty-five miles from London, she is taken to the rectory of a man named Staunton who as well as being a clergyman is a justice of the peace. "Who are you, young woman?" he grills her, "and what do you do in this country, and in such company? We allow no strollers or vagrants here." But when she replies that her father is David Deans, "the cow-feeder at Saint Leonard's Crags, near Edinburgh," he groans and hastens from the room, as well he might. For, as Jeanie is about to discover, he is the father of George Staunton, who is lying sick elsewhere in the house. It is he, apparently, who has got her sister pregnant, and it is his testimony that confirms Effie's innocence and reveals who is truly culpable for the murder of her child.

Newly supplied with the evidence that she hopes will reprieve her sister, Jeanie continues her journey. At Stamford, ninety miles north of London, she finds a place in a coach and soon arrives in the capital. Here she must first win over to her cause the Duke of Argyle, trusted in both England and Scotland at a period when the union between the two countries, formed in 1707, was still in a perilous state.

With the Duke's help, Jeanie is awarded the crucial audience with Queen Caroline. The Queen cannot help but be impressed and she assures Jeanie that she will speak to the King though there is no guarantee of the outcome.

In aligning the events surrounding the infamous Porteous riots with the tragedy of a young and foolish woman led astray, Scott—the inventor of the historical novel—brilliantly interwove the factual and the fictional to compelling effect. The public took the book and, in particular, Jeanie Deans to their hearts. She was a true heroine and her name is remembered at numerous sites throughout Edinburgh as if she were a real person and not a character in a novel. Meanwhile, the Tolbooth was demolished in 1817, a year before the publication of *The Heart of Midlothian*. Scott, a compulsive antiquarian, acquired its gateway, complete with door and padlock, which he had transported to Abbotsford, his mansion in the Scottish borders, where it remains.

STENDHAL

CHARTERHOUSE OF PARMA
(LA CHARTREUSE DE PARME) (1839)

Stendhal's young hero Fabrice discovers contemporary politics and the
brutality of war when he travels to Waterloo in 1815.

The Charterhouse of Parma, set in the early nineteenth century, relates the adventures of Fabrice del Dongo and his involvement in the court of Parma, presided over by a despotic prince. The court's habitués include Fabrice's aunt the Duchess of Sanseverina and her lover Mosca, a wily diplomat.

Politics are pervasive in Stendhal; they permeate characters' conversations, love-affairs, quarrels, and journeys, nowhere more obviously than when young Fabrice leaves his home by Lake Como to fight at Waterloo in Belgium. News of Napoleon's return from Elba in March 1815 reaches the Italian liberals, who retrospectively long for the French occupation of Italy: in 1796, Napoleon's invasion had been a means to throw off the Austro-Hungarian yoke. Impulsive Fabrice interprets the flight of an eagle, Napoleon's symbol, as an omen: he, Fabrice, must rally to the cause.

This is the longest journey in Stendhal's fiction and the most fraught with significance. Not least important is its break with the model of other literary journeys: it is a hyperbolic follow-up to all those eighteenth-century trips undertaken by naive heroes, ingenues, whose illusions vanish as they learn about society and themselves.

Stendhal pays tribute to, but also undermines, this "voyage of discovery" tradition. For Fabrice, geographical progress and fruitful life-lessons sometimes go hand-in-hand, sometimes do not: there is no easy equivalence. He doesn't grow up much: bumped off his horse by French soldiers commandeering it for a general, he loses sight of the military need and chases them in a fury, shouting Ladri! Ladri! (Italian for "thieves"—they would not even understand the word). Stendhal dryly comments: "A bit of a joke, running after thieves in the middle of a battlefield."

The journey also stands out for its incongruity between Fabrice's departure-point, Lake Como, and his destination. Como is peaceful, ravishing. By contrast, traveling through Switzerland and France on his way to Waterloo, Fabrice encounters brawling and low treachery and ugly sights. Though some of those he meets offer help, his money is stolen; he is suspected of spying; he's thrown into prison; and once free, he faces the reality of battle at Waterloo itself.

Stendhal was remarkable for his witty, fast-paced yet complex fiction, and broke new ground in his analysis of the interdependence between private feeling and historical circumstance.

The Charterhouse of Parma is the only famous nineteenth-century novel largely set in a country (Italy) different from the author's own. Stendhal uses this to compare so-called "French" characteristics with "Italian" ones, satirizing his French compatriots.

Stendhal was an atheist and feminist liberal. He supported women's education and created bold, clever, and unconventional heroines, including Fabrice's aunt Gina, Duchess of Sanseverina.

It has been said that Stendhal is the first European novelist to create, with his Waterloo, a modern depiction of warfare. Gone is the notion of glorious camaraderie (Fabrice is gently mocked for seeking this), gone any sense of purposeful strategy. Waterloo is chaotic, full of inescapable, excruciating, meaningless noises. Encounters with the conflict come in arbitrary fragments: generals incomprehensibly gallop by, tree-branches are suddenly split in pieces by explosions. Horror is here, too. Fabrice is quite literally introduced to it: in order to harden him, a camp-follower who has befriended him makes him shake the hand of a hideously disfigured corpse; and he sees with shock a bloody horse writhing in its own spilled entrails.

Stendhal's presentation of the Waterloo battle scenes paves the way for impressionist techniques in both literature and painting: the confused perception comes first, the explanation only second—if at all.

Fabrice is the "hero" of the novel; but how heroic is this hero? Rash as often as brave, he struggles to control his situation and fails. He sheds some

delusions—tongue-in-cheek, Stendhal asserts that blood loss from a wound frees him from the "novel-ish" ("romanesque") part of his character. But he still anxiously wonders if he has been at a real battle. His perplexity arises from the clash with the very different picture he had constructed beforehand. Stendhal, like other nineteenth-century authors, attaches importance to this strange, rich power of imagination, and highlights the disappointment that inevitably ensues when experience doesn't measure up.

Today, we can retrace Fabrice's footsteps from Como to Waterloo and back: Stendhal fills us in on his staging-posts, including Paris (outbound), and the road to Charleroi full of fleeing French soldiers (return). But twenty-first-century travelers arriving at the battle site—about eight miles southeast of Brussels—would have to resort to that prized faculty of imagination. The original landscape has not been preserved; the site is instead dominated by a huge artificial mound, the Butte du Lion.

Watercolor of Lake Como by Miles Birket Foster ca. 1870. Lake Como is Fabrice's departure point in the novel.

NIKOLAI GOGOL

DEAD SOULS (MORTVYYE DUSHI) (1842)

A tax-fraudster travels the potholed roads of the Russian countryside, visits a series of even more morally dubious provincial landowners, and then disappears in a swirl of rhetorical dust and lofty metaphor.

Gogol (1809–1852) wrote most of *Dead Souls* in Italy, in lodgings near the Spanish Steps (today marked by a plaque). Born in what is today Ukraine, Gogol had little direct acquaintance with the Russian provinces of which he writes.

Gogol claimed the idea for *Dead Souls* came from Pushkin, who incited him to write a work comparable to *Don Quixote*.

In 1845, Gogol burned the manuscript for a second volume of *Dead Souls*; in 1852 he burned a further version. A few weeks later, he died, having suffered from long periods of ill health and self-inflicted starvation.

Dead Souls confounded and divided its earliest readers and generations of those that followed. Was Gogol a Russian Homer? Was this a national epic celebrating the fullness of Russian life? A warts-and-all depiction that captured the contradictions of Russian reality? Or an exposure of vice through comic satire? That the novel remained unfinished did little to provide a certain answer. The projected trilogy was envisioned by Gogol as a Dantean progression from Inferno, through Purgatory, to Paradise. But Paradise remained unattainable: beautiful, redeemed Russia failed to materialize.

In this picaresque novel, set in the mid-nineteenth century, a rogue is on the road. A carriage rolls into the provincial Russian town of N.; its origin is unknown. Its occupant is Pavel Chichikov, a "traveling salesman from Hades," as Nabokov described. His get-rich-quick scheme? To buy up the dead serfs (or "souls") from local landowners (for the deceased remain a tax liability until the next census) and then "resettle" the serfs in the south so that they can be mortgaged back to the State.

Chichikov tours the surrounding lands to visit the estate owners and lay out his proposition. The result: a series of ever more morally moribund portraits. There is the cloyingly sweet Manilov, whose assent to the proposed transaction is clothed in the smooth language of decorum; the suspicious widow Korobochka, whose "principled" stance gives way when she realizes the fiscal benefits; the violent, menacing liar Nozdryov (his name means "nostril"); the bearlike Sobakievich, who resembles his heavy, rough-hewn furniture; and finally, the stingy hoarder Pliushkin, once a model landowner, now living among his ruined estate and overgrown garden, draped in filthy clothes.

Chichikov's journey has no clear beginning or destination. The flat, expansive Russian plains stretch out to a "horizon without end." Just as the journey is curiously directionless, so too does Gogol's prose often appear to lose its way. As he approaches Sobakievich's house, Chichikov spies two heads in a window, one of which resembles a Moldovan pumpkin, the kind of gourd, we are told, used by Russians to make balalaikas . . . and before we know it, an epic simile has unfolded, leaving Sobakievich's estate far behind, and we have been conducted to the scene of a jaunty courtship, where a winking lad strums a

balalaika, fashioned from a Moldovan pumpkin. . . . The original scene recedes from view and we are left in a curious virtual reality, far more alive and vividly specified than what is supposedly there before our eyes.

The novel ends with a passage that provided Russian culture with an iconic image. Chichikov's carriage flies along the road and is transformed into a winged bird–troika, the kind of vehicle "born only among a spirited people, in a land [. . .] that has flung itself, smooth-flat, o'er half the world." A symbol of ingenuity and of imperial expansion, the troika appears a celebration of Russia's soul and might. As the passage unfolds, the troika is figured as Russia itself and its journey as Russia's historical destiny:

> Art not thou too, O Rus, rushing onward like a spirited troika that none can overtake? Smoking like smoke under you is the road, thundering are the bridges, all falls back and is left behind. [. . .] Rus, whither art thou racing? Give an answer. She gives no answer. The bells set up a wondrous jingling [. . .] all that exists on earth flies by, and looking askance, other peoples and nations step aside and make way for her.

The novel ends without a destination in sight, resistant to clear interpretation: is this an ironic parody of a glorious national novel or does the closing bird-troika metaphor give voice to an imagination that conceives of Russia always as a distant, unobtainable dream?

Russian serfs listen to the proclamation of the 1861 Emancipation manifesto. Artwork by Boris Kustodiev, 1907. The "souls" in Gogol's title refers to serfs: workers who were considered the property of the landowner whose land they worked on. *Dead Souls* is considered by some to satirize the brutal system.

WILLIAM WORDSWORTH

THE PRELUDE (1850)

Meandering journeys through England and Europe are the catalyst for spiritual exploration and meditation on the relationship between man and nature in Wordsworth's autobiographical poem.

William Wordsworth (1770–1850) is regarded as one of the poets who helped launch the Romantic Age in Britain with the publication of his and Coleridge's *Lyrical Ballads* in 1798.

Wordsworth began writing *The Prelude* in 1798, at age twenty-eight, and continued working on it throughout his life. It was not published until three months after his death.

The poem was inspired by Coleridge who, in the introduction of the 1850 edition, wrote that he was "to whom the author's intellect is deeply indebted."

Wordsworth never called his epic-length blank-verse autobiography *The Prelude*. That title was attached to the work by Wordsworth's widow after his death in 1850. During his life, as he repeatedly revised and expanded the work, it was called "Poem (Title Not Yet Decided Upon) to Coleridge"— a better name for a poem that is about friendship, the undecidability of existence and, importantly, about "to"-ness—about going to places, about travel as metaphor and reality.

Young Wordsworth resolved to dedicate his life to one huge poem (the original plan was for something three times the size of *Paradise Lost*) about "Man, Nature, and Society" to be called *The Recluse. The Prelude* was to stand as a preface explaining how Wordsworth came to be Wordsworth—his youth, his development, and the growth of his poet's mind—so that readers could see why he was the right person to write *The Recluse*.

But as Wordsworth worked and reworked *The Prelude* all his long life, he never actually got around to writing *The Recluse*. Not that it matters: this eight-thousand-line excavation of youth, growth, beauty, and personhood is enough of an achievement.

That achievement is a pedestrian masterpiece. Not in a pejorative sense: whatever else it is, *The Prelude* is an epic of walking. Wordsworth composed poetry that way, turning lines over and over in his mind as he strode about the countryside, or sometimes simply walked round and round his yard.

This ambulatory poetic style very often produces a marching sort of verse that, if it has fallen a little out of favor nowadays, was revered by Victorians as the greatest modern literature could provide—not despite but because it steps so firmly, because it advances resolutely with healthful stride. And although *The Prelude* comprises many episodes from Wordsworth's early life—stealing a boat at night upon Ullswater, his schooldays and his time at Cambridge University, encountering beggars in London—it starts and ends with long walks (from London to the Lakes at the beginning, and up Snowdon at the end) and includes, in its central defining episode, an monumental trek through France, over the Alps and into Italy.

Previous:
Like Wordsworth, English
painters were also inspired to
cross the Alps. William West
painted the Simplon Pass in
1845, through which
Wordsworth and Robert
Jones must have traveled
more than fifty years earlier.

This episode recounts Wordsworth's 1790 walking vacation, undertaken with a university friend, Robert Jones. The French Revolution was one year old, and *The Prelude* gives us a groundling's view of those momentous historical events.

For all his later political conservatism, youthful Wordsworth was as enthusiastic a political radical as ever: "bliss was it in that dawn to be alive," he gushes in Book Ten, "but to be young was very heaven!" He rejoiced at the execution of Louis XVI ("this foul tribe of Moloch o'erthrown, / And their chief regent leveled with the dust") and his account of walking from town to town, in each of which revolutionary councils were reconfiguring French social and political life, is fascinating.

But the heart of the poem—formally, in that the episode happens in the middle, sixth book of the epic, and artistically in that it includes some of the most powerful poetry Wordsworth ever wrote—recounts his experience walking across the Alps. Wordsworth and Jones are thrilled at the prospect of the mountains' majesty but things don't go to plan. They get separated from their party, miss the way, trudge along in boredom, ask a local and discover they have already crossed the Alps. The sense of anti-climax is marvelously evoked, and leads, cannily, straight into a passage of extraordinary, towering sublimity. The two men retrace their steps:

> . . . The immeasurable height
> Of woods decaying, never to be decayed,
> The stationary blasts of waterfalls,
> And in the narrow rent at every turn
> Winds thwarting winds, bewildered and forlorn,
> The torrents shooting from the clear blue sky,
> . . . The unfettered clouds and region of the Heavens,
> Tumult and peace, the darkness and the light—
> Were all like workings of one mind, the features
> Of the same face, blossoms upon one tree;
> Characters of the great Apocalypse,
> The types and symbols of Eternity,
> Of first, and last, and midst, and without end.

They are walking through more than just a mountain range; they are walking through God, and by doing so, are opening their souls to grandeur of more than human scale.

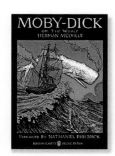

HERMAN MELVILLE

MOBY-DICK; OR, THE WHALE
(1851)

A nineteenth-century American whaling ship captain sails the globe driven by the consuming obsession of revenge against an albino sperm whale named Moby Dick.

The journey described in *Moby-Dick* by Herman Melville is inextricably and inevitably toward death. The book is treacle thick with its symbolism, and the death of man and beast is not far from any chapter. The ship for this doomed voyage, the *Pequod*, named after an Indian American tribe whose population had been killed, enslaved, and dispersed, is described solely with morbid references. Her tiller is the jawbone of a sperm whale and her bulwarks are pegged with the teeth of the sperm whale until the ship resembles an open jaw. The worn decking is described as "pilgrim-worshipped flag-stone in Canterbury Cathedral where Beckett bled." The shareholders of the ship are a mix of "widows, fatherless children, and chancery wards," all people who have been touched by death. Melville concludes his description of the vessel with, "A noble craft, but somehow a most melancholy! All noble things are touched with that." There is hardly better description of the book itself.

It took Melville eighteen months, twelve more than he expected, to produce one of the greatest contributions to American literature: a book that weaves together a romantic sea adventure; technical descriptions of nineteenth-century whaling practices and equipment; philosophical musings; parodies of the dry, academic treatise that served as reference material for the novel; the epic poetry of Milton's *Paradise Lost* and Virgil's *Aeneid*; the Old Testament; and Melville's assimilation and reinterpretation of the Shakespearean tragic hero and blank-verse style.

The narrator begins with the iconic sentence, "Call me Ishmael" and tells of his reasons for wanting to "see the watery part of the world." He evokes the martyring suicide of a Roman politician, and so "with a philosophical flourish Cato throws himself upon his sword; I quietly take to the ship."

Despite Ishmael's suicidal musings, with the farcical meeting and "marrying" of Queequeg, the Polynesian cannibal out late peddling shrunken heads, the first chapters are a Laurel-and-Hardy-esque buddy film. Once Ishmael and Queequeg set sail from Nantucket, the book's tone shifts dramatically. We are in the open sea of Melville's imagination. There are no landmarks to guide and chapters tack with the whim of Melville's imagination. Ishmael as character and narrator is the spirit of the book, meandering from

The original English publication, mostly likely due to a printer's error, omitted the epilogue, which confused initial reviewers.

Shortly after publication, Melville changed the title of the book from *The Whale* to *Moby-Dick*. It is unclear why Melville hyphenated the name for the title but not the whale within the book.

In 1841, Melville joined the crew of the whaling ship *Acushnet*. After abandoning the ship, taking part in a mutiny on another, and joining the U.S. Navy, he had gathered enough material for *Moby-Dick* and several other novels, most notably, *Typee* (1845), *Omoo* (1847), and *White-Jacket* (1850).

topic to topic. He is one kind of traveler, full of musings and openness but devoid of conclusions and direction. Terrible things will happen to the crew of the *Pequod* as they sail farther and farther from their home lives. Throughout the book, Melville explicitly draws out the dichotomies between sea and land, black and white, good and evil, man and nature, life and death, and here and there. The obverse to Ishmael's aimless near-suicidal ennui is Captain Ahab, the monomaniacal egotist whose sole purpose is revenge on the eponymous cetacean, the albino sperm whale Moby Dick. He is the other type of traveler: he sees nothing but the goal ahead. Melville rejects the temptation to use a physical journey as a metaphor for the psychological or emotional journey. With the tragic exception of Pip, the enslaved cabin boy, there is no growth, no movement or change for the characters in *Moby-Dick*. Once Ahab reveals his real purpose by nailing a golden doubloon to the mast, promising it to the sailor that first spots "a white-headed whale with a wrinkled brow and a crooked jaw," the characters are fixed. The tragedy of the story depends on it.

> Consider the subtleness of the sea; how its most dreaded creatures glide under water unapparent for the most part and treacherously hidden beneath the loveliest tints of azure.

Once sailing, the doomed *Pequod* never again reaches land or port, as would be normal for a whaling ship on a three-year journey. Land represents a return to reason and safety, the sea's opposite. Ishmael, who set off to avoid killing himself, is appalled as he is attracted by the sea and what it represents.

> ... consider them both, the sea and the land; and do you not find a strange analogy to something in yourself? For as this appalling ocean surrounds the verdant land, so in the soul of man there lies one insular Tahiti, full of peace and joy, but encompassed by all the horrors of the half-known life. God keep thee! Push not off from that isle, thou canst never return!

From the practical standpoint of plot, returning to port would mean the ship repaired, crew deserting—as Melville did during his career as a sailor—and chief-mate Starbuck, unbeguiled by Ahab, inevitably alerting port authorities to his captain's unfitness for duty. Instead, Melville introduces us to "the gam," the meeting of two ships at sea. In normal circumstances, gams were an opportunity for ships to socialize, and to trade information and correspondence. In *Moby-Dick* they serve several purposes. With each of the nine gams, Melville expounds on nineteenth-century whaling etiquette, lore, and practices, and provides Ahab with practical clues of the whereabouts of Moby Dick. Most importantly they serve as portents of the inevitable tragedy that will befall captain and crew.

As the *Pequod* nears the Pacific Ocean, having traveled through the Atlantic and Indian oceans, death becomes explicit. Several whales have

been killed. Pip has been psychologically destroyed after jumping from a whaleboat and forced to tread water until the day's hunt is finished. Queequeg and another harpooner have nearly drowned during the dangerous process of rendering a multi-ton mammal into a commodity. The sea is claiming the ship piece by piece, a physical manifestation of the toll exacted for this cursed voyage. Melville is not subtle with his symbols; the ship's life buoy has been replaced with Queequeg's lidded and caulked coffin.

In the final chapters, the narrative gains pace and Ishmael's musings fall away. The book turns into high-sea thriller and chapters zip past. Ahab seems on the verge of veering away from his self-imposed destiny. Confronted by Starbuck, he pauses with the thought, "What's that he said—Ahab beware of Ahab—there's something there!" But as with all tragedies, Ahab continues on his set course. Once the *Pequod* nears the equator, the farthest possible point from their home port and safety, Ahab destroys his quadrant; the ship's compass and the chip log's line are lost. Ahab fashions his own compass and the ship and its crew have no direction but Ahab's. It is Ahab who first spots Moby Dick, claiming the doubloon. For three days, the *Pequod* battles with the whale. Boats are destroyed, men are killed, and the whale is wounded. On the final day, Moby Dick breaches again and destroys the *Pequod* itself. Seeing that all is lost, Ahab strikes Moby Dick; his harpoon's line loops around his neck and drags him down with the stricken whale. Ishmael is the only survivor, floating on the sealed coffin. The biblical Ishmael, outcast into the desert by his father, was miraculously saved from too little water. Melville's Ishmael is miraculously saved from too much. The traveler who sought death was ultimately rejected from it.

Lithographers were quick to embellish the daring exploits of the whalers. This print, of a harpooner striking a whale while it attacks his boat, was already in circulation by 1859.

HARRIET BEECHER STOWE
Uncle Tom's Cabin (1852)

Uncle Tom's Cabin follows the perils of slaves, some escaping slavery to Canada and others suffering under cruel traders and masters in the Deep South.

Harriet Beecher Stowe (1811–1896) never lived in the Deep South. Her accounts were based on interviews with actual escaped slaves, some of whom made use of the Underground Railroad.

In its initial years of publication, *Uncle Tom's Cabin* was the most widely sold book in the United States after the Bible, and has been translated into at least twenty-three languages.

The novel has been widely regarded as helping to lay the groundwork for the American Civil War.

Uncle Tom's Cabin was responsible for much abolitionist fervor through the time of the Civil War by illustrating the cruelty of slavery in the American Deep South. These notions are commonplace about *Uncle Tom's Cabin* but the reality is much more complex. A reader new to the text may be surprised that significant journeys are the heart of the story. Characters, compelled by the need to escape slavery or in an effort to find a new life away from it, sojourn to Canada, to Louisiana, and eventually "back to Africa," reminding us that American slavery involved global travel, whether forced or voluntary. Questions of how to eradicate it and what to do with escaped and freed slaves—especially in states in which they were a significant portion of the population—resulted in journeys to establish colonies in Canada and purchase African land to create the new country of Liberia.

The novel opens in the farthest northern location for a slave to be owned, very near the banks of the Ohio River in Kentucky. This setting is crucial for Stowe to demonstrate that the Deep South cannot solely be implicated in the evils of slave ownership and torment. The Kentuckian Shelbys seem as gentle as slaveowners could be, but Mr. Shelby has few qualms about selling a child and an old man to a profit-seeking trader, forcing them to leave their home. Eliza's decision to escape with her young son Harry gives rise to the most dramatic visual from the novel: her barefooted and bloody escape across the Ohio on ice floes. The Ohio was both a symbolic and a literal marker for the enslaved; the fact of crossing less than half a mile at some points on the river was the difference between being considered chattel or human.

Quickly, however, the scope of the action spreads both north and south, as Eliza seeks and eventually finds her husband George, who had escaped for Canada, and Uncle Tom is sold "down the river" to masters in Louisiana. The action alternates between the two: Eliza and George are treated kindly by abolitionists, including a Quaker community, as they dodge the slave hunters on their trek north to cross Lake Erie. Disguised, they land in Amherstburg, Canada, which is presented as the heaven at the end of the journey by the magic of its moral superiority to their disunited home country:

... at last, clear and full rose the blessed English shores; shores charmed by a mighty spell—with one touch to dissolve every incantation of slavery, no matter in what language pronounced, or by what national power confirmed.

Color lithograph by Adolphe Jean-Baptiste Bayot, ca.1860, showing Eliza's dramatic barefooted and bloody escape across the cold ice floes.

The cruelty of plantation slave life is embodied by the rural Louisiana landscape, which Stowe repeatedly describes in graphically deathly terms: the swamps are slimy and infested with dangerous creatures, the Spanish moss is "funereal," the wind is "mourning." The sickly climate and the back-breaking agricultural work diminish the humanity of the slaves, creating "imbruted" beings who could only enact "animal selfishness."

Tom's role is not to survive this journey south, but to give his life protecting other slaves in their scramble to freedom. Escape for Cassy comes in a miraculous reuniting with her daughter Eliza in Canada. In a decision that has been unsatisfactory to many readers, Stowe neither leaves the little family to happiness in Canada nor returns them to a free life in the United States. In a lengthy letter to a friend, George explains that the family must reject the cruelties of America, or even the eventual possibility of repatriation, for an "African nationality." Written in the dark decade before the Civil War, *Uncle Tom's Cabin* takes readers on a global journey that explores the many evil facets of American slavery and the many roads to escape from it.

JULES VERNE

AROUND THE WORLD IN
EIGHTY DAYS (LE TOUR DU MONDE EN
QUATRE-VINGT JOURS) (1872)

Unflappable English gentleman Phileas Fogg and his excitable French valet Passepartout set out to win a bet by circumnavigating the globe in record time —unaware that they are being pursued by a detective from Scotland Yard.

According to UNESCO, Jules Verne (1828–1905) is the second-most translated author in the world.

Around the World in Eighty Days was serialized in "real time"—so that the last installment was published the day Phileas Fogg ends his journey, December 22, 1872. Some readers, believing it was a true story, placed bets on whether Fogg would make it in time.

At the age of eleven, Verne ran away to be a cabin boy on a sailing-ship (his father caught him before he could set sail); that yen for travel and adventure is at the heart of all his most famous books.

Around the World in Eighty Days is a paradox: a novel of hectic activity and breakneck speed, in which almost nothing changes. That is hinted at in the title: when you go around the world, you end up back where you started. But more than that, Phileas Fogg, the novel's hero, shows an almost pathological resistance to change: the perfect English gentleman, he is devoted to his routines. Utterly unflappable, he greets a typhoon, an attack by marauding Sioux warriors, a collapsing bridge, arrest, and imprisonment with cool indifference. His journey takes him across vast oceans, through jungles, and over mountains and prairies, but he barely glances at the scenery, preferring to play whist all day. He leaves it to his servant Passepartout, French and flammable, to supply all the emotion. Where Fogg rises above situations, Passepartout throws himself into them, making friends and getting into ridiculous scrapes (at one point, separated from his employer in Japan, he ends up at the bottom of a human pyramid of acrobats, wearing a six-foot false nose).

At the start of the story, at his gentleman's club on Pall Mall in London, Fogg bets £20,000, half his fortune, that he can circle the globe in precisely eighty days—an unprecedented feat, made possible by the opening of the Suez Canal, which cuts out the need to sail around Africa, and new railroad lines slashing the time it takes to cross India and the United States. An hour later he is on his way, with the other half of his fortune in cash for expenses: along the way he has to spend almost all of it on such things as buying an elephant, bribing a ship's captain, and toward the end, having missed a connection at New York, buying an entire ship; so that even if he wins the bet, he will be back where he started financially as well as geographically. At no point does Fogg waver in his certainty that he will pull off the journey; Passepartout, meanwhile, goes half mad with worry—and that seems saner.

The journey from London to Suez is smooth—at any rate, Verne doesn't bother to describe it—but from then on they face a problem in the shape of Inspector Fix of Scotland Yard: Fogg, with his bag of cash, fits precisely the description of a man who has robbed the Bank of England, and Fix has been

Illustration by the Russian novelist Leo Tolstoy. The novel was a favorite of Tolstoy's and he often read it aloud to his own children.

hard on their heels. In India, the brand new railroad that was a part of Fogg's plan turns out to be unfinished. This is where the elephant comes in, along with a detour to rescue a beautiful Indian widow who is being forced into suttee, being burned alive with her husband's corpse; Passepartout pulls off an ingenious rescue and Mrs. Aouda becomes their traveling companion. In the face of storms and Fix's machinations, they make it across the Pacific to San Francisco.

It's in America that they face their real adventure: hordes of buffalo, more hordes of Sioux, and scudding across an ice-bound prairie on a sled rigged with sails. The stop-start rhythm, the ratcheting of Passepartout's (and the reader's) anxieties, the sprinkling of exotic details, the extravagant descriptions of the places they pass through, and the bizarre contrast between this excitement and Fogg's indifference make it a thrilling journey. Right to the last pages, the big questions—will Fogg win his bet? Will he go to jail? Will he ever show a spark of feeling?—remain unanswered. But at the end, it seems that Fogg has shifted, that he is a more relaxed, more feeling person than he has allowed himself to be. It's a book about the shock of modernity and technology, but overall it has an old message: however hard you try to stop it, travel broadens the mind.

Previous: French theater poster for a production of the novel at the Théâtre du Chatelet, Paris. The featured hot-air balloon does not, in fact, appear in the original work but was added for the film version in 1956.

MARK TWAIN

ADVENTURES OF HUCKLEBERRY FINN (1884)

A meandering tale that traverses the American South, Twain's classic tries to do the impossible and capture the essence of the mighty Mississippi on the page.

Huckleberry Finn begins his eponymous adventures in comfort: safe and snug in the care of the Widow Douglas, in the relative civilization of the fictional St. Petersburg, Missouri. But civilization is a poor fit with Huck, and, before long, our hero casts himself out—not entirely unwillingly—into the wild.

Adventures of Huckleberry Finn is a peripatetic novel. Huck moves from one town to another, from Missouri to Mississippi, encountering increasingly absurd characters as he goes. The individual places he visits are all links in a chain—towns and farms, all demonstrating various facets of the absurd, chaotic life of the then-frontier of the 1840s. The chain that connects them is the Mississippi itself: not only the physical enabler of Huck's journey, but an omnipresent symbol of freedom and escape.

Huckleberry Finn is a rambling tale of a young man reaching maturity. Young Huck is often a proxy for Twain himself: his youth allows him a naive appreciation of the river, generous with praise, filled with awe, and free to make all the sentimental observations that the vehemently unromantic Twain could not.

Some of its sense of place stems from the way that it directly addressed issues in American society: this is, ultimately, a book railing against slavery, and attempting to explain the cultural divides that led to the Civil War. Twain also uses aesthetic elements to convey geography, the typographical assault on various Midwestern and Southern accents is similar to Sir Walter Scott's attempts to capture the Scottish burr. It can be difficult for modern readers, but still aids in capturing the novel's setting. But, above all, Huck Finn's underpinning Americanness—its indisputable sense of place—comes from the Mississippi River.

The American river has its physical peers only in the Amazon, the Yangtze, and the Nile, and, to Twain's contemporary reader, was as exotic and remote as any of those three. The Nile, with its deeply mythic presence, is perhaps the best comparison: Twain's Mississippi represents not only an untameable natural power, but also holds the power of life and death for the people clinging to its banks. Huck's descriptions of the towns clinging

Mark Twain, born Samuel Clemens, worked as a riverboat pilot in his youth and St. Petersburg, the home of Huck Finn and Tom Sawyer, was inspired by Twain's own childhood home of Hannibal, Missouri.

Since the first edition in 1884, the novel has appeared in more than 150 American editions alone and 200,000 copies are sold each year.

The Mississippi is 2,320 miles long. By comparison, the distance between Ireland and Ukraine—the entire breadth of Europe—is 1,700 miles, and between Brazil and Sierra Leone—the width of the Atlantic Ocean—is 1,850 miles.

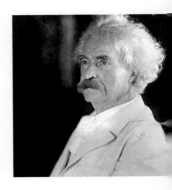

to the Mississippi's banks sound like lessons in prehistory: settlements of scavengers, living on what the river provides, completely at its mercy, with their fragile homes slowly eroding away into the water.

As if to further emphasize the Mississippi's incomparable nature, *Huckleberry Finn* freely taps into the rivers of myth. At times, the Mississippi is Styx, Lethe, or even the Acheron of the *Inferno*. It is as if Twain knows his readers cannot visualize the magnificence of the river in life, and that he needs to draw on legends to help visualize it.

Throughout the book, the river provides Huck and Jim with means of rescue and survival—but also claims the lives of others. Huck, throughout his titular book, keeps "dying." In a trick borrowed from Tom Sawyer, Huck fakes his own death to escape from his abusive father: after creating a false trail, he steps into the river, and floats away into the unknown. Huck comes "back to life" when he encounters Jim on an island—a patch of earth totally surrounded by the flowing waters. For the rest of the book, Huck shifts between the two states. While on the river, Huck remains "dead." But whenever he touches its shores, he is forced back to life. He must either be reincarnated (in one of his many ridiculous false identities) or be reborn (as when he encounters Tom Sawyer).

... right is right, and wrong is wrong, and a body ain't got no business doing wrong when he ain't ignorant and knows better.

Huck and Jim are not merely using the Mississippi to "die," they are using it to be *forgotten*—drawing from the river Lethe. The Widow Douglas, from whom both Huck and Jim are fleeing, is a "civilizing" influence—and there's nothing Huck fears more. On the shores, he must remember to wear clothes, remember his manners, remember all the arcane edicts around religion and honor. Here, Twain is at his most scathing, and the book is littered with peripatetic asides where Huck encounters strange cultures and societies: two feuding families, killing one another for reasons that no one recalls; an angry lynch mob, unable to complete their bloody mission because no one can "remember how to be a man." These are the evils of memory, the rituals of behavior without sense or meaning behind them.

Huck hopes the Widow doesn't mourn him. Jim hopes he's not caught and recaptured. To them, memory is a burden, freedom is in the forgetting. And, on the river itself, memory holds no sway: they make up their own stories, their own explanations, and are free to enjoy an unencumbered present. While on the river, Huck is free from decision: he can float, neutral, without worrying about his mortal affairs or immortal soul. But, again, when he steps to the *riva malvagia* ("evil shore"), he's forced into action: to ally with or betray con men, to aid or deceive runaway lovers, to help or hinder Jim's escape.

Right: The Mississippi River from Cairo, Illinois, to St. Mary's, Missouri, U.S. Coast Survey Map, 1865.

At the start of his adventures, Huck believes what his father told him: "the best way to get along with [evil] people is to let them have their own way." But his time on the river teaches him to trust himself.

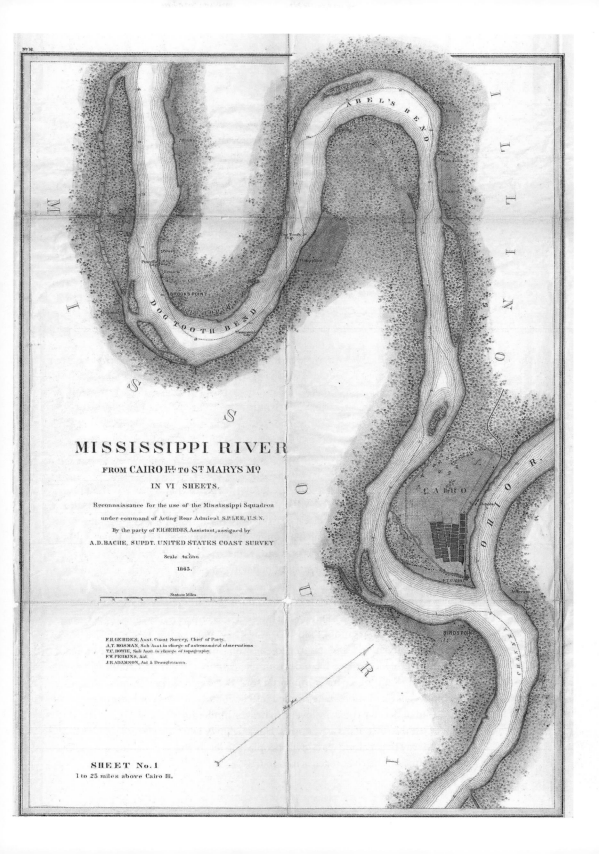

MISSISSIPPI RIVER

FROM CAIRO I^{LL} TO S^T MARYS M^O

IN VI SHEETS.

Reconnaissance for the use of the Mississippi Squadron
under command of Acting Rear Admiral S.P.LEE, U.S.N.

By the party of F.H.GERDES, Assistant, assigned by

A.D.BACHE, SUPDT. UNITED STATES COAST SURVEY

Scale 40.000

1865.

Statute Miles

F.H.GERDES, Asst. Coast Survey, Chief of Party.
A.T. MOSMAN, Sub Asst in charge of astronomical observations.
T.C. BOWIE, Sub Asst in charge of topography.
F.W. PERKINS, Aid.
J.R. ADAMSON, Aid & Draughtsman.

SHEET No. 1

1 to 25 miles above Cairo Ill.

JEROME K. JEROME

Three Men in a Boat (1889)

Inspired by a real trip, Jerome K. Jerome's comic novel recounts the journey three men (and a dog) take in a rowing boat from London to Oxford.

Jerome (1859–1927) was born in the West Midlands and started work very young after his parents died. In 1885 he began to have some literary success with a comic memoir about his early life as a touring actor.

Since *Three Men in a Boat* was published in 1889, it has never been out of print. It has been translated into numerous languages.

With its characteristically light and discursive voice, Jerome's writing has left its mark on many authors, P. G. Wodehouse and Nick Hornby among them.

Jerome K. Jerome married Georgina (known as Ettie) in June 1888, just nine days after she had divorced her first husband. Their honeymoon in a little boat on the River Thames inspired the comic novel *Three Men in a Boat (To Say Nothing of the Dog)*, which Jerome wrote as soon as they got home. In it, Jerome becomes J., the narrator, and his fictional companions are George and Harris, based on real-life friends of Jerome. Together with Montmorency the (invented) dog, they start from Kingston-upon-Thames, ten miles southwest of central London, and row a rented boat to Oxford, ninety miles upstream; they start to row their way back in the rain before deciding to catch the train to London, where they dine out and toast "old Father Thames."

The story starts in J.'s London flat with the three friends discussing their health, feeling they need a vacation and deciding to "go up the river." Boating on the Thames had become an especially popular pastime in the late nineteenth century as middle-class Londoners made use of their proximity to the great river. The number of registered boats on the Thames increased sharply from 8,000 in 1888 to 12,000 in 1889. No doubt the journey he recounts is one that would have been taken by many of his readers.

The three friends' planning and packing trigger reminiscences about Uncle Podger's catastrophic DIY, smelly cheeses, lost toothbrushes, and misleading weather forecasts. There is a timeless universal comedy in these tales of life in late Victorian England. And it is unexpectedly moving when one chapter ends seriously, with a pseudo-medieval allegory about encountering a vision of joy while lost in the dark forest of Sorrow.

Kingston, the busy market town where J. and Harris set off by boat, is the first of nearly forty riverside locations mentioned in the novel. It still has "quaint back-streets" and a station on the South Western Railway. Henley Regatta, the world's most famous rowing festival, began in 1839 and still runs almost every year. When J. and George wander into Henley for a drink, the town is preparing for the annual event and is "full of bustle." Jerome is cheerfully subjective in his accounts of the places on their route: the town of Reading is "hideous" while the village of Sonning is the "most fairylike little nook on the whole river."

Let your boat of life be light, packed with only what you need
—a homely home and simple pleasures, one or two friends,
worth the name, someone to love and someone to love you,
a cat, a dog, a pipe or two, enough to eat and enough to wear,
and a little drink; for thirst is a dangerous thing.

The travelers pass Hampton Court Palace, which prompts a story about Harris getting lost in the maze, and trespass into Kempton Park for a picnic, leading to a couple of virtuoso anecdotes about comic songs. The real journey described in the novel, with its glimpses of the riverside history and classic English scenery, is a springboard for the stories that have become the immortal laugh-out-loud legacy of *Three Men in a Boat*.

"I did not intend to write a funny book, at first," Jerome later confessed. He set out to write a travel guide, taking advantage of the late Victorian fashion for river trips and leisure tourism. The book was originally commissioned as a series of magazine features on "The Story of the Thames." In some of the remaining bits of historical info, Jerome playfully subverts the genre: "Henry VIII stole it from someone or the other, I forget whom now," he writes of one passing stately home.

Much of Jerome's humor lies in juxtaposing different registers: poetic digressions with plain-spoken realism, archaisms with slang, or mock-useful travel-guide-style sections with hilariously subjective asides. After a long lyrical passage near the start on the joys of camping ("lulled by the lapping water and the rustling trees"), Harris asks "What about when it rained?" Digressing on Elizabeth I's connections with the Thames and its waterside inns, Jerome comments: "She was nuts on public-houses, was England's Virgin Queen."

Details of the trip itself provide some of the funniest moments: cooking "Irish stew" over a campfire or searching for the elusive perfect hotel with honeysuckle over the door. Everyday objects take on lives of their own, like the tea kettle that will only boil if you studiously ignore it or the unopenable can of pineapple with its "mocking grin." In capturing its hilarious banalities, *Three Men in a Boat* celebrates everyday life, its trials and its triumphs in all their humorous profundity.

The real "three men in a boat": Carl Hentschel, George Wingrave, and Jerome K. Jerome.

H.G. WELLS
THE WHEELS OF CHANCE: A BICYCLING IDYLL (1896)

In this comic novel, a bicycling vacation through Surrey and Sussex becomes an endearing exploration of romance, gender, and the freedom of a bicycle.

Herbert George Wells (1866–1946) born in London, was a prolific writer, social reformer, and pacifist. Following World War Two, Wells's advocacy for human rights was instrumental in the creation of the United Nations. He coined the phrases "atom bomb," "time machine," "the war to end war" and "the league of nations."

The Wheels of Chance (1922), a silent movie directed by Harold M. Shaw, was only the second film adaptation of a Wells title ever made; the first was *Kipps* (1921). More than two hundred film versions of Wells's works have been made to date.

Young H. G. Wells, an enthusiastic bicyclist, based this early comic novel on his own experiences. Hoopdriver, a Putney draper's assistant (something Wells himself had once been) goes on a bicycling vacation around Surrey and Sussex. He keeps running into a beautiful young woman, Jessie Milton, who has run—or bicycled, rather—away from her Surbiton stepmother, believing a man called Bechamel will help her set up as an independent woman. In fact the fiendish Bechamel hopes only to seduce and ruin the toothsome Jessie, and Hoopdriver helps her escape him. Smitten himself and hoping to impress her, Hoopdriver pretends to be aristocracy and spins tales of his enormous South African wealth. But the deception preys on his conscience and he soon comes clean. They end the story friends—not lovers, since Jessie decides that "she was going to Live her Own Life, with emphasis." It's an immensely charming story, and genuinely funny, from droll apprehensions of the indignities of getting flies up your nose as you pedal along, to the larger humor of the mismatch between humble Hoopdriver and his soaring, pseudo-poetic desires to escape, to be high-born and rich, and to win the heart of the beautiful girl.

Wells plots his story topographically: the two youngsters bike from London to Cobham and from there southward to Ringwood, Stoney Cross, and the Rufus Stone, where the two part ways. Then Wells's humble hero drives his hoops back through Hampshire and Surrey to his Putney home. That is a long way but not uncharacteristic of the bicycling boom of the 1880s and 1890s. For young Wells, the bicycle represented freedom in several senses. It was a machine that literally freed-up that lower-middle and working class majority of people who could not afford horses and carriages, gifting them a new actual mobility. But it also represented a new social mobility, with a particular gender component. The "New Woman" of the 1890s was often characterized, and satirized, as seizing the destabilizing empowerment of this new mode of transport. "Woman, until recently, was for ages regarded as a dependent being in the family," noted *The Lady Cyclist* magazine in 1896; "she was looked upon as almost helpless." The bike changed all that: "Tens

To ride a bicycle properly is very like a love affair—chiefly it is a matter of faith. Believe you do it, and the thing is done; doubt, and, for the life of you, you cannot.

of thousands of wheelwomen of the country have demonstrated that their sex are not an inferior portion of the human family," that magazine declared, "in this wonderful form of outdoor sport and have rendered untold aid to the cause of equal suffrage, by dispelling the mistaken idea of women's dependence and helplessness." Wells's novel several times refers to Jessie's dress and manner as "rational," 1890s code for what we nowadays might call "feminist." But although the story toys with our readerly expectations as to the mode of rationality she espouses, in the event she does not go the full "liberated New Woman" and have sex with either of the men pursuing her. She is a fast woman in the literal bicycle-assisted sense but not a fast woman in the sexual sense. But she is mobile, and her journey is both a scenic tour of the British home counties and a voyage toward personal freedom.

Freedom of the open road —illustration from the first edition, 1896.

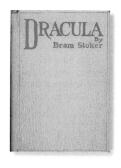

BRAM STOKER
DRACULA (1897)

Dracula tells the story of blood that is drawn from its intended path, and with it Stoker's characters are pulled in endless, circular movement. Travel in Dracula *not only charts where we are: it shows how we are made.*

Dracula was immediately a bestseller and has remained popular since its 1897 publication.

Though Bram Stoker (1847–1912) traveled widely, he never actually visited Eastern Europe.

Known in his own day as the manager of one of London's most successful theaters, Stoker's most important influences were not only playwrights like Oscar Wilde, whom he counted as a friend, but also the American poet Walt Whitman.

Dracula tells the story of a vampire—an ancient Transylvanian count—who comes to England and wreaks havoc on a circle of friends. After leaching the lifeblood from the beautiful Lucy Westenra, and nearly doing the same to Lucy's virtuous friend Mina, Dracula is finally defeated—driven back to Transylvania and killed—by the men who love these women. Thirst for blood draws Dracula to England, and the blood he draws there moves the novel's characters in strange patterns they don't fully understand.

Nothing about the novel is simple. Not even its central journey—Dracula's trip from Transylvania to England, and back again—is witnessed. Like the blood he desires, Dracula travels under the surface of everyday life.

Dracula has no omniscient narrator who can tell or see all the workings of the vampire's dark magic. Instead, the book presents readers with journals, letters, telegrams, and newspaper clippings. Because the major characters are rarely in the same place, their messages to each other travel, too, via telegram and post. The story of Dracula—which the character Mina works to compile as the novel goes on—moves as mysteriously as the vampire himself.

In the novel's opening journey, the reader encounters a travel diary kept by Jonathan Harker. Harker believes he is making deliberate and informed choices about his movement, but this is not the case. A young English lawyer, Harker is on the road to Transylvania, where he will provide counsel to a count planning to immigrate to London. He keeps detailed track of his journey—writing down recipes, for instance, to bring home to his fiancée Mina—and notes with interest the increasingly strange and superstitious behavior of the "peasants" he meets in Hungary and Romania.

For a time, the garlicky food and aggressive religiosity he finds only serve to increase Harker's confidence in his own modernity. Everything looks primitive to him, especially the means of travel: "it seems to me the farther East you go the more unpunctual are the trains." After a final carriage-drawn journey through the Carpathians, Harker finally meets the sophisticated-seeming Count. But his castle is full of mysteries—locked doors, strange sights—and soon it becomes clear to Harker that this is not so much the launching pad of his career as a jail, from which it is hard to escape. The

A fifteenth-century portrait of Vlad Tepes, also known as "Dracula of Wallachia" (1431–1476), reputedly painted from life. This copy hangs in the Ambras Castle, Innsbruck, Austria.

progress he thought he was making is anything but, and the journal he is keeping "for Mina" gets lost; when finally it emerges, Mina has no idea what anything written in it means.

The confusion increases as the novel goes on. While Mina frets about the sudden lapse in Jonathan's letters, the novel's perspective shifts to another perplexing movement: Mina's friend Lucy, in the English seaside town of Whitby, has begun to sleepwalk. No one connects this to the other strange event in town: the arrival of a ship, washed upon the rocks, with no sailors but a corpse tied to the masthead. Dr. Seward and his adviser, Van Helsing, are consulted. Why is the ebullient Lucy so pale? She seems to be losing blood: in turn, all her suitors give her transfusions. Their blood travels into her. After each transfusion, they are confident she is better and return to their homes—they take trains, ships—only to be drawn back to her side.

What the reader pieces together, although the characters themselves

TRAN

Riuuli
Rodna
Kalberg
Durchestritz
Georg
CI

Torfalu
Metersdorff
Waldorff
Zum lot.
Wenbe
Petersdorff
CAR

Berckes
Milstorff
Schippersdorff
Treppen
BISTRICIA Bistercze H.
Budeck
Seilendorff
Botz
Regen
Bircke
Vilack

Kerestur
Herckdorff
Saltz
NOSNER LAND.
Sthy
Kirlegiß
Pache

Banfa
Bayersdorff
Mintzdorff
S.Ioan
Durbach
Wela
Neumarck
Petlestof

Czizo
Sesarma
Lechnitz
Vnda
Teckedorff
Nereu
Hogitorff
Schmigen

Yeteck
Biclern
S.Georgen
WEINLANDT.

Viuar
Nemechi
Pontstorff
Prostorff

Galata
Burglos dees
Busaten
Naglack
Kockelsbury
Keßel
Frauenhoff

Koroffeu
Ville Walachie
Feck
Boncida
Bogatz
Ziden
Feigendorff
Kleynschelke.

Almas
Apehie
Torrenburg Torda
Blasendorff
Balcos
Lang.tal
Apistorff.

Sebesuar
Buda
Mikelsdorff
Kalterbrig
Schinen
Scharesflen

Hunad
Fenisch.
Teleck
Kazara
Gereng
Groß Kockel A.
Ludis
Schaen

CLAVDIOPOLIS.
Clausenburg.
Kolosuar. H.
Kerest mezo
Mönua
Reysdorff

NIGRA PALVS
Feketetho. H.
Plan
Arasma fl.
Oberwintz
Pered
Weingarten
Humlisch
Großaw.

OCCIDENS.
Ofemburg Pfriboma
Diod
Engetin
Rotkirch
Niderspold
Oberspold
Blechi

Krezk
Ysemberg.
Dujnen
S Emerich
LAND VOR DEM WALDT.
Dobrica

Capolna
Koroshania
Borband.
ALBA IVLIA
Weißenburg.
Gulaseyruan.H.
ZABEVS Millibach.
Kelbing
Vrbegen
Rakzes F.

Schaeten a prug.
Zalom
Zalatne rudera.
S.Michel
Vardia.
Petter sdorff
Sabesus fl.
S.Francisco.

4.Bergstet.
Borbrig
Wintz
Kazir

Altenberg
Therme
Kinermezo
MONS VVLCANI

Cum priuilegio
Zazuaros Broß.
S.Giory
Siriy fl.

HANC VLTRA VEL TRAN
SILVANIAM, QVAE ET PANNO
DACIA, ET DACIA RIPENSIS,
VVLGO SIBEMBVRGEN DICITVR,
ediit Vienne A: 1566. Nobiliß. atq Doctiß.
Ioes Sabucus
Pannonius.

S.Kiras
Deua
Varheli

Illie
Branizka
47
Orle angus Fie
Morfenes
Hunad Vaida
Vallis Hatzag vbi
Iofy.

VANIA.

MOLDAVIAE TERMINVS.

Tartroß

Pog Hauas

Pretz

SED CHVL.

SED Vever hel.

Aluta fl.

Neumarck

SED KISDI.

SED ORBAI

LI.

Beserenfalo.

Aderhel.

S.Merten

Zum Kreutz

Warugch

Dayla

Asyto.

S.Georgen

Pagi Sicu:
lorum.

Teufelsdorff.

Meburg.

Drausz

Radlen

Katzendorff.

SED
SCEPSI.

Schesburg.

Segesuar. H.

SED Kysdy.

Budendorff

Hamerod.

schees

Vellendorff

SED Reps.

Plamendorff.

Honsberg.

Armdorff

Tarten.

Trapold.

ALTLANDT.

Schuerse

Dopich

Gest.

M.ergenburg

Bren:
dorff.

Petersberg.

7 dorffer

Pendorff

Neustadt

Maypch.

Rocuback.

BVRZELAND

Burcia

Neudorff

CORONA. STEPHANO:
POLIS. Cronstatt.

Nethusen

CENTVM COLLES.

Stein

Seesling

Heloden

Brasso. H.

Iacobsdorff.

Schamberg.

Seligstad

Felmer

Herbrig
Einsidel

Seidyn

Nenstad

Agnetlin

Mergental.

Schars.

Halmegn

Seerkengen

Seydes Wald.

Molkendorff.

Rosenau.

Rosenthal.

Maywod

Torsyl.

Fogaras

Fried.

Cerne.

Birgetz.

Brokyn.

Kleyn
Schebel

Scharkan.

Turtzfest.

Leiskirch.

Rotberg

Holtzmenge.

fl.Alt.

Blechisdorffer.

H.Litera in hac ta:
bula nonnullis voca:
bulis adiuncta sig:
nificat ea esse Hun
garica.

Baugarten

Zacabad.

Kertz. Abbat.

Kastenholtz.

Schellen:
berg.

Grissaw

Kertzeberg.

Rudbom.

Michelsberg.

Calmisch.

Eeck

Rot:
thurn.

Alpes.

Campolongum.

Langenaw.

Chernesse

Schaid.

Irgisch templum

Teltz.

VALACHIAE

TERGOVISCIA.
Teruisch.

PARS.

Greyf.

Reduitz.

Pitesi Coenobium

Bocaretz

Dambouitz fl.

Pinie.

Gierusch.

Saluata fl.

Zorga

Sarmysethusa.

ES.

Danubius fl.

don't see it, is how the story of Lucy's mysterious blood loss is also the story of Dracula himself. His presence on the ghost ship at Whitby is only discovered in the ship's log, as the captain anxiously watches his sailors disappear one by one. Dr. Seward does not recognize Dracula as he sees Lucy mysteriously getting weaker. He does not recognize that the strange marks at Lucy's throat are the answer to both Lucy's illness and his own movement, as Dracula pulls blood through Lucy, and as he—Dr. Seward—returns to her, again and again.

What is most curious about *Dracula* as a journey story is that while the characters are nearly always on the move, they get nowhere. Characters go to the cemetery and back, to London and back, to Amsterdam and back, even, finally, to Transylvania and back—but these trips work more like traps. This is one of the ways that the novel's many passages mimic the course of blood: circulation holds more sway than destination. The characters circulate like blood because blood is Dracula's vehicle, and for most of the story they are trapped in Dracula's will. Lucy's blood, and all the blood transfused into her, has gone astray into Dracula's monstrous body.

Why are these wise men so slow to realize Dracula's power? It's not just Dracula's monstrous energy; it's also that they are "modern," scientific, lawful. These very qualities—which are a source of pride for them, and, in 1897, a rationale for England's tremendous global power—make them vulnerable to the vampire, who they only painfully come to believe exists.

He can transform himself to wolf . . . he can come in mist which he create . . . he comes on moonlight rays as elemental dust . . .

It's as if they are trying to defeat a monster with a train schedule. While Dracula flows erratically around the novel, his pursuers catch trains on unchangeable timetables that Mina has memorized. It is no small matter that British orderliness seems like a limit to our heroes. One of the questions of *Dracula* is whether modernity—science, timekeeping—can defeat the dangers of the barbaric, dangerous past. If trains—a literal and figurative vehicle by which England shaped its rapid progress—were an obstacle rather than an asset in slaying the monster, what else might England turn to?

Everything that might have helped them (garlic, superstition) seems to them the thing they should cast off. It's only Van Helsing who recognizes that British rationalism cannot be the key to defeating the vampire. The problem is that Dracula's movements are not limited as humans' are: "He can [. . .] appear at will when, and where, and in any of the forms that are to him," Van Helsing says, in his broken English. "He can transform himself to wolf . . . he can come in mist which he create . . . he come on moonlight rays as elemental dust—he become so small, come out from anything or into anything, no matter how close it be bound." How can they stop a power so various?

In the novel's conclusion, the characters blend their reason with the

strategies of the past. Armed with crucifixes and holy wafers, the characters begin using Dracula's power against him. Slowly, with great human cost, they pursue him back to Transylvania. But what remains? How have these journeys changed them, or their understanding of the world?

Van Helsing claims that the difference between vampires and humans is that vampires "are not free": they move powerfully but—like blood—only within their prescribed course. But the novel's attention to its characters' circulation seems to challenge his sense that humans have the freedom they desire. They, too, are dependent on the unconscious, primal circulation of blood within them: their biological drives are not a disease Dracula introduced but simply a part of themselves Dracula made them see. The journeys in *Dracula* show to the reader what it means to be human: that it can be difficult to tell the difference between moving and being trapped: that there are forces within us, moving us, which we may learn to track but can never completely control.

Bram Stoker stayed at Whitby Abbey in 1890 and first read of the exploits of Vlad the Impaler from papers in the town library. The town of Whitby is now famous for being the site where Dracula first arrives in England.

Previous: A 1570 map of Transylvania, now in the west of Romania and the legendary home of Dracula.

2 THE AGE OF TRAVEL

While ocean-going liners opened up new territories for tourism, the arrival of the railroads brought undiscovered inland places into reach.

The Pennsylvania Railroad sold tickets to the Midwest, while the Ford Tri-Motor heralded the arrival of new air travel. Poster by Grif Teller, 1931.

JOSEPH CONRAD

HEART OF DARKNESS (1899)

Marlow, a seasoned seafarer, recounts a trip he once made to the heart of the Congo in search of the brilliant but mad ivory trader Kurtz—a journey that confronted him with the horrors of imperialism and the fragile limits of civilization.

Joseph Conrad, a titan of English literature, was born Józef Teodor Konrad Korzeniowski. English was Conrad's third language, after Polish and French; he only started learning it at twenty-one.

Heart of Darkness is set during the Scramble for Africa, when European powers vied to take control of resource-rich territories on the continent.

Heart of Darkness is based on a trip Conrad took in 1890. Like his main character Marlow, he captained a river steamer and returned from the journey with his health permanently damaged—to the extent that he decided to give up his career in the merchant navy and devote himself to writing.

Heart of Darkness is a novel that punches above its weight: it has managed to lay a solid claim to a place in the Anglophone literary canon in under a hundred pages (in most editions, at any rate). And, as is often the case with literary classics, it is a book we feel we know even without having read it: there is a river, an impenetrable jungle, and a mythical, mad figure at the end of it: Kurtz. A figure whose mythical status is incidentally enhanced by Conrad's novel having inspired an equally classic film, Francis Ford Coppola's *Apocalypse Now*, which moved the action from the Congo during colonization to Vietnam during the war, and offered Marlon Brando an opportunity to give a legendary performance as Colonel Kurtz. As, however, is equally often the case with literary classics, the reality of the text as a whole is actually quite different to the impression made by the fragments that have made it into our collective imagination.

The journey at the heart—to coin a phrase—of this novel is indeed an ascent of the Congo River in search of Kurtz, a renegade ivory trader who his bosses back in Europe want taken home; but this journey itself does not actually start until the middle of the narrative. Just as important a part of the story is the journey that takes the main character, Marlow, to his starting point on the Congo—or rather, "the journeys," plural. . . . The first of which is one that will not begin: we are on a "cruising yawl," the *Nellie*, sitting on the River Thames and waiting for the tide to turn before the ship can set off upriver. An unnamed narrator is on board with three of his friends, all seamen, though only one of them is still actively involved in the trade. This is Marlow, who decides, while they wait, to tell them about a trip he made to the Congo. *Heart of Darkness* is thus a tale within a tale, a journey within the pause in another journey, a seaman's yarn—a reminder, perhaps, that ever since the *Odyssey*, peregrination has always been one of our main sources for a good story.

Marlow explains the fascination he had felt for Africa since he was a boy, which pushed him to lobby for a job that would take him there; and thus the first half of the novel is taken up with the journey before the journey, first in Brussels as Marlow charms his way into a position as captain with a Belgian

trading company, then traveling on someone else's ship to the Congolese coast, then trekking by foot to the station where he is to find his boat. Except that said boat needs repairs, so that just as Marlow thinks he is finally going to be able to set off on his great trip, he finds himself stuck in an outpost waiting for spare parts that the corrupt colonial officials on which he is dependent seem determined to prevent him from getting. At last, however, Marlow does set off on a nightmarish river trip, deeper and deeper into the jungle, dodging death from a treacherous nature and hostile native tribes, until he finds the much-vaunted and despised Kurtz, a once brilliant man who has descended into madness, violence, and barbarism. Marlow extracts Kurtz from the natives who have adopted him as a kind of demigod and falls under his spell, too, as they make their way back downriver; but Kurtz is too far gone and dies on the journey, with Marlow the only witness to his final, terrible words: "The horror! The horror!"

Literary classics have a journey of their own through the culture they are defining, and it is difficult to write about *Heart of Darkness* today without acknowledging the criticism the novel has received for the way in which it describes the inhabitants of the Congo, most notably by the Nigerian novelist Chinua Achebe, who accused Conrad of being a "bloody racist" and of "reducing Africa to the role of props for the breakup of one petty European mind," thus being complicit in "the dehumanization of Africa and Africans, which this age-long attitude has fostered and continues to foster in the world." Since Achebe made these comments in 1977, critics have stepped

Mixed-media illustration by Max P. Häring—entry for a competition to illustrate the 2014 Folio Society edition of the book.

Following: A hand-colored woodcut depicting explorer Henry Morton Stanley's camp on the Congo River in the 1870s. Stanley is considered one of Conrad's inspirations for the novel.

up both to defend Conrad and to condemn him further, and the debate is sure to continue, since there is no denying that Conrad's treatment of the African figures is problematic. They are represented as suffering cruelly at the hands of their European invaders, so that they provide a mirror held up to the Europeans that reveals how thin the boundary is between civilization and barbarism, but in so doing, Conrad portrays them as unknowable, wild, completely other—and thus as somehow fundamentally different from his European protagonists.

Yet, at the time of its publication, *Heart of Darkness* was used by anti-imperialist activists to oppose the Belgian hold over the perversely named "Congo Free State," as it painted such a damning picture of the Europeans involved in plundering Africa. *Heart of Darkness* is both anti-imperialist pamphlet and relic of the colonialist mindset, and this journey taken by the novel in terms of its reception is worth pondering. It is a book that, while critical of the hypocrisy and brutality of colonialism, nevertheless is not free of the racist and dehumanizing perspective behind the very thing it criticizes. In short, *Heart of Darkness* has from the start confronted Western readers with the racism and brutality that underpin their supposed "civilization"; but while early readers could feel they were being spoken to directly by Conrad himself, we who read him now must uncomfortably navigate what attitudes he may be betraying in spite of himself—and in so doing, question how we ourselves may be complicit in these attitudes.

The journey on which this book has been is, of course, partly a journey on which the whole world has been. Marlow explains thus why he was so desperate to get a job in Africa:

> Now when I was a little chap I had a passion for maps. At that time there were many blank spaces on the earth, and when I saw one that looked particularly inviting on a map [. . .] I would put my finger on it and say, When I grow up I will go there.

By the time Marlow grows up, most of the blanks have been filled in, but only roughly—there is still a sense of much of the world being, from a European perspective, unexplored, unknown, truly remote, and other. And thus there is a sense of a journey as offering the opportunity of coloring in the blanks for the first time, of discovering things that are truly new. What neither Marlow nor Kurtz realized, perhaps, is that there is also a blank within themselves that the journey will color in, and that the excitement we feel upon setting off at the prospect of all the new experiences that await us ignores the risk that these experiences may color us in ways we might not want. For both Kurtz and Marlow, the darkness they journey toward is not just that of the jungle but that within themselves; and for us as readers too, *Heart of Darkness* confronts us with some uncomfortable truths about the world we live in.

PÍO BAROJA

ROAD TO PERFECTION
(CAMINO DE PERFECCIÓN) (1902)

Road to Perfection recounts the physical and spiritual journey of the fictional artist Fernando Ossorio, a self-diagnosed degenerate who leaves Madrid to travel through Castile and the Levante, finally freeing himself from neurosis in the fertile province of Castellón.

Road to Perfection follows the travels around Spain of the tormented artist Fernando Ossorio as he moves toward psychological reintegration and resolution for his perceived degeneracy, manifested in debilitating symptoms including synesthesia and pseudo-mystical visions.

Madrid is described as a decadent city from which he sets out on a physical and spiritual journey through Castile. The imperial city of Toledo marks the crisis-point in his progress; from there he moves southeast to address his past and seek redemption in Yécora, the location of his oppressive Catholic education. Finally, Fernando reaches the province of Castellón, where he finds solace in marriage to Dolores and a resolution to his journey. At times resplendent, at other points hostile, the portrait of Spain on Fernando's travels reflects Baroja's compelling critique of his homeland.

Baroja studied medicine in Madrid and Valencia, submitting a doctorate on "Pain: A Psychophysical Study" in 1893; he practiced briefly as a doctor in the Basque town of Cestona before turning definitively to writing. These autobiographical experiences are reflected in the character of Fernando Ossorio, who abandons university to devote himself to painting. Since Fernando produces only a handful of artworks over the course of the novel, most memorably the anguished scene of mourning in *Hours of Silence*, Baroja's technique for exploring his protagonist's creative vocation relies primarily on other strategies.

As we move through the varied landscapes of central Spain, we encounter myriad references to illustrious artists (Titian, Rubens, El Greco) and terms such as "brushstroke," "painting," and "altarpiece." The key to understanding Baroja's experimental techniques is the projection of Fernando's changing vision onto the world through the description of successive locations as works of art. The view from Madrid, for example, evokes a panoply of colors at sunset:

Pío Baroja (1872–1956) was a prolific author in early twentieth-century Spain and one of the group of writers labeled the "Generation of 1898," although he rejected the term. Born in the Basque Country, he wrote more than sixty novels, and numerous journalistic articles, short stories, and memoirs.

Critically acclaimed from the outset, *Road to Perfection* has appeared in several major editions and has been translated into many languages.

Inspired by artists such as Santiago Rusiñol and Darío de Regoyos, Baroja regarded himself as a literary impressionist.

When the sun went down, the mountain range took on a more violet hue; its last rays still illuminated a faraway peak in the west and the other mountains remained swathed in a splendid rose-colored mist, of carmine and gold, which seemed to have been wrested from some apotheosis of Titian.

Following a turbulent sexual relationship with his Aunt Laura, Fernando leaves Madrid believing himself to be a degenerate, and sets off around Spain to overcome his neurotic symptoms and achieve equilibrium. The protagonist believes that he has inherited the pathological traits of family relations, especially a tendency to hysteria and sexual excess, which he seeks to overcome through psychological progress and physical travel. Both the depiction of the neurotic artist and the decadent urban environment of Madrid draw vividly on Max Nordau's sensationalist work *Degeneration* (1892), published in Spanish translation in 1902. Irony is ever-present in Baroja's works, though, and the author was careful to distance himself from any consistent ideological position.

First Fernando heads north from Madrid on foot, through the towns of Fuencarral, Colmenar, and Rascafría, encountering inhospitable people and desolate scenery along the way. Upon reaching El Paular and the Guadarrama mountains, he converses with a German traveler, Schultze, who advises him to take exercise and read Nietzsche to remedy his nervous temperament. From Segovia, he rides to Illescas in a cart driven by Polentinos, who conveys his own pessimistic vision of the world. Moving on to Toledo, the protagonist suffers from an inflammation of the eyes, a reaction to the harsh sunlight and a symbol of his distorted vision. On a nighttime visit to see El Greco's painting *The Burial of the Count of Orgaz* (1586–88) at the Church of Santo Tomé, the hypersensitive protagonist feels overwhelmed and is forced to close his eyes. As he walks along the banks of the river to calm his mind, the sinister silhouette of a cross seems to beckon to him in the moonlight, providing an ironic reminder that his journey to perfection is far from complete.

Now Fernando travels southeast to the location of the Piarist school he attended in Yécora (based on Yecla, in Murcia), described as a prisonlike institution that has instilled a psychological burden of sin and guilt. The damning critique of the Catholic Church is achieved through the description of this hostile place and disparaging portraits of priests whom Fernando meets along the way. In Yécora, Fernando is refused forgiveness by a young woman, Ascensión, whom he once brutally seduced. Having confronted his past, however, Fernando's neurasthenia begins to abate in the barren, monotonous setting of Marisparza. The protagonist's recovery takes place in the Valencia region, described in the novel through images of warmth and fertility in the natural world as his journey reaches an outcome of sorts. After a series of dysfunctional encounters with women over the course of the novel, in Castellón he marries Dolores who represents a spiritual refuge through union

with nature. Although resolution is achieved through the birth of a healthy son in the hospitable setting of the Levante, the deeply ambiguous ending is characteristic of Baroja's early fiction. The novel's conclusion provides an ironic twist on the journey narrative by depicting the devout grandmother sewing a page of the gospel into the baby's swaddling band, an obvious reference to the enduring constraints of Catholicism from which the protagonist has tried to free himself. The physical and spiritual journey thereby culminates in an ambivalent solution. The restless protagonist reaches psychological equilibrium but can no longer paint, as spiritual reintegration is only partially achieved. Fernando Ossorio's troubled psyche, projected on to his geographical travels, functions as a symbol of the Spanish nation at the turn of the twentieth century, a period of introspection and national soul-searching expressed so powerfully by Baroja and his contemporaries.

El Greco's *The Burial of the Count of Orgaz* (1586), which Fernando visits at the Church of Santo Tomé in Toledo. The visit provokes a profound spiritual and physical reaction in Baroja's protagonist.

JACK LONDON
THE CALL OF THE WILD (1903)

The story of a dog's journey to become a wild animal, The Call of the Wild *follows Buck from California to the hinterland of the Alaskan Yukon Valley, tracking his encounters with both good and cruel humans along the way.*

Jack London's short life —born in 1876, he died in 1916 at the age of forty —was one of much travel and adventure. From a young age, he worked in many different jobs, such as seaman and coal heaver, and even ran for Mayor of Oakland, as well as traveling all over the United States and the world.

The Call of the Wild was first published in four installments in *The Saturday Evening Post,* which paid $750 dollars for it.

The story was met with immediate success and since its publication by Macmillan in 1903, has never been out of print.

In 1897, Jack London sailed to Alaska to join the Klondike Gold Trail, following the hundreds of thousands of people who took this same journey to look for gold in the Klondike River, between 1896 and 1899. London immortalized the hardship of this journey in his 1903 story *The Call of the Wild*, making his protagonist not a man but a dog.

Buck, a half-St. Bernard and half-Scotch shepherd, lives a comfortable and free life in Santa Clara, California, as "neither a house-dog nor kennel-dog" but quietly ruling the land and gardens of his owner as a "country gentleman." He is stolen by one of the poor gardeners who sells him to a man who supplies sled dogs for those heading north. Because of his enormous size and heft, Buck is quickly sold and so begins his life as a sled dog. He soon gains a love of the hard work of running through the snow, though he meets with mixed fortune with his owners, and endures many hardships traversing the Yukon landscape. His life is saved one day by a man named John Thornton, for whom he develops a real love, but at the same time, Buck begins to hear the "call of the wild," the sounds of his ancestors urging him to become a truly wild animal. When John Thornton dies after an attack by Native Americans, Buck finally loses the last thing tying him to domesticity, his love of man, and joins the wolf pack for good.

Buck's journey from his life in sunny and mild California to cold and snowy Canada transforms him from a domestic animal to a wild beast. During his initial capture, he is beaten by a man with a club in an attempt to "break" him and make him compliant, but Buck learns a different lesson: "The club was a revelation. It was his introduction to the reign of primitive law." Buck learns the lesson of violence, and from then on, London traces the "decay of his moral nature" as he embraces the awakening of his deep instincts. Buck feels the inheritance of his true wolf nature in his body, and firstly hears the call metaphorically—". . . it was his ancestors, dead and dust, pointing nose at star and howling down centuries and through him,"—and then hears the real calls of wolves that lures him to finally abandon his previous life and take up a new wild one.

Many people were making journeys from all parts of America, and indeed the world, to try their luck in Canada as part of the gold rush. London shows many different kinds of traveler in his story, and when Buck is bought by Mercedes, Charles, and Hal, he shows how many of these people were making journeys for which they were unprepared. These difficulties contrast to the way that Buck takes to his new rugged life so easily, marking him out as a special and unique animal, and suggesting that he is fulfilling his true nature.

In making his main character a dog, London exposes the proximity between civilization and brutality. Though Buck gets in many fights with other animals, he is also subject to starvation and beatings by his human masters, showing that the human world is just as violent and cruel as the animal, and in fact, the threat of violence is how society operates. The quick descent of Buck's life from a comfortably domestic one to a harsh and brutal one suggests that within all apparently "civilized" societies, violence is never far away.

Four men—from left, Marshall Bond, Oliver H. R. La Farge, Lyman R. Cold, and Stanley Pearce—sit at a cabin with their dogs. Marshall's dog on the left was the inspiration for Buck.

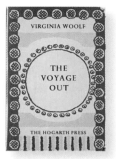

VIRGINIA WOOLF

THE VOYAGE OUT (1915)

In her first novel, Virginia Woolf explores the social conventions of her time through the lens of a young woman's journey across the Atlantic.

In 1905, Virginia Woolf traveled with her brother by boat to Portugal, an experience that possibly informed her depiction of the journey in *The Voyage Out*.

The novel went through several incarnations. In 2004, scholar Louise DeSalvo published a reconstruction of the book's original version under the title *Melymbrosia*.

A review of *The Voyage Out* in *The New York Times* in 1920 ended with the following prescient words: "With the cleverness shown here, crude as most of it is, there should be a possibility of something worth while from the same pen in the future."

A boat, the *Euphrosyne*, sits on the Thames at the start of *The Voyage Out*, preparing for a journey to South America. It is peopled by a diverting cast of characters—among them the novel's twenty-four-year-old protagonist, Rachel Vinrace, who is traveling across the Atlantic with Helen and Ridley Ambrose, her aunt and uncle. As the voyage begins, and London is left behind, the cast expands: at Lisbon, Clarissa and Richard Dalloway come aboard. Later, when the *Euphrosyne* delivers Rachel and the Ambroses to Santa Marina, a fictional port in South America, they meet a number of other Britons at a nearby hotel—one of them is Terence Hewet, with whom Rachel falls in love. An expedition is undertaken up the "great river" and there, bathed in the green light of the rain forest, Rachel and Terence confess their love to each other. But Rachel contracts an illness during this expedition; back at her villa, she becomes feverish and dies with Terence by her side.

These are the bare bones of Virginia Woolf's first novel, a strange, sometimes dreamlike, satirical book, which contains within it the seeds of much of her later work. But *The Voyage Out* is more than merely its bones. The chapters are packed with sardonic social commentary on subjects such as male chauvinism, British politics, and colonialism. It is a many-layered, complicated novel, about which Woolf later felt negatively: she rewrote it before publication, toning down its biting commentary, but would continue to be displeased by the result.

The book's title is misleading; there are many voyages contained within its pages. The most obvious is the passage of the *Euphrosyne* from England to South America, and the movement away from the stifling social norms of the characters' home; in the middle of the ocean, they all feel "the same exhilaration at their freedom." Despite the distance the journey gives them from their own country, however, they continue to be inhibited by social convention and share a pervasive inability to communicate properly. (This is echoed in the subject of Terence's book on "silence [. . .] the things people don't say," a subject that is invested with darker significance with the "profound silence" that follows Rachel's death.)

The second voyage is a figurative one: Rachel's journey from naivety to knowledge. She is the daughter of an absent father, brought up in cloistered confines in the home she shares with her aunts in Richmond. The behavior of men, their passions, their relations with the "sumptuous women" in Piccadilly, are foreign to her. On board the *Euphrosyne*, Richard Dalloway kisses her, unsettling her with previously unknown emotions. These emotions find a more socially acceptable subject in the form of Terence Hewet, who is "good-looking in the sense that he had always had a sufficiency of beef to eat and fresh air to breathe." They fall in love and dream of a life together in England (the sultry South American climate, the huge alien landscape, makes them feel "insignificant," even "raving mad"—they rhapsodize instead about "muddy lanes, with brambles and nettles").

Here, a conventional bildungsroman might meet its conclusion: with Rachel's successful navigation from girlhood to womanhood and the young couple's intended return to England. Yet, as E.M. Forster wrote of *The Voyage Out*: "Wedded bliss is promised [Rachel], but the voyage continues, the current deepens, carrying her between green banks of the jungle into disease and death."

The novel seems to encapsulate the passage of Woolf's life, as well as Rachel's. Many of Woolf's later themes and ideas—including those about society and women and the spaces they inhabit—are expressed

Virginia Woolf on the beach with her brother-in-law Clive Bell in 1910.

here in nascent forms. *The Voyage Out* clearly stayed with its creator: not only are its themes returned to, but also are some of its characters (Clarissa Dalloway would be resurrected in other short stories and in *Mrs. Dalloway* a decade later, as would the name "Euphrosyne," which Woolf later recycled in *Orlando*). Woolf would even revisit one of the book's most poignant ideas at the very end of her life. At Rachel's deathbed:

[u]nconscious whether he thought the words or spoke them aloud, [Terence] said, "No two people have ever been so happy as we have been."

Previous: The Cunard Line began ocean cruises as early as 1840, selling the romance and adventure of foreign travel that inspired Virginia Woolf.

It is moving to note the similarity this sentence bears with the final line in Virginia Woolf's suicide letter: "I don't think two people could have been happier than we have been," she wrote to her husband on March 28, 1941.

The Voyage Out is often overlooked today, jostled into the background by its more famous successors. But it warrants a revived interest for the precision of its prose and the brilliance of its characters, as well as for the rich and intriguing insight it gives us into the mind of its creator.

KATHERINE MANSFIELD

The Voyage (1921)

Following the sudden loss of her mother, a little girl's boat journey to live with her grandparents reveals unexpected glimmers of hope in a time of darkness.

Katherine Mansfield is roundly celebrated as one of the most important short story writers of the twentieth century. She is considered an important voice in modernist writing, exploring ideas of self, place, and home. Mansfield traveled from New Zealand to Europe, moving between England, Germany, and France, before her death in 1923, and we can see this focus on travel and its disruptions reflected in many of her works. In a letter to her friend, the writer Virginia Woolf, dated from 1919, Mansfield wrote, "what the writer does is not so much to solve the question but to put the question." In many of her stories about journey and traveling, Mansfield writes of the ambiguous feelings that moving between places can provoke, without seeking to resolve or simplify them through her narratives.

One such story which shows travel as both exciting and full of uncertainty is 1921's "The Voyage." It tells the story of Fenella, a little girl whose mother has recently died, as she takes a boat journey with her grandmother, from Wellington Harbour to Picton port on the South Island. Mansfield writes in the third person, but the narrative is definitively from Fenella's perspective, and so the language she uses is simple and often descriptive, representing the way that the young child sees and knows the world around her.

Because of this perspective, the emotional resonance of the story slowly emerges over its few pages. Mansfield gradually reveals the death of the mother, hinted at the opening of the story through details such as the black mourning clothes. Though Fenella seems to accept the separation from her father, she does not seem to have any idea about her future: "'How long am I going to stay?' she whispered anxiously." Her father does not respond but in giving her shilling, she finds her answer. Fenella watches the exchange between her grandmother and father closely, but finds seeing their tears too much, "Fenella quickly turned her back on them, swallowed once, twice, and frowned terribly at a little green star on a mast head." Later, as they pull into the harbor, Fenella wonders "Oh, it had all been so sad lately. Was it going to change?" We see the little girl's worries through the forms of questions, a child's method of interrogating a complicated world. But Mansfield shows that though she may be young, and cannot adequately vocalize her feelings

Born Kathleen Mansfield Beauchamp, Mansfield (1888–1923) is one of the most well-respected short story writers of the twentieth century, publishing four collections before her death, and several collections posthumously.

"The Voyage" was first published on December 24, 1921 in *The Sphere*, a newspaper aimed at British citizens living in abroad in the colonies.

Mansfield's parents were of the first generation to be born outside of England, in Australia, before moving to New Zealand. This meant that her family felt a deep connection to England, and lived in a way that reflected and replicated the Victorian values of the time.

Picton Harbour in 1912 from the east featuring a yacht race with spectators cheering from the launches and the steamship decks. Artist unknown, part of the New Zealand National Collection which first opened in 1920.

as yet, she is beginning to be aware of the complex emotions of other people around her, and indeed her own, too.

Though the title of the story indicates a journey, the actual trip on the boat is rendered very briefly, and the arrival to this new place does not seem to provoke much anxiety in the little girl: "now a gull flipped by; and now there came a long piece of real land." The "journey" she takes then, is not only the physical one on the boat but the physic journey into a new world without her mother's presence. But though this loss is clearly emphatically felt by the family, Mansfield does not suggest that this is wholly negative, and she describes the home of Fenella's grandparents in hopeful terms. Fenella is greeted by a white cat, and her grandfather sits cheerfully in the bed with a "white tuft." This contrast to the gloom of her black mourning clothes indicates a shift in the little girl's life: this will clearly be a loving home.

But, as Mansfield suggests in her letter to Woolf, in only "putting" the question to us, we cannot know with any certainty what will happen to Fenella. Mansfield often places her characters in moments of change or shift: her novella *Prelude*, for example, published by Virginia Woolf's Hogarth Press in 1918, follows a family as they move from their home in the city to a sprawling house in the country. These moments of shift are made all the more complex by the short story form. Rather than giving extensive description, Mansfield's stories give an insight into that particular moment in time. Through the brevity of this journey, Mansfield suggests that every journey we make is rich with the possibility for change.

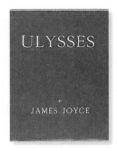

JAMES JOYCE

ULYSSES (1922)

A pioneering work of the modernist genre, Joyce's novel mirrors Homer's Odyssey *in both its structure and its characters. In a series of eighteen episodes, the novel's protagonist, Leopold Bloom, travels a meandering route through the streets of Dublin.*

Born in Dublin in 1882, Joyce sought to escape the stifling conservatism of contemporary Irish society. He lived in mainland Europe from 1904 until the end of his life.

Ulysses' first appearance in print was in American journal *The Little Review*, where it was serialized in parts from 1918 to 1920, when publication ceased due to a prosecution for obscenity. The book was first published in its entirety in Paris in 1922, though it remained effectively banned in the United States until 1934.

An annual pilgrimage, known as Bloomsday, is held in Dublin every June 16, retracing Bloom's route through the city.

Joyce called Dublin "the last of the intimate cities." It was a higgledy-piggledy assemblage of villages, which had somehow been joined together. Each of Dublin's micro-villages still had a rural feel in those days, with cattle being herded through the streets down to the city docklands for live export.

Many of the 200,000 citizens of the Irish capital had come in from the countryside, bringing with them a love of storytelling and gossip. In Dublin there were no ultimate strangers—only friends who one hadn't yet met. *Ulysses* celebrates the chance meeting of a bourgeois adman and a bohemian postgraduate student, suggesting that one of the main functions of a modern city is to connect people with their own inner strangeness. Hence its protagonist, Leopold Bloom, is a part-Jewish wanderer, a flaneur, the outsider-insider.

Dublin is a city of walkers. Bloom spends most of June 16, 1904 meandering through its streets. Some readers have understandably wondered whether he is "trying to walk something off"—the troubling knowledge that, back in his home at 7 Eccles Street, his wife Molly has taken to bed a lover named Blazes Boylan.

At a time of dire overcrowding, with constant evictions of tenants by bailiffs and death rates close to those of the slums of Calcutta, many people preferred the streets as places of glamour and mystery. Joyce believed that the free circulation of bodies in a city's streets was a sign of social health, much like the unimpaired circulation of blood in the hale human body. Each episode of *Ulysses* is dedicated to an organ of the body—lung, heart, kidney, etc. The restored human body may have been his image of the reconquest of Ireland by its own people, achieved finally in the year of the novel's publication, 1922.

The book is justly famous for its interior monologues, especially those which render the stream of consciousness as experienced by Bloom. It is a narrative in which little enough happens at the level of plot. Instead, the strolling of characters in city thoroughfares provides endless prompts to thought. If, in Renaissance poetry, the rhythm of iambic pentameter recapitulated the movements of a rider on a horse, here the cadences of

thought itself are keyed to the rhythm of walking . . . A book that is famous for its private ruminations and personal daydreams is largely set in public spaces: streets, beaches, libraries, churches, a maternity hospital, hotels, and —most of all—pubs. *Ulysses* celebrates Dublin's friendliness, musicality, and expressiveness of language (the rainy weather being "as uncertain as a child's bottom"). In the course of his long day, Bloom moves from the cemetery, through pub and beach, to the maternity hospital, as if to echo Joyce's notion of literature as an affirmation of life against death.

Joyce lived all of his adult life in exile from this city of his youth. But it was a place to which, in the end, he gave unconditional love.

A statue of James Joyce in the famous Temple Bar Pub in Dublin.

Following: Cyclops by Aidan Hickey, 2022. Hickey's collection, "Painting Ulysses," a series of works based on Joyce's novel, was featured at the James Joyce Cultural Centre to mark the 100th anniversary of the book's publication.

Signatures of all things I am here to read, seaspawn and seawrack, the nearing tide, that rusty boot. Snotgreen, bluesilver, rust; colored signs. Limits of the diaphane.

JOSEPH ROTH

FLIGHT WITHOUT END
(DIE FLUCHT OHNE ENDE) (1927)

Crisscrossing Europe from east to west, this "lost generation" novel presents the postwar odyssey of a former soldier and a homeward journey that, even after a decade, has no end in sight.

Austrian journalist and novelist Joseph Roth (1894–1939) is best known for his elegiac novel of the end of the Habsburg empire, *Radetzkymarsch* (1932).

The novel is narrated by a playfully fictionalized version of Roth himself, who names himself in the text. Born in Galicia, he was multilingual and, like his character Tunda, could speak Russian.

It was inspired by Roth's trip to the Soviet Union in 1926. The daily *Frankfurter Zeitung* newspaper published his reports from several of the locations in the novel, including Moscow and Baku.

Unlike the majority of Joseph Roth's later works, which look back to the world as it existed before 1914, *Flight Without End* brings the 1920s to vivid life. Franz Tunda's odyssey begins with his capture by the Russian army in August 1916 and continues through the following decade, with no real end ever in sight. The novel presents the condition of interminable "flight"—from commitment, from everyday life, and ultimately from oneself—as an existential state.

This is a fast-paced novel in which journeys are both structurally and symbolically important, and which is written in a style that is reminiscent of the observational essays for which Roth was famed. Tunda's travels through temporal, existential, political, and cultural boundaries provide a thematic link through the episodic narrative.

The story begins with his escape from Russian captivity, after which he spends three years living in the Siberian wilderness. Hearing that the war is over, Tunda makes a first attempt to return to the West, only to find himself caught up in the Civil War in Russia and the Ukraine. Alongside the revolutionary Natasha—one of several emancipated female characters in the novel who represent a modernity that Tunda feels both attracted to and threatened by—he spends another two years fighting for the Bolsheviks, but without ever really believing in their cause. When Natasha leaves he moves to the Soviet oil metropolis of Baku in Azerbaijan, and is eventually inspired to return to his old identity following a brief erotic encounter with a visiting French woman, who mistakes him for an officer of the secret police.

The novel charts the stations through which Tunda passes, carrying a fading photograph of the woman to whom he had been engaged in 1914, as he wanders through a Europe he barely recognizes. In chapters set in Vienna, an unnamed city on the Rhine, Berlin, and Paris, the misfit Tunda's bemused gaze exposes the pretentions of postwar metropolitan society. The account of Tunda's train journey from Vienna to the Rhineland is vivid:

> Of Germany he saw only the stations, the sign-boards, the posters, the churches, the hotels by the railroad, the silent gray streets of the suburbs, and the suburban trains looking like tired animals emerging from their stables.

Tunda, an antihero who anticipates the alienated protagonists of Camus and Handke, is an embodiment of the same "lost" and traumatized generation that haunts other works of the 1920s, notably those of Hemingway and Fitzgerald. Standing before the grave of the unknown soldier in Paris, Tunda reflects on his own existence, and that of his generation:

The West Pier train station in Paris Saint-Germain. Pencil, watercolor, and gouache by Victor Marec, early twentieth century.

> Tunda sometimes felt as if he himself lay there in the ground, as we all lay there, all those of us who came back but never came home—for it is a matter of indifference whether we are buried or alive and well. We are strangers in this world, we come from the realm of the dead.

By the conclusion, Tunda is considering a return to his starting point in Siberia, and thereby resetting his "flight without end." The final paragraph finds him alone in Paris, feeling utterly redundant: "He had no occupation, no desire, no hope, no ambition, and not even any self-love. No one in the whole world was as superfluous as he." Bleak as this seems, this is a novel that brims with sly humor and the joys of travel and place, written at the peak of his powers by one of the greatest of German-language travel writers.

HALLDÓR LAXNESS

THE GREAT WEAVER FROM KASHMIR (VEFARINN MIKLI FRÁ KASMÍR) (1927)

Modeled on a medieval pilgrimage, The Great Weaver From Kashmir *is a metaphorical and literal quest that sees Steinn travel from Iceland to mainland Europe in search of truth, love, belief, and peace.*

Halldór Laxness is the only Icelander to have won the Nobel Prize in Literature, in 1955.

He worked on drafts in many of the European locations in the novel. The book has parallels in Laxness's own life, most notably his conversion to Catholicism in 1923.

Laxness intended to take orders but had changed direction by the time he started working on *The Great Weaver;* the novel has been read as his retreat from the monastic mountaintop.

It is 1921 and Steinn Elliði is eighteen years old. Brilliant, passionate, debauched, egomaniacal, he is newly reborn and pledged to chastity after a divine revelation on the outskirts of Reykjavík. "I've made a pact with the Lord about becoming the most perfect man on Earth," he announces to sixteen-year-old Diljá, the childhood friend who has grown up with his grandmother. "God himself has told me that if I am pure enough, I can inspire a new era in world literature, like Dante Alighieri."

The Great Weaver from Kashmir is a book about the search for perfection, and the agonies of such a journey. Steinn Elliði sails from Iceland the next day: the years that follow see him travel between England, France, Belgium, Italy, Sicily, and Switzerland while Diljá remains at home in Reykjavík. A few years later Steinn Elliði has lost his way. He ends up traveling to Belgium where he seeks refuge at the top of a mountain within the walls of the Benedictine monastery of Sept Fontaines. Here, Steinn Elliði confesses the sins of his life and converts to Catholicism, but temptations crowd his mind and he decides to visit Iceland before taking orders. At the family summer house at Þingvellir (site of the ancient Icelandic parliament and symbolic heart of Iceland) Steinn Elliði and Diljá go over the past. They admit their love for each other but Steinn Elliði is still resolved to choose God over human love and he leaves Diljá and Iceland for a second time. A "wretched pilgrim of love," Diljá follows Steinn Elliði to Rome where he is staying at a seminary. In the final scene, she leans against a column in St. Peter's Square as church bells ring in the new day.

Laxness was in his early twenties when he wrote *The Great Weaver from Kashmir* and not yet twenty-five years old when it was published in 1927. He first left Iceland himself in 1919 and spent several years exploring damaged and febrile postwar Europe. He wrote to his mother during this trip that, "It is clear to me that this journey of mine is a great step in the direction that I have been seeking, namely, to gain knowledge of people and the world, so that I can become a real writer, which is where my heart truly lies."

Laxness's literary and intellectual influences included August Strindberg and Otto Weininger; his avant-garde style and treatment of his subject matter

had almost no precedent in Icelandic literature. Unsurprisingly, reception was mixed. Some reviewers defended the work, seeing how necessary creative experiment and new forms were for Icelandic literary culture. More conservative voices expressed shock at its philosophical and religious ideas and the perceived moral degeneracy of its characters with just the kind of bourgeois narrow-mindedness derided by Steinn Elliði in the novel.

Laxness himself conceived *The Great Weaver of Kashmir* as "a great and remarkable book for the whole world," a book that proclaimed "the newest movements that characterize our time in the art of form." Iceland's great medieval literary legacy—the eddas and sagas—had played a key part in Iceland's progress toward gaining independence from Denmark in the late nineteenth and early twentieth centuries. Laxness was determined to break free from the past, however, although later he would openly acknowledge that an "Icelandic author cannot live without constantly thinking about the old books."

Even though his early ambition was to do something utterly new, Laxness could not distance himself from his literary heritage categorically. He refers to and quotes directly from several sagas and from *Völuspá* (a mythological poem that describes Ragnarök, the end of the world, and its subsequent rebirth). The influence of the sagas also seems to manifest itself in the narrative structure of *The Great Weaver of Kashmir*. Several sagas, for example, tell of Icelandic poets who leave their girlfriends behind while they go abroad to make their name and fortune, and sometimes convert to Christianity; on return, the girlfriends are no longer available though feelings remain between the old lovers.

Þingvellir by Þórarinn B. Þorláksson (1900). Þingvellir was the site of the Alþingi, the annual parliament of Iceland from 930CE. It remains a place of huge spiritual and historical significance for Icelanders.

Iceland is an island, and perhaps inevitably, therefore, the rite-of-passage storyline of a young Icelandic man leaving home to seek out worldly and spiritual truths in the wider world is a fundamental narrative structure. The sagas as a genre wrestle with questions of identity and explore the place of Iceland and Icelanders in the world: the fact that the motif of home runs throughout *The Great Weaver of Kashmir* is worthy of note in this context. Steinn Elliði is said on several occasions never to have really had a family home but the prior of Sept Fontaines welcomes him by saying, "Imagine that you have come home." When spring comes though, he begins to think of Iceland and becomes sad with homesickness "like an ancient Icelander." It is Iceland's landscape that exerts the most powerful influence on Steinn Elliði's mindset and Laxness's descriptions of Icelandic nature are among the most lyrical and bewitching passages in the book.

> He thought of the blue bays of Reykjavík, and the mountains that watch over the bays. He saw these things in his mind's eye in the same glory as they had appeared to him in his youth, and he dreamed of the wilderness like a young man who dreams of the bosom of his lover; he could not sleep for their songs. He thought of the peaks, the tranquility of the peaks, the glaciers, the light of the glaciers, because he loved the godlike purity of the natural wilderness at home, the depth and expansiveness of the sky vaulting over that royal world.

It is, of course, Diljá that Steinn Elliði wants most to see, but his longing for the mountains, for the idea of home, for illusion of timelessness, all fuse together: "The enchantments of the land of memory are powerful," comments the narratorial voice. What does it mean to be an Icelander? How can an Icelander know about and reach the world if they stay at home? How can an Icelander survive away from home? Halldór Guðmundsson, one of Laxness's biographers, wrote that, "throughout his life he was pulled in two directions, to be an Icelander and a man of the world, and it was never easy." Perhaps what the theme of the journey lays bare most intriguingly in *The Great Weaver from Kashmir* is the dialectic between Iceland and the wider world: the relationship between Icelanders—their history, culture, beliefs, values, outlooks—and other nations, other countries. Iceland, an island on the periphery of maps and international consciousness, is the center of the world for Icelanders.

WILLIAM FAULKNER

AS I LAY DYING (1930)

The most famous of Faulkner's Yoknapatawpha County stories, a novel that established him as a giant of twentieth-century American fiction, through a portrait of the Deep South as powerful as a biblical tale.

As I Lay Dying is a short, dark, and compelling novel set in Yoknapatawpha County, Faulkner's "apocryphal county," a fictional rendering of his native Mississippi. Faulkner, steeped in the Deep South, conscripted his experience of the slave-state and its darkness to his purposes as a writer. His fiction became the deeply expressive part of his life's journey.

It was written in extremis, the place from which many great novels have come. Faulkner claimed he composed it from midnight to first light in six weeks while working at a coal-fired power plant to make ends meet, and moreover, that he did not change a word. This boast is as apocryphal as Yoknapatawpha County itself.

The title of the novel was inspired by the passage in *The Odyssey* where, with "As I lay dying . . . ," Agamemnon tells Odysseus about his murder. This classical allusion underpins the elegiac, valedictory spirit of the novel, but it remains a fundamentally American classic. No U.S. writer before Faulkner had ever immersed his readers so completely in the vernacular language and culture of a society that was—possibly still is—so foreign to American experience. He is also inspired by its religion. The language and sonority of the Bible is braided into many of the short chapters that drive his tale to its climax. "When they told me she was dying," says the preacher Whitfield, "all that night I wrestled with Satan, and I emerged victorious."

The death and burial of a southern matriarch, Addie Bundren, is told from some fifteen viewpoints, including that of the dying woman herself. The Bundren family's stream-of-consciousness narrative is intercut with the voices of the local doctor and preacher, together with neighbors and friends. From the first line, the reader is pitched into the Deep South:

> Jewel and I come up from the field, following the path in single file [. . .] anyone watching us from the cotton-house can see Jewel's frayed and broken straw hat a full head above my own.

Addie's dying wish is to be buried among her own people, "a hard day's

William Faulkner (1897–1962) was born and lived most of his days in northern Mississippi, which was the setting for most of his writing. He won the Nobel Prize for Literature in 1949.

As I Lay Dying helped found the Southern Renaissance—a revival of literature emerging from the American South throughout the 1920s and 1930s. Much of this literature —produced by the likes of Tennessee Williams, Zora Neale Hurston, and Margaret Mitchell, among others—was concerned with existentialism and the metaphysics of everyday life.

ISSETIBBEHA'S

TALLAHATCHIE RIVER

FISHING CAMP,
WHERE WASH JONES
KILLED SUTPEN, LATER
BOUGHT AND RESTORED BY MAJOR CASSIUS DE SPAIN

CHICKASAW

McCALLUM'S, WHERE YOUNG
BAYARD SARTORIS
WENT WHEN HIS
GRANDFATHER'S
HEART FAILED IN
THE CAR WRECK

SUTPEN'S
HUNDRED,
12 MI.

GRANT

JOHN SARTORIS' RAILROAD

To MEMPHIS JUNCTION

PINE

SARTORIS PLANTATION
& GIN. 4 MI.

CHURCH WHICH THOMAS
SUTPEN RODE FAST TO

WHERE OLD BAYARD SARTORIS DIED IN YOUNG BAYARD'S CAR

JOHN SARTORIS' STATUE & EFFIGY, WHERE HE CAN WATCH HIS
RAILROAD, AND
CEMETARY WHERE THEY
BURIED ADDIE BUNDREN AT
LAST.

'REVEREND HIGHTOWER'S
WHERE CHRISTMAS WAS
KILLED

HOLSTON HOUSE

BELLE MITCHELL'S

BENBOW'S

MISS JOANNA BURDEN'S, WHERE CHRISTMAS KILLED
MISS BURDEN, & WHERE LENA GROVE'S CHILD WAS
BORN

JAIL WHERE GOODWIN WAS LYNCHED

COURTHOUSE WHERE TEMPLE DRAKE TESTIFIED, & CONFEDER-
ATE MONUMENT WHICH BENJY HAD TO PASS ON HIS LEFT
SIDE.

COMPSON'S, WHERE THEY SOLD
THE PASTURE TO THE GOLF CLUB
SO QUENTIN COULD GO TO HARVARD

SAW MILL WHERE BYRON
BUNCH FIRST SAW LENA
GROVE

OLD BAYARD SARTORIS' BANK,
WHICH BYRON SNOPES ROBBED,
WHICH FLEM SNOPES LATER
BECAME PRESIDENT OF

MISS ROSA COLDFIELD'S

S

To MOTTSTOWN,
WHERE JASON COMPSON
LOST HIS NIECE'S TRAIL,
AND WHERE ANSE BUNDREN
AND HIS SONS HAD TO GO
IN ORDER TO REACH JEFFERSON

PINE

JEFFERSON,
YOKNAPATAWPHA CO.,
MISSISSIPPI

HILLS

SURATT'S

ARMSTID'S

AREA, 2400 SQ.MI.

POPULATION, WHITES, 6298
NEGROES 9313

TULL'S

WILLIAM FAULKNER,
SOLE OWNER & PROPRIETOR

VARNER'S STORE, WHERE
FLEM SNOPES GOT HIS
START

BRIDGE WHICH WASHED
AWAY SO ANSE BUNDREN
AND HIS SONS COULD NOT
CROSS IT WITH ADDIE'S
BODY

FRENCHMAN'S

BEND

YOKNAPATAWPHA RIVER

OLD FRENCHMAN PLACE,
WHICH FLEM SNOPES UNLOADED
ON HENRY ARMSTID AND SURATT, AND WHERE
POPEYE KILLED TOMMY

BUNDREN'S

"ride" away. The family is carting her coffin to Jefferson, Mississippi, for the funeral. Faulkner's narrative, energized by his command of movement, inspired by the drive and intensity of Homer, tracks the mourners' journey: "the wagon came up the road with the five of them in it." At times, Faulkner consciously mythicizes their travels: "On the horse he rode up to Armstid's and came back on the horse, leading Armstid's team. We hitched up and laid Cash on top of Addie."

The Bundren family's journey to these last rites becomes itself a rite-of-passage punctuated with fire (a burning barn) and water (a dangerous river crossing). While conscious, as a writer, of a timeless narrative key, Faulkner never lets us forget, as readers, that we are in the modern United States:

we have been passing the signs for some time now, the drug-stores, the clothing stores [. . .] the mile-boards diminishing . . .

The brilliance of a sometimes difficult novel lies in Faulkner's compulsive unfolding of Addie's bleak history, and her relationship with her beloved son, Jewel, the result of her affair with Rev. Whitfield, the minister. The reader also meets her family, a cast of weird southerners—Cash, Darl, Dewey Dell, and Vardaman Bundren. Faulkner's originality makes this novel seem incomparably more contemporary than Hemingway and Fitzgerald. For some, he is greater than both.

A section of Thomas Hart Benton's 1930 mural *America Today* depicting the riverboat way of life immortalized by Faulkner. The original ten canvases are held by the Metropolitan Museum of Art in New York.

Left: A map, hand-drawn by the author, of Jefferson, part of Yoknapatawpha County —the fictional setting for almost all of Faulkner's novels and at least fifty short stories.

ANTAL SZERB

Journey by Moonlight
(UTAS ÉS HOLDVILÁG) (1937)

A man has gone on his honeymoon to Italy. It is the 1930s, a time when fascism is exerting its ever more pernicious grip across Europe.

Antal Szerb (1901–1945) was a noted scholar of literature and a polyglot, who received his doctorate at twenty-three. He died in a Hungarian concentration camp in January 1945.

Journey by Moonlight did not find its way into English translation until 2001, when it became an instant and enduring classic, leading to the worldwide translation of many of his other works.

Szerb traveled through Italy in wrote the summer of 1936: he a series of short personal essays published that same year, which form the basis for the novel.

Mihály is in early middle age, working for his father's firm in Budapest. Life is that of the comfortable, moneyed professional with ample leisure time and now, marriage, to the virtuous Erszi. On honeymoon first in Venice, next in Ravenna and then Florence, Mihály feels, instead of blissful exhilaration, the weight of oppression—the demands of the family business, his father's control and now that of his bride. As they reach their next departure point, he inadvertently—or is it on purpose?—abandons his wife by boarding the wrong train, leaving Erszi traveling south without him to Rome while he heads in the opposite direction on a express to Siena.

Journey by Moonlight is an ambiguous, modernist masterpiece. Mihály's journey of flight and self-discovery reveals itself to be a form of seductive death wish. In Szerb's playful and capricious telling, his antihero recklessly pursues his past self in order to make sense of his future—and obliquely, that of a civilized world, which is fast disappearing into the maw of history.

Szerb's disaffected protagonist inhabits the same world of ardent personal nostalgia that Szerb evokes in personal essays he wrote after traveling through Italy in the summer of 1936: in Mihály this manifests itself in a nostalgic longing for the past.

The recesses of the mind, of memory and imagination, are powerfully at work; once he and Erszi meet up and reach Ravenna, with its "famous Byzantine mosaics," Mihály again feels the urgent need for solitude. Later, at an outdoor cafe, Mihály and Erszi are confronted by the demonic János Szepetneki, who roars up to them on a motorcycle demanding that Mihály accompanies him in a search for their old friend Erwin, who has become a monk and is somewhere in a monastery in "Tuscany, or Umbria." Refusing, Mihály is unsettled by this encounter, which will later have consequences for his soon-to-be-forsaken marriage.

Traveling almost as a fugitive, without money or possessions, moving from shabby room to shabby room, meeting strangers, the heights of ecstasy that he first experienced as a feeling of reprieve lead to deflation. As he persists with his crisscrossing of Italy, the ravishing external landscape changes to one of internal suffering:

He knew that the traveler had been journeying through that increasingly abandoned landscape, between tumultuous trees and stylized ruins, terrified by tempests and wolves, for an immense period of time, and that he, and no one else in all the world, would come abroad on such a night, so utterly alone.

Journey to the Mediterranean (Traveler and Moonlight) by Hungarian artist Gyula Batthyany.

This stark scene is a profound foreshadowing of Szerb's own tragic end; as the 1930s darkened into the 40s, his Jewish origins led various of his works to be banned and the loss of his job. Finally, after Germany invaded Hungary in 1944, Szerb was sent to a concentration camp in Balf. As *Journey by Moonlight* ends, all is not lost, however. Szerb's summing up of a generation's despair at the vanishing not only of their youth but also of Europe's recent enlightened past, is embodied in the physical and spiritually saturated Mihály, who finally accepts the need to conform, to face responsibility:

Mihály stared out of the window, trying to make out the contours of the Tuscan landscape by the light of the moon. He would have to remain with the living. [. . .] And while there is life, there is always the chance that something might happen . . .

JOHN STEINBECK

THE GRAPES OF WRATH (1939)

The Grapes of Wrath is John Steinbeck's signature work, a powerful novel about dispossessed families in the 1930s traveling along Route 66 from Oklahoma to California, hoping for a new start.

Steinbeck traveled on Route 66 from Chicago to California in the fall of 1937; he may have also driven on Route 66 with migrants when he researched the book in 1937–38.

When published in 1939, the book was an immediate success but also controversial and banned in some communities because of its salty language and depiction of Okies and selfish California farmers.

John Ford was so worried about filming the adaptation of this controversial book that when he sent a film crew to Oklahoma, he called the work "Route 66," not *The Grapes of Wrath*.

The journey undertaken by the Joad family in *The Grapes of Wrath* never ends. In this magisterial novel about the dispossessed of the 1930s, everyone is on the road looking for a new start, whether physical or emotional. "It's like a whole country is movin'," muses Jim Casy. As the novel opens, life in drought-stricken Oklahoma has become unsustainable:

> To the red country and part of the gray country of Oklahoma, the last rains came gently, and they did not cut the scarred earth. [. . .] The sun flared down on the growing corn day after day until a line of brown spread along the edge of each green bayonet.

Steinbeck invokes a national crisis as an environmental failure. Throughout the 1930s, sharecroppers and impoverished families abandoned farms in the southwestern United States as dust swirled and crops failed. Former prairie land had been exhausted by years of single-crop farming and extensive plowing followed by years of drought. And so, as Steinbeck tells it, "owner men" representing "monster" banks came to reclaim the tenants' tired land. The "dusted out" farmers took to the road, seeking jobs and new homes in the west, especially California—the visionary destination of Americans for decades—a promised land with "plenty work," sun, "little white houses in among the orange groves," and white-sand beaches.

In alternating chapters, Steinbeck's novel captures both this national saga of displacement and one family's plight, the Joads, as they travel from Oklahoma to California. The first Joad we encounter, Tom, is newly released from prison and heading home, hitchhiking on the book's first road. Beside that road he meets Casy, a fallen preacher restlessly seeking a new calling. The two shamble down a dusty byway to locate Tom's family, who, having been tractored out, are living on his uncle's place and are frantically packing a beat-up Hudson Super Six for the car trip west. Eleven Joads, Casy, and a dog are sardined into the vehicle. The overstuffed car, furniture piled on top, tarpaulin over the load, would become one of the signature images of 1930s migration, captured in Farm Security Administration (FSA) photographs

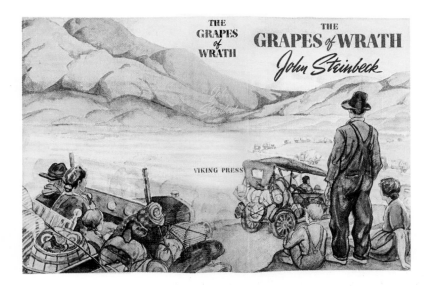

by Dorothea Lange and Russell Lee, who also documented this regional upheaval. More than 500,000 southwest migrants, it is estimated, drove to California during the decade.

Dust jacket for the first edition, published in 1939 by Viking Press, featuring the iconic illustration by Elmer Hader.

The Joads' road west, U.S. Highway 66, runs from Chicago to Santa Monica, a two-thousand-two-hundred-mile artery connecting half of America. Steinbeck called it "the Mother Road" and "the road of flight," an iconic, almost mythical route west for the fictional Joads and the historic dispossessed. (Route 66, also called the Will Rogers Highway, became legendary, the stuff of songs—"Get your Kicks on Route 66"—a 1960s television show, road races.) Over a third of this novel follows that tortuous journey west, detailing the dangers and comforts of the road. After the Joads leave the Oklahoma farm, highways and back roads are the novel's spine, the narrative a series of roadside stops.

Vehicles—cars and trucks and tractors—are vital signifiers. Tractors that reclaim the migrants' land are monsters put in motion by bankers, driven by a soulless "machine man." A "closed car," a "new big car," a Lincoln Zephyr, or a "big swift car" belong to powerful, detached owners—"shitheels," sniffs Mae the waitress. On used-car lots, migrants are swindled into buying broken-down cars. Salesmen screech: "Goin' to Califorina? Here's jus' what you need. Looks shot, but they's thousan's of miles in her." The Joads choose carefully, and their ancient Hudson Super Six sedan, top cut off and truck bed fitted on, becomes their "new hearth, the living center of the family." Vehicles register characters on scales of empathy. And for families in flight, "the highway became their home and movement their medium of expression," suggesting escape, dreams, tenacity, and despair.

For each character in decrepit cars or working jobs along Route 66, the road means something different. This novel hums with American voices. For Grampa, for Al Joad, and Connie—Rose of Sharon's husband—the destination is

A family in Pittsburg County, Oklahoma, are forced to leave their home during the Great Depression, June 1938. Photograph by the American documentary photographer, Dorothea Lange, most famous for her iconic portrait of a migrant mother and her children.

everything: a rosy future in California, perhaps night school, a car, a job in radio. For Tom, who is breaking parole when he leaves Oklahoma, it's a dangerous road, police to be avoided. Pa looks backward, to the Oklahoma land that defined him. And Ma Joad simply endures. A gas station attendant voices puzzlement: "Ever' person I talked to is on the move for a damn good reason. But what's the country comin to?" Others are openly hostile to the migrants: "There ain't room enough for you an' me," snarls a tire salesman, "for your kind an' my kind, for rich and poor together all in one country, for thieves and honest men. [. . .] Whyn't you go back where you come from?" California border patrols threaten the same, as was, in fact, exactly what the L.A. police attempted in 1936.

Both the novel and John Ford's film released a year later, are heavily dialogic, capturing voices of the dispossessed, the marginalized, and the powerful who exploit the powerless. "Stay with the detail," Steinbeck's wife Carol, also his editor and typist, kept reminding her husband as he wrote the book from May through October 1938, in a hundred "working days." Steinbeck concurred. He wanted the novel, like a long road trip, to move slowly, details of the way west precisely noted: the truck's steady whir and desert heat; hamburger stands and signage, and mileage between towns. The names of towns, Shamrock and Alanreed, Groom and Yarnell and Amarillo.

A large drop of sun lingered on the horizon and then dripped over and was gone, and the sky was brilliant over the spot where it had gone, and a torn cloud, like a bloody rag, hung over the spot of its going. And dusk crept over the sky from the eastern horizon, and darkness crept over the land from the east.

In addition to its historic heft, Steinbeck's novel has a biological dimension: migrations, after all, are endemic to many species. A few migrants don't survive the trip west. Uprooted from the land that defined them, Granma and Grampa Joad perish before they reach California. The family dog is killed by a powerful, indifferent vehicle. Noah Joad, the eldest son with a troubled mind, sinks into the Colorado River, refusing to continue the journey past Needles. And Rose of Sharon's husband, Connie, feels like he won't succeed in California and scuttles back to Oklahoma.

For Steinbeck, "survivability" is one measure of species adaptability. Those who adapt will make it, and those who can't, fall by the wayside. Chapter 3, the justly famous turtle chapter, suggests as much, when a turtle crossing a highway is missed by one car, struck by another, and yet spins, flops upright, and "jerked itself along," planting a seed as it crawls down the embankment—a gesture of hope, suggesting the book's emergent properties.

Another quality that humans share with other species is group behavior. Early in the trip, the Joads meet the Wilsons on the road and together the families sustain one another with food and material aid—there is nothing more essential on the road than fixing a broken car, and Tom, Al, and Casy replace the Wilsons' con-rod. The unit that the two families create suggests

the novel's central thrust, from "I" to the far more potent "we." When "I lost my land" morphs into "we lost our land," something powerful is born, perhaps even revolutionary, as Steinbeck suggests again and again. The novel's potent "we" created the impression, among some 1939 readers, that Steinbeck had written a dangerous, communist book.

What he had written was "history as it was happening," a story of dislocation and social crisis: homelessness in California, low wages, and too few jobs along roads that have no end, even after the Joads reach California. Steinbeck insisted that the novel had five levels and sensitive readers would plumb those depths. The novel's roots are journalistic. In the fall of 1936, the *S.F. News* asked Steinbeck to write articles about sub-standard housing for California field workers and migrants, and some of that material is incorporated into descriptions of roadside camps, Hoovervilles, and the government camp near Bakersfield, which existed at Arvin. Another layer is mythic: as in the biblical Exodus, the exiled seek the land of milk and honey. Yet another taps into American history: the title is from "The Battle Hymn of the Republic," a Civil War anthem, and Steinbeck insisted that all words to the song be printed in the endpapers. American conflicts, he suggests, continue. And the novel propels itself into the future, as Tom Joad exits the novel vowing to fight injustice wherever found. In 1995, Bruce Springsteen produced an album called *The Ghost of Tom Joad*, the title song about a contemporary homeless man, camping along a highway.

In the twenty-first century *The Grapes of Wrath* remains deeply relevant because the issues endure: environmental degradation, migration, job insecurity, homelessness, and the pain that the powerful inflict on the powerless. In this novel, "on the road" means out of work, hungry, and desperate.

Cars and trucks make their way across the desert toward Los Angeles. During the Dust Bowl exodus in the 1930s, 2.5 million people left the Plains states, with many seeking fortune in California.

ANNA SEGHERS

TRANSIT (1944)

Written soon after Seghers's arrival in Mexico, this is a dislocated story of displacement, influenced by her friend Walter Benjamin's suicide in Spain after failing to obtain the necessary travel visa to go on to the United States.

Anna Seghers (1900–1983) was born into an upper-middle-class Jewish family in Mainz, Germany. By 1929 Seghers had joined the Communist party and received the Kleist Prize for her first novel *The Revolt of the Fishermen*.

After moving to France in 1933, the 1940 Nazi occupation forced Seghers to flee to Marseilles where, with her Hungarian husband and two children plus other noted intellectuals she found safe passage to Mexico in March 1941.

After the war, Seghers returned to Germany, settling in East Berlin. Her novel *The Seventh Cross* (1939) was one of few books to depict Nazi concentration camps in the contemporary period.

They're saying that the *Montreal* went down between Dakar and Martinique. That she ran into a mine. The shipping company isn't revealing any information. It may just be a rumor. But when you compare it to the fate of other ships and their cargoes of refugees which were hounded all over the oceans and never allowed to dock, which were left to burn on the high seas and never permitted to drop anchor because their passengers' documents had expired a couple of days before, then what happened to the *Montreal* seems like a natural death of a ship in wartime.

One of the great fictional accounts to emerge from World War II, Anna Seghers's beautiful, caustically rendered autobiographical novel is simultaneously a political thriller, a piece of existential art, and a work that recounts the daily minutiae of lives in flight and in exile, capturing not only the adrenaline rush of fear, but also the deadly boredom of bureaucracy and endlessly waiting for a visa with which to travel, the alternative being staying put and certain death.

The plot is simple—refugees attempting to flee Europe for safer havens as the German army advances. In this case the country is France, and the story begins just before the war in 1937. A young unnamed man, like Seghers a Communist, and therefore an enemy of the Nazi regime, has managed to escape a concentration camp in Germany, scaling a wall and swimming across the Rhine by night: France was at this time a natural destination for exiled Germans. He and his fellow escapee eventually join scores of refugees heading for Paris:

Like most people in those days we had the simplistic goal of getting across the Loire. We avoided the main road, walking instead across the fields, passing through deserted villages where the unmilked cows were bellowing, we would search for something to sink our teeth into, but everything had been consumed, from the berries on the gooseberry bushes to the grain in the barn.

It seemed as bare and white as an African city. At last
I felt calm: it became the same calm I felt when I like
something very much . . . I walked with the crowds,
buffeted by a wind that knew first sunshine, then
showers over us in rapid succession.

Once in Paris he meets a German writer, Paul, who asks him to deliver
some documents to a man named Weidel. Arriving at the hotel where
Weidel is staying, the narrator finds he has committed suicide: as well as
his documents which will enable a visa to Mexico (Seghers's own eventual
destination), Weidel's belongings include the manuscript of an incomplete
novel. Traveling to Marseilles, where he will find, meet, and fall in love with
Weidel's wife, the narrator assumes another identity, that of a man called
Seidler—although to the authorities he is officially Weidel, a Kafkaesque
mutation of identities and anonymity—but Marie, Weidel's wife, is unaware
her husband is dead and continues to search for him ceaselessly.

The narrator's first sighting of Marseilles is unforgettable. The extreme
southwestern port had become, since the fall of France in June 1940, the final
place of departure for those with the elusive transit visa with which so much
of the novel is preoccupied.

The changeable Marseilles weather—at one point Seghers has the Mistral
symbolically blow out the candle on a church altar—reflects the situation of its
weary travelers: by turns hopeful and despairing, frenzied or paralyzed by ennui.
The narrator, passing through these fractured lives, has, with his adoption of
otherness through assumed names, more options than one. His choice to stay
and live out another's identity, another version of life, leaves him in constant
apprehension, "a scrap of shadow" in a suffering world in which the "fabled
cities of other continents" are just that—fabular.

PAUL BOWLES

THE SHELTERING SKY (1949)

Bowles's novel follows the journey of three aimless travelers whose relationships are tested as they wander across the remote North African desert.

For more than fifty years, writer and composer Paul Bowles lived outside of the United States: in his autobiography *Without Stopping*, published in 1972, he wrote, "I had always been vaguely certain that sometime during my life I should come into a magic place which in disclosing its secrets would give me wisdom and ecstasy—perhaps even death."

In many ways, the first novel that he wrote, *The Sheltering Sky*, expounds upon this promise of finding a "magic place," and the failure of travel to give meaning to life. The narrative follows three Americans, a husband and wife, Port and Kit, and their friend Tunner, as they travel in the Algerian Sahara, moving to increasingly remote areas and difficult living circumstances. Having traveled together for twelve years, Port and Kit seem to have come to an impasse in their marriage, and Tunner seems to desire to profit from this rift by seducing Kit. As the three move from town to town, without any real direction or desire, Port looks to get rid of Tunner to have Kit to himself in the hopes that this will patch up their relationship. But once they are on their own, Port quickly takes ill and eventually dies from typhoid. Kit is left, immeasurably bereaved and alone, wandering in the desert.

Though much of the plot is ostensibly about the breakdown of the relationship between husband and wife, the novel is a finely wrought exploration of travel and the identity of the traveler. Early in the novel, we read Port's manifesto of sorts:

> He really did not think of himself as a tourist; he was a traveler. The difference is partly of time, he would explain. Whereas the tourist generally hurries back home at the end of a few weeks or months, the traveler, belonging no more to one place than the next, moves slowly, over periods of years, from one part of the earth to another. Indeed, he would have found it difficult to tell, among the many places he lived, precisely where it was he had felt most at home.

Paul Bowles lived for most of his life in Tangier, Morocco, but traveled extensively around the world, and even bought an island of his own, Taprobane in Sri Lanka, where he and his wife, the writer Jane Bowles, would spend their summers.

The Sheltering Sky spent ten weeks on the *New York Times* best-seller list in 1950, and sold more than 200,000 paperbacks in 1951.

Port wants to make a clear distinction between himself as a traveler and those less serious tourists. He has, very consciously it seems, chosen to dedicate himself to a kind of travel without an end point, always moving on, without thinking about where he has come from, or looking back. The traveler is also a seeker, looking for authentic experiences, and throughout the novel Port goes off on his own, walking around the towns they are staying in but seemingly never quite satisfied with what he finds.

But this also poses another question: if one is always traveling, then where exactly is home? And what drives this need to travel in this way? Bowles does not answer either of these questions, though it seems for both writer and his character, a singular home does not exist. The three Americans restlessly move from one town to another, it seems, for the sake of traveling itself, without any real enjoyment or engaging with the places they come to. In this way, Bowles's book asks many questions about the journey away from somewhere, so that, rather than a novel about the process of travel, it is really about the fact that ceaseless travel can become a way of avoiding the real problems and complexities of life.

Crossing the Sahara in search of a "magic place"—still taken from the 1990 movie version, directed by Bernardo Bertolucci and starring Debra Winger and John Malkovich.

VILHELM MOBERG
THE EMIGRANTS (1949)

In the late nineteenth and early twentieth century, almost a quarter of Sweden's population left their homes to move abroad, with many choosing to settle in North America. Moberg's novel sees a small group of protagonists, fleeing poverty, head for pastures new in Minnesota.

This is the story of a group of people who in 1850 left their homes in Ljuder Parish in the province of Småland, Sweden, and emigrated to North America. They were people of the soil and they came of a stock which for thousands of years had tilled the ground they were now leaving.

With those words, the Swedish author Vilhelm Moberg (1898–1973) began *The Emigrants*, the first of his four epic novels about Swedish settlement in Minnesota. Suffering from famine, poor schooling, and primitive transport, his fictional emigrants embarked on a journey that freed them from Old World poverty but presented lingering questions about self-fulfillment in their new land.

Writing his novels proved as arduous for Moberg, a self-described stay-at-home Swede, as emigration was for his fictional characters. In Sweden the four volumes are described as The Emigrant Novel, a gargantuan work of nearly 1,400 pages. In English the titles are: *The Emigrants* (1951); *Unto a Good Land* (1954); *The Settlers* (1961); and *The Last Letter Home* (1961). They depict humble Swedes stricken by natural disasters, who also bow to religious persecution, class discrimination, and frequent alcoholism.

The fates of individual characters dramatize collective social problems. Karl Oskar Nilsson is an embattled farmer in Småland, called the Kingdom of Stones. He removes boulders from his farmland single-handedly. By dint of such hard work, he and his wife Kristina have maintained family life. Only when one daughter dies and lightning strikes his barn does Karl Oskar curse God and decide to emigrate. Though ever faithful to Sweden and the Almighty, Kristina obediently follows Karl Oskar. Robert, Karl Oskar's younger brother and an inveterate dreamer, is ill-fit for farm labor, so he too defects from Sweden, as does Ulrika, the village prostitute providing sexual services to the State Church clergy, who denounce her as a whore. Likewise, Per Danjel, a Free Church pastor, opts for America when he learns of religious freedom there.

As the group leaves Sweden, Karl Oskar predicts his sons one day will thank him for taking them to America. Long days by oxcart to Göteborg

Between 1825 and 1930, 1.2 million Swedes emigrated to escape poverty at home. (Approximately 4 million was the country's largest population at any time during this period.) Vilhelm Moberg termed this exodus the most significant happening in Swedish history.

As a Social Democrat and a critic of Sweden for its monarchy, Moberg was often out of favor with the political and literary establishments in Sweden, which he felt cost him a chance at a Nobel Prize for literature. He was much beloved by the general reading public and remained a prolific writer for fifty-five years. In illness and exhaustion he drowned himself in 1973.

are followed by ten weeks on the Atlantic, when many become sick and others die. The travelers pass through America's Great Lakes. At last, the newcomers go by riverboat up the Mississippi to the budding settlements of the Minnesota Territory, which true to actual history, has few Europeans in 1850 and only a handful of Swedes. Iced-in each winter by frozen waterways, Minnesota is still eight years from statehood when Karl Oskar's group arrives. Ahead is free land in Chisago County, whose rolling hills remind them of southern Sweden. Karl Oskar and Kristina claim a homestead. Their family grows. Per Danjel meets like-minded believers. Ulrika gains respectability and ironically marries a pastor. Chisago County becomes quintessential Swedish America.

Here the story might end, but as one Swedish critic has commented, the serpents soon slither into paradise. Robert and others succumb to wanderlust or disappear seeking gold mines out West. Some fail at farming or give in to drink. Still in her thirties, Kristina is unable to adapt. Clinging to dreams of long-lost Småland, she dies after childbirth. Once more, Karl Oskar curses God, blaming Him for taking Kristina's life. Karl Oskar spends his last years in melancholy, tracing on a map of Ljuder Parish places where they courted when young. Kristina and his youthful spirit are equally irretrievable. Their sons prosper in America, but at a price. Fully Americanized, they speak no Swedish and know of Sweden only as their homesick mother's fairy-tale land. To the boys, now grown, their father is a quaint American, now known as Charles O. Nelson, whom they never thank. Slow to fathom irony, Karl Oskar is increasingly isolated in the America he himself chose. Having twice denied God, abandoned his homeland, and lost Kristina, he clings to his Minnesota farm until he dies in 1890.

Unlike Karl Oskar, Vilhelm Moberg understood life's ironic turns acutely. Himself a native Smålander, he spent 1948 to 1965 crisscrossing America to prepare materials for The Emigrant Novel and dreaming of literary success there. He praised post–World War II America as the world's greatest bastion of freedom and progressive thought. Only the Joseph McCarthy political witch hunts of the 1950s, the arrest of Charlie Chaplin for Leftist sympathies, and the Vietnam War gave the author doubts about his romance with America, and he returned to Sweden. Moberg wrote later that he, like his aging persona Karl Oskar, was too like an unyielding block of ancient Swedish granite to adapt to America's size and diversity.

Asked in an informal survey during the 1990s to choose The Most Important Swedish Literary work of the Twentieth Century, Sweden's general reading public chose The Emigrant Novel, a tribute to Moberg's understanding of Swedish sensibilities and universal patterns in human experience.

… And beyond their eyes' reach their thoughts struggled further, their thoughts ventured on roads never traveled, down to a sea never seen, and across the waters of the ocean.

ALEJO CARPENTIER

The Lost Steps
(LOS PASOS PERDIDOS) (1953)

In the middle of the twentieth century, Cuban author Alejo Carpentier set out to discover if it was still possible to explore uncharted territory in the forests of South America; his book The Lost Steps *reveals what he found out.*

Alejo Carpentier lied about his place of birth his entire life. He was born in Lausanne, Switzerland, but always claimed to have been born in Havana. A Cuban birth gave him greater credibility in writing about Latin America and the Caribbean and was useful in securing him government positions.

Santa Elena de Uairén, upon which Carpentier based the remote Venezuelan outpost featured in *The Lost Steps*, was founded in 1927 by a Spanish gold prospector named Lucás Fernández Peña; by 1935 there were four diamond mines in the vicinity.

The South American jungle has long held the appeal of the unknown for travelers: for centuries, Spanish conquistadors were sure the lost kingdom of gold known as El Dorado lay hidden in its depths. By the end of World War II, however, the dense tropical forests of South America were on the cusp of losing their mystique. Venezuela's oil boom was fueling interest in air travel and opening up parts of the forest that had previously been almost unknown to outsiders.

The Cuban writer Alejo Carpentier, who was working in publicity in the glittering, oil-rich city of Caracas, wanted to catch a glimpse of Venezuela's wilderness while it still existed. In 1947, he traveled to the remote outpost of Santa Elena de Uairén near the Venezuelan border with Brazil and Guyana. The question he seemed to be asking himself was "In this modern era, is it still possible to have an adventure in the wilderness?" The book he published about the experience in 1953 became *The Lost Steps*.

The unnamed protagonist of *The Lost Steps* is a failed composer and musicologist who is fed up with his hectic yet soulless life in a thinly veiled New York City. On a lark, he undertakes a journey to the South American hinterlands at the behest of a North American museum to locate rare native Amerindian musical instruments. He travels by plane, bus, and eventually canoe through Venezuela's great plains and sinuous rivers. Along the way, he imagines he is traveling back through time as he travels into the dense forest at the center of the continent. He plays at being a conquistador, pretending he and his companions are seeking El Dorado, also known as Manoa:

> We all felt the impulse to rise, set out, and arrive before the dawn at the gateway of enchantment. [. . .] Once more the towers of Manoa arose. The possibility that they might exist came alive anew, inasmuch as the myth persisted in the imagination of all those who lived in the vicinity of the jungle—that is to say, of the Unknown.

While Carpentier never did find a kingdom of gold, he did reach places in a matter of hours by plane that had previously taken weeks or even months to reach by boat or on foot.

In *The Lost Steps*, the protagonist eventually finds the musical instruments, but decides to stay in the hinterlands forever, enthralled by the simple pleasures of life in a recently established settlement called Santa Mónica de los Venados. Carpentier based his description of this town on Santa Elena de Uairén, where, he recorded in his diary, humans and their technology were so rare that it was possible to hunt deer on the plains from a moving car. From Carpentier's vantage point, in this wilderness utopia it was still possible to start a new civilization.

Yet what makes *The Lost Steps* a compelling novel is not its repetition of commonplaces about a forest Eden, but rather the protagonist's realization that his jungle paradise is a chimera of his own fabrication. Carpentier's diary records his passage through oil fields and diamond mines en route to the forest. In fact, the town of Santa Elena de Uairén was a site of extensive diamond mining; plane service to Caracas operated three days a week. Similarly, in *The Lost Steps* the mirage of a pristine wilderness community soon evaporates: a large diamond is found near Santa Mónica de los Venados, a harbinger of what is to come. Carpentier's protagonist finds himself whisked back to his quotidian reality of the job, the bills, and even the wife he left behind. He is unable to trace his "lost steps" back to the wilderness idyll. The virgin territory Carpentier and his protagonist imagined was no longer accessible, except in literature. In the contemporary era, the end of *The Lost Steps* implies, the best adventures may lie on the page, rather than in the landscape.

The Lost Steps would be translated into more than twenty languages after its first edition in 1953. *From Left to Right Above:* 1979 Spanish edition, 1979 English edition, and 1976 French edition.

3 POSTMODERN MOVEMENTS

1954-1999

The era of the car brought new horizons closer to home and spawned a whole new infrastructure of paved highways, gas stations, and motels.

Reflection of a Woman Behind the Wheel. . . by documentary photographer Homer Sykes, Los Angeles, 1969.

VLADIMIR NABOKOV

LOLITA (1955)

Much of Vladimir Nabokov's first American novel is an extended road trip back and forth across the United States of his newly adopted homeland —while in the company of its criminally insane narrator and captive stepdaughter: the eponymous Lolita.

Vladimir Nabokov reportedly received the "first little throb of Lolita" in Paris, 1939, having read a news story about an ape who, "after months of coaching by a scientist, produced the first drawing ever charcoaled by an animal: the sketch showed the bars of the poor creature's cage."

After emigrating to America in 1940, Nabokov (a keen lepidopterist) undertook extensive road trips in search of rare butterflies. Much of *Lolita* was written during these road trips, often while actually in the car, with wife Véra driving.

The narrator of Vladimir Nabokov's most notorious novel is one Humbert Humbert: European émigré, would-be sophisticate, arch narcissist, and, most notedly, an utterly deranged monomaniac driven by an erotic obsession with a certain type of young girl aged between nine and fourteen years of age (or, "nymphets," to use Humbert's own rarefied neologism).

Recuperating from the most recent of his mental breakdowns, Humbert moves to the sleepy New England town of Ramsdale where he lodges with the lonely widow Charlotte Haze and her precious twelve-year-old daughter, Dolores (a.k.a. Lolita). Humbert promptly marries Charlotte with the plan of murdering the mother to gain sole access to the daughter—with whom he has fallen hopelessly in love. But when Charlotte uncovers her husband's diary and learns of his duplicitous nature she is so grief-stricken that she is killed in a traffic accident (panic, collision), leaving Humbert free to embark upon the first of two exhaustive road trips across North America with his captive young ward. Each of these road trips has its own distinct texture, and each chronicles the (further) decline of one of literature's most monstrous creations.

A road trip forces its participants into a state of close proximity—and Nabokov's analogous use of the road trip to examine his characters' abusive relationship is a stroke of creative genius. For not only is Humbert and Lolita's state one of unnatural (and, indeed, illegal) intimacy, but having crossed the line from thought to deed means there is no going back for Humbert. To stop traveling would be to risk discovery and shatter the notion the devious Humbert has instilled in Lolita's young mind that she bears a degree of culpability for their situation. It is also possible that by "putting the geography of the United States into motion" Humbert is subconsciously attempting to outrun time itself. After all, Lolita's desirability to Humbert is strictly finite.

Like his loquacious narrator, Nabokov was also an émigré from the Old World to the New. This shared sense of strangeness saturates the novel. It is a strangeness that is further heightened by Nabokov's employment of a mentally unbalanced, morally bankrupt narrator who is cruising far beyond the pale of civilized society's accepted norms and values. Thus an "Uncanny America" (of real and fictional locales) is vividly evoked via a kind of shorthand.

Behind the slick glibness of Humbert's patter, behind every Sunset Motel and U-Beam Cottage, lies another night of sexual abuse for Lolita. That the sex act itself is never graphically described by Nabokov has the curious effect of making the novel an even more uncomfortable read. Instead, Nabokov eroticizes Humbert's language to such an extent that the abuse becomes semi-abstract; something that is implied through metaphor and allusion; so that even a simple travelogue is perverted by Humbert's seemingly subliminal choice of verb, adverb, and adjective. Their route began with "wiggles and whorls," "meandered south," then "dipped deep" into Dixieland. They "zigzagged through corn belts and cotton belts" and "crossed and recrossed the Rockies," an exploration that finally ends when they "return to the fold of the East."

After a year on the road Humbert starts to grow fearful that their "guilty locomotion" may be "instrumental in vitiating our powers of impersonation." But, after months of strained attempts at "normal" cohabitation in the town of Beardsley, Humbert's paranoia eventually gets the better of him and once again the pair take to the road.

This time they head west, with Humbert nursing the secret hope to "spin on to California, to the Mexican border, to mythical bays, saguaro deserts, fata morganas" in the reasoning that a "change of environment is the traditional fallacy upon which doomed loves, and lungs, rely." Because if Humbert's first road trip was a giddy fever-dream of forbidden fruit and requited lust, his second is an unending nightmare of paranoia and dankest dread. Not only is time against him, but Humbert's paranoia has become petrified in the *idée fixe* that they are being pursued. And as our unreliable narrator becomes more unreliable by the mile, Nabokov instills a delicious ambiguity as to whether this pursuer actually exists or is but a figment of Humbert's deranged mind. And so the novel careens drunkenly on to its inevitable denouement.

But for all of Lolita's wicked humor and dazzling displays of linguistic virtuosity, there are a few crucial moments when Nabokov allows Humbert's mask of solipsism to slip—and it is in these moments that the chuckling reader is pulled up short and afforded a stark and sobering glimpse into the heart of darkness that lies behind it:

> We had been everywhere. We had really seen nothing. And I catch myself thinking today that our long journey had only defiled with a sinuous trail of slime the lovely, trustful, dreamy, enormous country that by then, in retrospect, was no more to us than a collection of dog-eared maps, ruined tour books, old tires, and her sobs in the night—every night, every night— the moment I feigned sleep.

"The Friendly Place

U.S. HIGHWAYS 60 and 70 . . . East Cit

op"
its . . . BLYTHE, CALIFORNIA

"Cheap room to rent, $1.25 a night"—the arrival of motels, the first originally called the Milestone Mo-tel, catered for a new generation of travelers.

JACK KEROUAC

ON THE ROAD (1957)

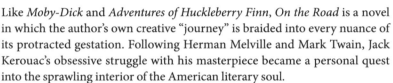

The book that established Kerouac, overnight, as the voice of the 1950s American beat generation,

Kerouac was born and raised as Jean-Louis Lebris de Kerouac and didn't speak English until he was six years old.

The original typescript of *On the Road* was sold to the owner of the Indianapolis Colts football team in 2001 for $2.2 million.

On the Road was recognized as an all-American classic from the moment of publication. It has never been out of print, and expresses for every generation a sublime version of the American Dream.

Like *Moby-Dick* and *Adventures of Huckleberry Finn*, *On the Road* is a novel in which the author's own creative "journey" is braided into every nuance of its protracted gestation. Following Herman Melville and Mark Twain, Jack Kerouac's obsessive struggle with his masterpiece became a personal quest into the sprawling interior of the American literary soul.

On the Road is a lyrical evocation of childhood, adolescence, and the "excelsior" spirit of the eternal pioneer that becomes a delirious eulogy to its author's coming of age. Steeped in the aspirations of the New World, it also speaks to readers and writers alike with a feverish excitement for all the frontiers of the human mind and spirit. It is also an immigrant novel whose hero Salvatore "Sal" Paradise has ethnic roots. Sal's narrative opens during the depths of winter in New York City, 1947, with young Paradise "feeling that everything was dead." An Italian American, and would-be writer, Sal is hanging out near Columbia University with some fellow "beats," restless and disaffected bohemians, who include Carlo Marx (a.k.a. the poet Allen Ginsberg) and Dean Moriarty (a.k.a. Neal Cassady, the original beat).

When Jack Kerouac began hammering out his first draft, he was inspired "to express the inexpressible," an ambition that announced itself in a book that became an urtext for the James Dean decade. A great journey mobilizes its readers' imaginations. Kerouac's repeated use of "the promised land" recalls the hopes of America's pioneers as well as of the postwar generation that longed to push the horrors of World War II into the past.

On the Road pulsates to the rhythms of 1950s America: jazz, sex, drugs, and the desperate hunger of young men and women for experiences that are passionate, exuberant, and alive to the potential of the present moment.

Kerouac was not immune to the charms of the American Dream. The "road" is always democratic, but *On the Road* is also a timeless national romance, a new version of Huck Finn's longing to "light out for the territory." Indeed, although acclaimed as a prophet of 1960s counterculture, Kerouac's own idea of himself and his work was to reclaim the gritty individualism of the pioneer past.

In these pages, every character feels the call of the wild, aches to hit the

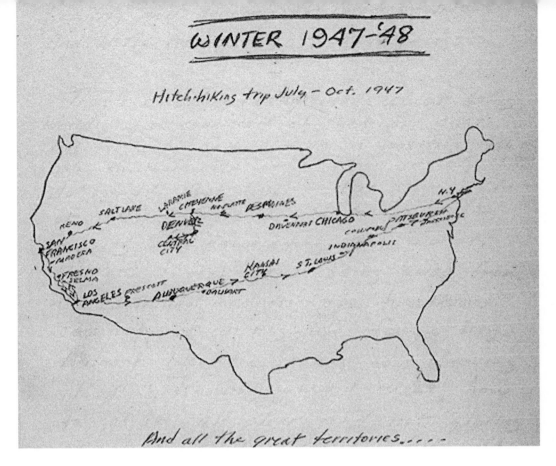

WINTER 1947-'48

Hitch-hiking trip July – Oct. 1947

And all the great territories.....

Jack Kerouac's hand-drawn map of the trip to "all the great territories."

road and head out West. This is what *On the Road* is all about: the quest for ultimate fulfillment before the sun goes down. Kerouac called this magic moment "It," and devoted his life to the pursuit of ecstatic inspiration. For Kerouac, Ginsberg, and the Beats, it's the journey, not the arrival, that matters. Sal Paradise will chase girls, drink late into the night, and walk on the wild side, but this mystical "It" will always elude him. The reader follows him (and the charismatic Dean Moriarty) as poignant reminders of lost youth, those sublime years when everyone feels immortal.

The first of the five journeys to the far West, and finally Mexico, that fuel the narrative of *On the Road* was forged in a language that insists on the veracity of Kerouac's version, incredible as that sometimes might seem: "this was really the way that my whole road experience began, and the things that were to come are too fantastic not to tell." Once Sal is hitchhiking toward "the so-longed-for West," he's meeting every kind of postwar pioneer:

> The greatest ride in my life was about to come up, a truck, with a flatboard at the back, with about six or seven boys sprawled out on it, and the drivers, two young blond farmers from Minnesota, were picking up every single soul they found on that road . . .

But it's Dean Moriarty, "the Holy Goof," to whom Sal's in thrall, a character with "the tremendous energy of a new kind of American saint." It is Moriarty, above all, who animates the greatest pages of *On the Road*: "He was BEAT— the root, the soul of Beatific." Once the boys have met up with Carlo Marx, the book becomes literary history on a stick. When this first trip is over, and Sal is back in New York, another year passes before he sets off to find Moriarty, ending up in Frisco, in search of "the same old thing [. . .]—gurls, gurls, gurls." They head to Mexico, the ultimate trip for postwar American youth, hunting booze, "gurls," and drugs. Eventually, the road comes to an end in Newark. To Sal, facing "the forlorn rags of growing old," Moriarty has become "the father we never found."

The inner journey of *On the Road* is to do with its torturous composition. Few manuscripts of any classic had such a strange history. Kerouac began to write as a merchant sailor during World War II. His first fiction, *The Town and the City*, was published in 1950, got poor reviews, but introduced him to Neal Cassady. Their meeting in Harlem early in 1947 became the opening of Kerouac's second book.

At this stage in its long gestation, *On the Road* (the title hardly ever varied) was planned as a quest like Bunyan's *The Pilgrim's Progress*. In June 1949, Kerouac headed out to San Francisco to join Cassady, an excursion that became Part Three of his work in progress. In 1950, Cassady took him to Mexico (Part Four). Meanwhile, Kerouac slogged away at *On the Road*, developing friendships with William Burroughs and Allen Ginsberg, both of whom had a decisive influence on the final text. As part of his journey, Kerouac invented a nonstop typing style, "kick-writing," to achieve the headlong literary momentum he wanted. It was here, famously, that he taped together twelve-foot-long pieces of drawing paper, trimmed them to fit and fed them into his typewriter as a continuous roll. In this pre-digital era, it was essential to his nonstop method not to have to pause to insert new paper. This, declared Kerouac, was the start of "a new trend in American literature." Sweating profusely, fueled with pea soup and Benzedrine, he embarked on a typing marathon—three weeks in April 1951—in which the essential draft (nearly ninety thousand words) of *On the Road* was completed.

After that spring frenzy, Kerouac continued to retype the original manuscript roll. In 1956, after many vicissitudes, Kerouac rewrote his text (again) for publication in September 1957. His publishers, dealing with a writer trapped within an obsession, never sent him any galley proofs for fear of further revisions.

On publication, Kerouac awoke to find himself famous. *The New York Times* declared that the book's publication "a historic occasion in so far as the exposure of an authentic work of art is of any great moment in an age in which the attention is fragmented and the sensibilities are blunted by the superlatives of fashion." The rest is history.

DOWN TOWN CARWASH 9
ON THE ROAD
Liquor
Girls
Fun
BUS STOP
LOANS
len deighton
JACK KEROUAC

PATRICK WHITE

VOSS (1957)

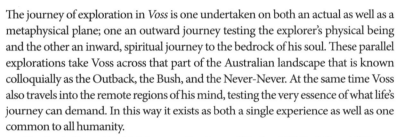

Based on the real-life expedition of Prussian explorer Ludwig Leichhardt, White's titular protagonist delves deep into the harsh landscape of the Australian interior in this psychologically provoking novel.

Although born in London, Patrick White's parents were Australian, and the family emigrated back to the continent when White was six months old. He lived in Sydney for most of his life.

Ludwig Leichhardt, the real-life inspiration for Voss, disappeared without a trace in the Australian Outback in 1848.

Voss has been translated into twenty-three languages and was also adapted into an opera of the same name, which premiered in 1986 and was written by Richard Meale, with the libretto by David Malouf.

The journey of exploration in *Voss* is one undertaken on both an actual as well as a metaphysical plane; one an outward journey testing the explorer's physical being and the other an inward, spiritual journey to the bedrock of his soul. These parallel explorations take Voss across that part of the Australian landscape that is known colloquially as the Outback, the Bush, and the Never-Never. At the same time Voss also travels into the remote regions of his mind, testing the very essence of what life's journey can demand. In this way it exists as both a single experience as well as one common to all humanity.

To Australians, the highly evocative terms "Outback," "Bush," and "Never-Never" are such a towering presence in their imaginations that they are rendered with capitals. And beyond the mere civilized fringe of this island continent, the overwhelming spread of landscape is as arid and hostile to settlement as these metaphors might suggest. Even so, to the first white settlers this alien landscape exerted a magnetic allure, both fearful and fascinating. It challenged them to conquer its vast spaces and to name its furthest reaches as if this act alone could confer authority and dominion.

Patrick White enshrined this dichotomy in his novel *Voss*, which first appeared in 1957 and received wide international acclaim. When White was awarded the Nobel Prize for Literature in 1973, the citation specifically celebrated his depiction of the unique Australian landscape by an "epic and psychological narrative art which … introduced a new continent into literature."

In its home country, however, White's dislocated syntax (which one critic called "over-literary arabesque"), alienated many readers. Yet White was forging a new style in an attempt to convey the metaphysical; in his own words striving "to create completely fresh forms out of the rocks and sticks of words." The writer himself therefore became an explorer, wrestling with new stylistic territory as, seemingly, out of the very landscape itself, he struggled to give it a voice. Others found the book's unapologetic German mysticism, which depicts a central character consumed by Nietzschean pretensions and Hitlerian megalomania, impenetrable. And thus, with distinct echoes also of Melville's Captain Ahab, Voss sets off with heaven-storming arrogance to conquer the landscape by sheer will.

> I am compelled into this country. [...] I will cross the continent from one end to the other. I have every intention to know it with my heart.

His retort, when asked if he had studied a map, is that he will "first make it." In his godlike stance Voss bestows animus upon this landscape, considering it his only worthy opponent.

By White's own admission the novel was conceived during the London Blitz and anchored in his wartime experiences in the Western Desert. Its specific inspiration was as much the Australian landscape as the Prussian explorer Ludwig Leichhardt (1813–1848) who perished while attempting to cross the continent from east to west. In White's retelling, the inner landscape of Voss becomes manifest in the outer landscape he traverses: alien, prickly, unforgiving, and inexplicable. By "winding deeper into himself, into blacker thickets of thorns" Voss internalizes the landscape, which assumes mythic, even gothic dimensions. The Outback becomes a protagonist itself as Voss travels to the very horizon of his known self and into an equally "disturbing country."

While White's desert metaphors have biblical overtones they also resonate with the archetypal myth of Odysseus's wanderings. Ultimately, however, the land becomes a place of dispossession rather than one that man can possess. Voss's arrogance cannot conquer the landscape.

When the expedition sets out, Leichhardt's men begin an apotheosis into mythical status. Initially, the explorers set out from a fertile coastal landscape, which devolves into "the approaches to hell" where they are "writing their own legend." The first setting epitomizes the superficial and the finite, the other the mystical and the infinite and critics responded to this vision of landscape. Some discerned it as Wordsworthian or as individual in character as Thomas Hardy's Wessex.

Cover art for the 1957 first edition designed by Sidney Nolan—one of Australia's most internationally celebrated artists and Patrick White's lifelong friend and collaborator.

Ultimately, any wisdom wrung from Voss's wrestling with landscape is vouchsafed to Laura: "Knowledge was never a matter of geography . . . it overflows all maps that exist [and] . . . only comes of death by torture in the country of the mind." The explorer becomes a metaphor for all men whose lives are an unexplored desert and where suffering and humility are the preconditions of his spiritual quest.

BORIS PASTERNAK

DOCTOR ZHIVAGO (1957)

During World War I, a gifted doctor from Moscow falls for a nurse searching for her soldier husband. Over the years, as he travels halfway across Russia and back, it becomes a love that transfigures and destroys him.

Boris Pasternak (1890–1960), born in Moscow, was destined to be a composer but turned to poetry instead. His work was so popular that it was learned by heart by several generations.

When he fell out of political favor, the manuscript of *Doctor Zhivago*, his only novel, was smuggled to Italy, where it was published in 1957.

It won him the Nobel Prize in Literature, but because of the outcry he refused the honor. When the Russian public demanded his deportation, he told the president that "leaving the motherland will equal death for me."

Doctor Zhivago is filled with journeys, as its characters cross Russia in pursuit of ideological or personal dreams, or in search of safety. The pivotal voyage is a three-day train ride through snow in carriages so basic that Tonya Zhivago thinks it "no better than a stable on wheels." For the young doctor, Yuri Zhivago, who is fleeing poverty-stricken revolutionary Moscow with Tonya and their son, the many discomforts are a price worth paying for reaching Tonya's former family estate in Varykino, Siberia. Even though it is now a collective, they hope to find food and shelter there, and avoid the scrutiny of the capital's paranoiac revolutionaries.

These are desperate times: following the revolution of 1905, the horrors of World War I, and with the Russian Revolution of 1917 gathering pace. Zhivago is broadly in sympathy with the Bolsheviks, but he reserves his deepest passion for poetry and for Lara Antipova. An inscrutable but gentle nurse in the front-line hospital where he was a medical officer during the war, she had seemed impervious to "his honest endeavor not to love her." Only when they accidentally meet again, after he reaches Varykino, do they give in to their feelings.

As war and revolution rage—"shell-bursts like fiery umbrellas opening over the fields"—Pasternak describes a love story like few others. Scrupulous in evoking emotional turmoil and angst with a realistic lack of glamour, Pasternak is unsparing—yet understanding—of all his characters, even the most venal or cruel. Zhivago is essentially a good man and, while he loves his wife, he and Lara have an intellectual and spiritual connection that cannot be denied. Lara, too, loves her absent spouse Pasha. She had gone to the battle front in search of him, when he was with the Russian army, and heard he was presumed dead in action. Eventually, however, he is discovered to be alive, and leading a rebel group. His reckless military actions are his way of winning his wife's love.

Wretched at betraying Tonya, and resolving to end his affair, Zhivago is captured by the Partisans. By the time he is released, Tonya and her family have been deported, probably to Paris, and Lara is in desperate danger, because her husband is now on the authorities' hit list. Zhivago's unresolved

Julie Christie and Omar Sharif head for the train in the 1966 film version.

torment over these two women could be read as representing being torn between old White Russia and its Soviet successor.

Pasternak's own relationships hover over the book. He was twice married, but his literary assistant and lover, Olga Ivinskaya, is widely believed to have been the inspiration for Lara. After publication of *Doctor Zhivago*, she denounced him to the KGB.

The plot of *Doctor Zhivago* crisscrosses Russia, but its protagonists' travels reflect both their personal crises and the country's rush toward a new and unforgiving future. Love and loss are at its core, yet *Doctor Zhivago* is also a manifesto for art. Zhivago reflects, "Art has two constant, two unending preoccupations: it is always meditating upon death and it is always thereby creating life." This novel, whose message has grown even more insistent with time, is the embodiment of that belief.

And remember: you must never, under any circumstances, despair. To hope and to act, these are our duties in misfortune.

JOHN UPDIKE

RABBIT, RUN (1960)

A washed-up high school basketball star briefly flees his dreary life as a small-town husband and father, only to return and take up with another woman.

Updike wrote four Rabbit books: *Rabbit, Run* (1960), *Rabbit Redux* (1971), *Rabbit is Rich* (1981), and *Rabbit at Rest* (1990). In 2000, he wrote a novella, *Rabbit Remembered*, about Rabbit's children.

At Harvard University, where Updike graduated *summa cum laude*, he was twice turned down for the university's prestigious creative writing class, English S, taught by poet Archibald MacLeish.

As a young man, Updike dreamed of being a cartoonist and spent a year studying at the Ruskin School of Drawing and Fine Art at Oxford University before returning to the United States to write for the *New Yorker* magazine, his literary home for the next five decades

"The only way to get somewhere, you know, is to figure out where you're going before you go there." These words of wisdom are spoken to Harry "Rabbit" Angstrom, the young, libidinous hero of John Updike's 1960 novel *Rabbit, Run*, by a surly gas station attendant with whiskey on his breath. Rabbit has just fled his pregnant wife and young son, slipping out of town in a 1955 Ford with the half-baked idea of driving all night through "the broad soft belly of the land" toward Florida's white sand beaches. Ignoring the whiskey-scented advice of the gas station attendant, Rabbit drives on and quickly gets very, very lost.

Updike once said that he wrote *Rabbit, Run* partly in response to the romanticized heroes of Jack Kerouac's *On the Road* (see page 140) to show readers "what happens when a young American family man goes on the road —the people left behind get hurt." Six decades after its publication, that is how Updike's novel reads today, as a finely wrought morality tale demonstrating the futility of escape as a means of self-actualization. Rabbit can run all he wants, Updike seems to be saying, but he can never escape himself.

In the novel's opening pages, Rabbit, an aging high school basketball star, is spending his days hawking kitchen gadgets at five-and-dime stores and his nights trapped in a loveless marriage to his mousy, alcoholic wife Janice. He yearns for a life that will match his exalted sense of his own potential, but without an education or the imagination to make use of the few marketable skills he has, he sees no way to free himself from the tangle of familial responsibilities weighing him down. So he runs.

Behind the wheel of the 1955 Ford, he skips his hometown of Brewer, Pennsylvania—a thinly disguised version of Updike's own Reading, Pennsylvania—and heads south. But Rabbit Angstrom is no Dean Moriarty. He's a small-town kid who has never really been anywhere, and before he has driven twenty miles he is disoriented and worried that the state police are on his tail.

Navigating more or less by feel, Rabbit passes through Lancaster, Pennsylvania, into rural Maryland, listening to small-town radio stations and dreaming of waking under "the white sun of the south like a great big

pillow in the sky." But he's already hopelessly lost, and the more he drives the more lost he gets. Somewhere in West Virginia, looking for a shortcut, he impulsively takes an unmarked road, which narrows and narrows until it abruptly dead-ends in a secluded lover's lane.

Lost, lonely, frustrated, and afraid, Rabbit turns back, his great escape having become a humiliating fiasco. But instead of returning to his pregnant wife, he takes up with an erstwhile prostitute who lets him into her life and eventually has his child. Rabbit is himself something of an overgrown child, a prisoner to his insatiable sexual hunger and his monstrous ego. But like a spider trapped in a web spun of his own misplaced ambition, each move he makes ties him more tightly to his ineluctable ordinariness.

Updike would go on to write three more Rabbit books, chronicling his most famous character through heartbreak and financial success, ending at last in Rabbit's premature death by heart attack in Florida. But as readers of the novels can attest, the direction of Rabbit's life is forever set in motion on that reckless night early in the first book when he dreams of escaping his humdrum life and instead runs headlong into the realization that he is guilty of the greatest sin an American fictional hero can commit: he is an ordinary man.

Heading south: *The Gas Station* by Edward Hopper, 1940.

CHARLES PORTIS

TRUE GRIT (1968)

It is 1870 and fourteen year old Mattie Ross is looking to track down the man who shot her father. With an unlikely partner, she ventures from the frontier city of Fort Smith into the "Indian Territory" of post-civil war Oklahoma.

Charles Portis began his career as a journalist, working for a time at the New York Herald Tribune alongside Tom Wolfe, Jimmy Breslin and before he quit to devote himself to writing novels.

True Grit was Portis' second novel and by far his best seller. It was first published as a serial within *The Saturday Evening Post* before being picked up by Simon & Schuster.

The 1969 film adaptation starring John Wayne was shot not in Oklahoma but the Colorado Rockies, while the 2010 remake by the Coen Brothers was shot in New Mexico.

Mattie Ross is admirably forthright about her intentions: "I am looking for the man who shot and killed my father, Frank Ross, in front of the Monarch boarding house. The man's name is Tom Chaney. They say he is over in the Indian Territory, and I need somebody to go after him." So begins the perilous and eventful journey of one of the most memorable odd-couple partnerships in American literature.

The man she finds to avenge her father's death is a one-eyed Deputy U.S. Marshall named Reuben "Rooster" Cogburn— "a pitiless man, double-tough, and fear don't enter into his thinking"—gets by as a freelance lawman of shaky ethics, motivated by the adrenaline rush of adventure far more than by any passion for justice. Tom Chaney is thought to be holed up with a band of thieves and killers in the mountains of the Choctaw Nation, in what is now Oklahoma. For one hundred dollars Rooster agrees to go and smoke him out.

Accompanied by a boastful Texas Ranger called LaBouef (pronounced LaBeef), the duo travel across the Arkansas River, into the "well timbered" hills of present-day eastern Oklahoma, and up the steep grades of the Winding Stair Mountains, where Chaney is hiding. Mattie's trusted pony, Little Blackie, must work hard to keep up with the men on horseback. It is winter and the wind and snow are relentless, but Mattie is resolved to endure the cold and rough terrain without complaint so that she's not teased by the men as a "tenderfoot."

Mattie's hardheaded determination motors *True Grit*, and indeed, this novel is partly about the unlikely kinship that forms between two of the most stubborn cusses ever put on the page. Rooster has the reputation as a man of "true grit"—the phrase suggests a fearless refusal to give up—and Mattie is possessed by a similar tenacity, what she calls "spunk." Though Rooster and LeBouef repeatedly try to leave her behind, her persistence earns their respect. The gruff camaraderie that develops between the severe, churchgoing teenage girl and the weathered, hard-drinking gunman is both very funny and wonderfully affecting.

Their quest to catch Chaney takes them into the wilderness of Oklahoma. At that time Oklahoma was designated as "Indian Territory," effectively

placing it outside the jurisdiction of state authorities and making it a refuge for criminals. Bounty hunters like Rooster and LeBouef supposedly represented the federal government but, in reality, were simply a different class of outlaw. Mattie's coming-of-age into this world of vigilantism is suitably epic. She fords the racing Arkansas River on her pony, a kind of renegade baptism. She is educated in the fine art of the ambush. And the thrilling ending involves a snakepit, a bite from a rattler and a desperate race against time back to Fort Smith.

People do not give it creedence that a fourteen-year-old girl could leave home and go off in the wintertime to avenge her father's blood but it did not seem so strange then, although I will say it did not happen every day.

Charles Portis spent nearly all his life in Arkansas and his deep knowledge of the region, its people and its vernacular made him a local icon. Not long ago, the state paid tribute to him by establishing the True Grit Trail, a stretch of rural roadway that symbolizes the route Mattie might have traveled from her farm near Dardanelle to Fort Smith, and eventually curling through the verdant foothills of Oklahoma's Winding Stair Mountains, where the novel's grand finale takes place. It's a singular landscape in an often-overlooked part of America—and it's the setting of one of the greatest Westerns ever written.

Mattie Ross pulling her father's gun in the 2010 adaptation of *True Grit*. Hailee Steinfeld received an Oscar nomination for her performance in the role.

VENEDIKT YEROFEEV

MOSCOW TO THE END OF THE LINE (MOSKVA-PETUSHKI) (1970)

Ride the train with erudite and vulgar drunk, Venichka, and chase after the hair of the dog in the stagnant Brezhnev-era Soviet Union on a journey as spiritual as it is spirit fueled.

Written in 1970, *Moscow to the End of the Line* circulated unofficially in manuscript (*samizdat*) throughout the Brezhnev years. It was first published in 1989 in the journal *Sobriety and Culture*.

Yerofeev was expelled from Moscow State University and the Vladimir Pedagogical Institute (for unclear reasons, which may include non-participation in military preparation classes and possessing a Bible). At the time he wrote *Moscow to the End of the Line*, he was working as a telephone line repairman in Moscow.

Petushki is an entirely prosaic suburban town to the east of Moscow, still served by the electric commuter train.

Consummate alcoholic Venichka (who shares his name and his propensity to drink with the author) narrates his attempt to cover by suburban train (or *elektrichka*) the 125 kilometers (78 miles) of track that separate him from the town of Petushki, a mythical land where the jasmine always blooms and where his beloved and child await.

The account of the journey is wildly funny and desperately tragic. Venichka's drunken monologue gives way to ever more hallucinogenic scenarios (including conversations with angels, a Sphinx, and Satan among others), and by the end of the novel he has failed to reach Petushki. It's unclear exactly why, or, indeed, whether he ever left Moscow in the first place. He is wandering near the Kremlin when he is attacked by four assailants—reminiscent of the four horsemen of the apocalypse—and killed.

The subjects of Venichka's drunken discourses are various and include, among other things: existential musing; sexual desire and romantic longing; Kantian philosophy; an analysis of the hiccup; Soviet workers' productivity; the composer Modest Mussorgsky (another great drunk of Russian culture); and recipes for noxious cocktails of perfume and sock deodorizer bearing names such as Canaan Balsam, The Tear of a Komsomol Girl, and Dog's Giblets (disclosed between stations Electro-Coal and Kilometer 43 [mile 27]).

What happened between Hammer & Sickle and Karacharovo is deemed unspeakable; between Kilometer 61 (mile 38) and Kilometer 65 (mile 40), passengers (or imaginary interlocutors) share love stories à la Turgenev. The chapter titles name the stations along the route (some of which are merely the kilometer-post marking the distance from Moscow) but the narration frequently runs over these divisions. There is no landscape beyond Venichka's language and visions. "For isn't the life of man a momentary booziness of the soul?" he asks.

The journey itself has many cultural touchstones. Ascribed the genre "poema" (long narrative poem), the work recalls Gogol's *Dead Souls* of 1842, another "poem in prose" and parodic twist on the picaresque. In the tradition of Russian travelogues, Yerofeev's work might also be understood as a rewriting of Alexander Radishchev's *Journey from St. Petersburg to Moscow*

The Moscow metro map from 1964.

(1790), a drunken counter-statement to that Enlightenment reformer's faith in reason. Beyond Russian culture, Laurence Sterne's *A Sentimental Journey* is another point of reference, and Venichka even produces some Sternean squiggles akin to those of *Tristram Shandy*.

A journey that fails to reach its goal and appears circular when it returns Venichka to where he started, *Moscow to the End of the Line* undoes the model of the Marxist progression of history that underwrote officially sanctioned socialist-realist art. Also running counter to the tenets of official Soviet culture is the spiritual dimension: punctuated with allusions to the Gospels, Venichka's journey is a blasphemous revisiting of the stations of the cross.

The text is a dense weave of citation and reference to other works of literature, culture, and philosophy, incorporated—alongside vulgarisms and deliriums—into Venichka's anecdotes and offhand remarks. Such rich allusion restores the fullness of intellectual inner life that had been hollowed out by Soviet culture and makes of its reader an understanding intimate of Venichka. At the same time as it brims with cultural reference and imaginative freedom, the text is also marked by emptiness and despair. Moscow is a hollow center where Venichka has never seen the Kremlin despite living there for many years, and Petushki is an unattainable Eden. *Moscow to the End of the Line* stands as an indictment of and monument to the penultimate chapter of Soviet history, the period dubbed by Gorbachev the "era of stagnation."

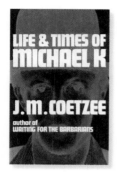

J.M. COETZEE
LIFE & TIMES OF MICHAEL K.
(1983)

A gardener tries to take his elderly mother back to her childhood home, through a landscape ravaged by civil war.

J.M. Coetzee is only the second South African to have won the Nobel Prize in Literature, in 2003. Born in Cape Town in 1940, his first novel, *Dusklands* (1974), was followed by a succession of highly original, hard-hitting novels, memoirs, and literary criticism.

Life & Times of Michael K. won the Booker Prize in 1983, a prize Coetzee won again in 1999 with *Disgrace*.

Outspokenly anti-apartheid as a younger writer, Coetzee is also a passionate advocate of animal rights. Often inaccurately described as a recluse, he lives in Australia.

Michael K. was born with a cleft palate, which so repulsed his mother that she packed him off to an institution. When the novel opens, he is a gardener for the City of Cape Town. He is not stupid, but his intelligence functions at an unusual level. Devoted to his mother, despite her early neglect, he agrees to take her back to the countryside, where she can live out her life in peace.

Peace, however, is a distant prospect. The country is at war with itself, although who is fighting whom is not entirely clear. Police and army attempt to keep control as rebels taunt and defy a crumbling government, leaving ordinary citizens trapped between them—and sometimes caught in the crossfire. Constructing a box on wheels, Michael K. sets out to push his mother home. The nightmarish quality of this venture deepens when his mother sickens and dies, although "he did not miss her, he found, except insofar as he had missed her all his life." Instead of returning to the city, Michael heads into the safety of the mountains. Here he lives a feral existence, planting melons and pumpkins in the wilderness and living like a creature of the night for fear of being captured. He survives on water, grubs, and the occasional slice of melon, but this already emaciated man is a walking skeleton by the time he is discovered and thrown into an internment camp for guerrillas.

Coetzee's writing is so clean and unfussy that he can make the intolerable sound banal. His style seems effortlessly fluid but he once admitted: "I don't like writing so I have to push myself. It's bad if I write but it's worse if I don't." There is sly humor in this tragicomedy of a homeless pauper so out of kilter with the rest of society that, even though he is as weak as a kitten, he is seen as a danger. As Coetzee writes, "he was so obscure as to be a prodigy."

Michael's route takes in the various staging posts of the conflict, from rebels in hiding, to the army intent on capturing them, to the medical officer at the so-called rehabilitation camp who tries to coax Michael into eating. As he refuses sustenance, it becomes clear that Michael's priorities are elemental and his journey more spiritual than geographical. Escaping confinement, he somehow manages to make his way home. As a result, by the novel's end he has returned to the same place from where he set out. By now the city is

in an even worse state of turmoil than when he left but, while he is barely alive physically, his journey has awakened an awareness of the meaning of life, and its many complicated relationships and transactions. Traveling at a snail's pace has also connected him viscerally with his homeland. It is no coincidence that he is a gardener, capable of making the earth bloom and feed its people. His self-imposed starvation is a searing indictment of a country that has lost touch with its roots.

Illustrated book covers from editions published by Penguin Random House.

He thought of himself not as something heavy that left tracks behind it, but if anything, as a speck upon the surface of an earth too deeply asleep to notice the scratch of ant feet, the rasp of butterfly teeth, the tumbling of dust.

LARRY MCMURTRY

LONESOME DOVE (1985)

The Pulitzer-winning western about men unable to stand still, McMurtry's Lonesome Dove *follows the turbulent journey of two Texas Rangers heading north.*

Lonesome Dove took a long journey of its own. First written as a script (with Peter Bogdanovich, McMurtry's collaborator on *The Last Picture Show*), it spent over a decade in development hell before McMurtry eventually bought back the rights and adapted it into a novel.

Although there are similarities with historical figures such as Charles Goodnight, McMurtry insists that Gus and Call were not modeled after them —instead, he took inspiration from Don Quixote and Sancho Panza.

McMurtry founded Booked Up (in Archer City, Texas), one of the largest used bookstores in the world.

The great cattle drives of the nineteenth century changed the very shape of America. The drives carved paths across the country, built new towns, displaced the existing population, and reshaped the physical environment. Symbolically the drives became—and still are—the ultimate metaphor for both manifest destiny and manful coming of age.

Yet against this very background of political, geographic, and cultural significance, Larry McMurtry's *Lonesome Dove* features a cattle drive that is no more than a self-indulgent failure.

McMurtry's Pulitzer-winning novel is set in the 1870s and features a cast of dozens, led by the hedonistic Augustus "Gus" McCrae and stoic Woodrow Call, both retired Texas Rangers. McCrae and Call have set up in the titular town, a half-dead hamlet on the Mexican border. Lonesome Dove is a purgatorial place. Call toils all day on the failing ranch but never makes progress. Gus, lazier, is trapped in his own recurring routine— baking biscuits, drinking, gambling, and whoring. Call wrestles with a dawning self-awareness, feeling "pressed in, [. . .] bound in" by the endless unproductive labors of the ranch. The more extroverted Gus is lonely for human contact. For both cowboys, life "just seemed smaller."

When an old comrade comes riding in with stories of the vast grasslands in Montana, it takes little convincing to set the cowboys into action. They promptly steal a herd from Mexico and begin the journey north.

The drive turns sour quickly, as a promising young cowboy is swarmed by a nest of poisonous snakes. He is only the first to die. *Lonesome Dove* spends hundreds of pages raining Biblical terrors on Gus and Call, down to the proverbial locusts. Virtually every encounter—with the elements, with other people—ends in horror.

The cattle drive is relentless, and it is cruel. It is also futile. By the time the company reaches Montana, only a few of the original number remain. Call, seeking material success, realizes he no longer wants it. Gus, desiring meaningful companionship, has been spurned by an old lover and dies after a meaningless skirmish. After less than a year in Montana, Call picks up and heads back to Texas.

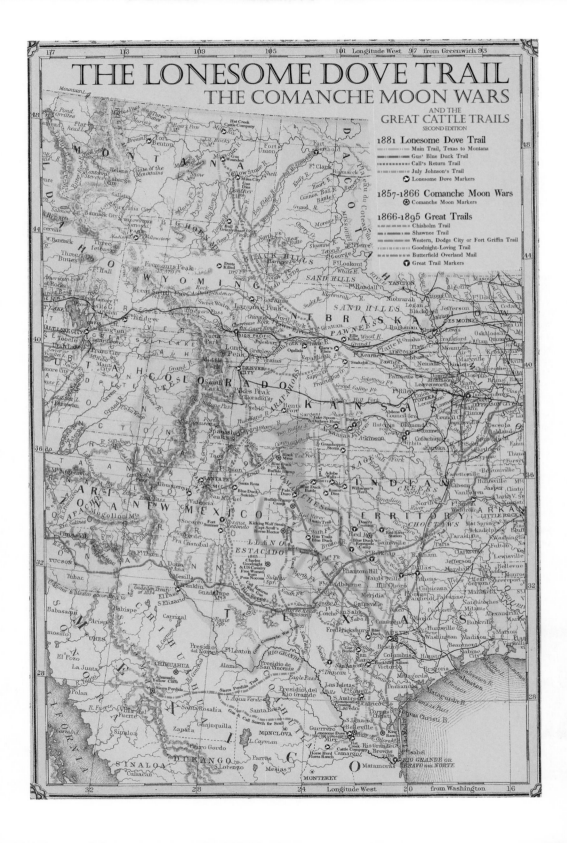

THE LONESOME DOVE TRAIL
THE COMANCHE MOON WARS
AND THE
GREAT CATTLE TRAILS
SECOND EDITION

1881 Lonesome Dove Trail
- Main Trail, Texas to Montana
- Gus' Blue Duck Trail
- Call's Return Trail
- July Johnson's Trail
- Lonesome Dove Markers

1857–1866 Comanche Moon Wars
- Comanche Moon Markers

1866–1895 Great Trails
- Chisholm Trail
- Shawnee Trail
- Western, Dodge City or Fort Griffin Trail
- Goodnight-Loving Trail
- Butterfield Overland Mail
- Great Trail Markers

A hand-colored woodcut depicting cowboys driving a herd from Texas to Kansas on the Chisholm Trail, 1870.

The grave's our destination. Those who hurry usually get to it quicker than those who take their time. Now me, I travel , and when I'll get anywhere is anybody's guess.

The return journey is ironically uneventful. Even as Call slowly tows Gus's corpse back across the country, he faces none of the dangers from the previous drive. Arriving back in Texas, he buries his friend and returns to Lonesome Dove. Which begs the question: did their journey matter at all? They have sacrificed their bodies, lives, minds, and souls, and for what? Gus and Call are right back where they started, and one of them is dead.

The answer is buried within *Lonesome Dove* itself. In one of the book's many chance encounters, a wandering entomologist, Mr. Sedgwick, notes that "the grave's our destination. Those who hurry usually get to it quicker than those who take their time." As proved by *Lonesome Dove*'s course of events, every ambition is coupled with risk. To go searching —for land or for love—is to put yourself in danger. Yet death is inevitable for everyone; the question is how you meet it. As Gus himself says, "Life's a short affair. Why spend it here?"

For men such as Gus and Call, stasis is the true futility. It is neither the journey nor the destination; it is the traveler. There are those that must hurry, that have to seek, that drive because they themselves are driven. The consequences may be brutal, and the mission itself futile, but that was not, and never will be, the point. When the world "just seems smaller," you can reduce yourself or choose to make it bigger again, whatever the price.

JEANETTE WINTERSON

THE PASSION (1987)

Set during the tumult of the Napoleonic Wars, Henri and Villanelle's stories intersect at an army camp in Russia, and stay intertwined.

"I read three books about Venice before I wrote *The Passion*, and twenty years later, those three books are still the ones I would choose above all others to find the place as it needs to be found—imaginatively," Jeanette Winterson wrote in 2011.

The word "imaginatively" encompasses much of the journeying that occurs in Winterson's second novel *The Passion*, which is set in France, Russia, and Venice during the Napoleonic Wars. But even with such large swaths of the map covered, Winterson makes clear that the most important journeys happen imaginatively: "the cities of the interior do not lie on any map."

The Passion—which was awarded the 1987 John Llewellyn Rhys Prize —alternates between two voices. The story begins in 1804 with Henri, a Napoleon acolyte so devoted to the Little Corporal that he foregoes his dreams of being an army drummer for the opportunity to be Bonaparte adjacent, even though that means being a chicken-neck-wringer in Bonaparte's kitchen. As Napoleon's passion for war leads his army across Europe, Henri's passion for Napoleon sees him following after. "We are in love with him," Henri says, explaining France's devotion to the soon-to-be emperor. "If Bonaparte had asked us to strap on wings and fly to St. James's Palace we would have set off as confidently as a child lets loose a kite."

The second narrator is Villanelle, a bisexual, cross-dressing casino worker with magical properties passed down through the generations of Venetian boatmen. Villanelle and Henri's stories intertwine in frigid Russia where Villanelle has been sold into prostitution by the husband she wronged, and Napoleon's *Grande Armeé* is wavering as the wars reveal themselves to be endless.

Henri quickly falls for Villanelle, trading his blind devotion to Bonaparte for an equally blind devotion to this mysterious Venetian. The two of them, along with a defrocked priest, desert Napoleon's camp, setting off on foot from Moscow to Venice.

This epic trek along borders, through Poland and Austria, across the Danube, and into Italy is the most literal journey in *The Passion*. The destination matters, but Winterson makes clear that this destination is not

Jeanette Winterson published her first novel, *Oranges Are Not the Only Fruit*, when she was only twenty-six. *The Passion* was published two years later.

Winterson was raised in an evangelical household and says her style is heavily influenced by the Bible. In a 1988 radio interview Winterson said, "If you think of the way the Bible is written, always in very few words and a few verses you get the whole story: You know who the people are, you know where the place is, and something miraculous has happened."

Projections indicate that by 2200 Venice could be permanently underwater.

The irrational Venice, as it was in the eighteenth century—hand-colored illustration, 1750.

one easily mappable. Once in the labyrinthine city, Winterson's plot turns and twists, mimicking the city's geography and the nonlinear journey of life—even for those who do everything in their power to make it so. "Where Bonaparte goes, straight roads follow," Henri says. But "not even Bonaparte could rationalize Venice." Indeed, not even Bonaparte could rationalize any of life's journeys: he was ultimately captured and imprisoned, and died on a remote island with only his interior map to navigate. Straight roads end.

The end of *The Passion* commits that truth to the page. Villanelle is destined to live out her days navigating the waterways of Venice. "Where I will be will not be where I am," she says cryptically. Henri, like his former hero, is ultimately imprisoned. "I don't want to see any more of the world," he says. They have both ended their physical journeys, opting instead for the mapless world of the interior.

But there is one more element to the journeys in *The Passion*: time travel. In a 1988 radio interview, Winterson explained her desire to set this novel in the past. "Setting things in the past allows you to enter into almost a fairy-tale world where the constraints of the present are missing. It's like

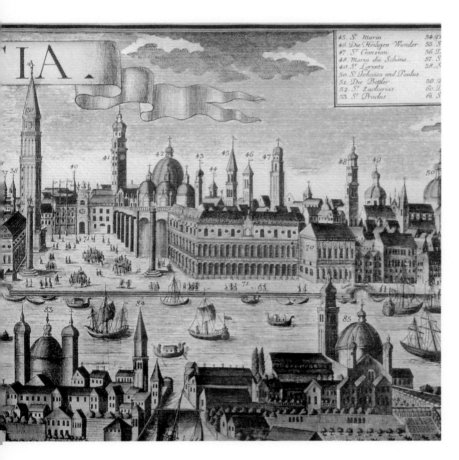

swimming—your usual sense of gravity is gone. You go somewhere different and you can learn lessons that would not be possible if you were there in your own home, in your own front room, reading about people who were contemporary with you," she says. "If you do follow your heart's desire, you could end up anywhere."

The city I come from is a changeable city . . . It is not always the same size. Streets appear and disappear overnight, new waterways force themselves over dry land.

PAULO COELHO

THE ALCHEMIST
(O ALQUIMISTA) (1988)

In this simple fable, a Spanish shepherd travels from the Spanish coast to Egypt in search of a treasure after being prompted in a dream.

Like the main character Santiago, Paulo Coelho had a religious education and challenged his parents' plans for him; he dreamed of becoming a writer. Instead of giving him their blessings, his parents committed him to a mental institution to treat his depression and anger problems until the age of twenty.

The Alchemist holds a curious entry in the *Guinness World Records*: "most translations [53] of a single title signed by the author in one sitting," during the Frankfurt Book Fair in 2003.

The Alchemist follows Santiago, a shepherd from Andalusia, Spain, who stops to rest with his sheep at an abandoned church one night. When he sleeps, he has a recurrent dream: a child takes him by both hands and transports him to the Egyptian pyramids. "If you come here, you will find a hidden treasure," the child says. Intrigued, Santiago visits a gypsy woman in Tarifa. She simply tells him to follow his dream. Moments later, an old man—actually, King Melchizedek from the biblical city of Salem—encourages him further by explaining that the dream contains Santiago's Personal Legend: "It's what you have always wanted to accomplish. Everyone, when they are young, knows what their Personal Legend is." As time passes, however, most people forget about these dreams, which are each person's *raison d'être*, he continues. With the king's blessings, Santiago embarks on a trip from the Spanish coast to Tangier and then to the Giza pyramids despite great hurdles that will test his resolve. When a tribal war forces Santiago's caravan to wait in the Al Fayoum Oasis, he finds love and a mysterious alchemist, whose teachings may help him survive the rest of his trip.

Coelho's language is straightforward, as if he were a storyteller spinning his yarn around a campfire. The result is a fable with many twists and apparent contradictions along the way. Thus, Melchizedek warns Santiago about "the world's greatest lie": "at a certain point in our lives, we lose control of what's happening to us, and our lives become controlled by fate." However, the king also describes the Personal Legend as someone's mission on Earth, which was "originated in the soul of the universe." Later, he even instructs Santiago with details of a god in the machine: "In order to find a treasure, you will have to follow the omens. God has prepared a path for everyone to follow."

No wonder an Arabic word appears repeatedly in the novel: *Maktub*, or "it is written." Still, these seemingly discordant ideas are imbued with a universal conflict at the heart of formative narratives: the hero's struggle against a received fate in order to make his own choices into a new fate—what was written must be rewritten.

To learn how to find his good omens, Santiago needs to understand what traveling entails. He is presented with two perspectives about the subject.

After he builds up the courage to tell his parents that he wants to explore the world, his father seems unmoved. "People from all over the world have passed through this village," he remarks. "They come in search of new things, but when they leave they are basically the same people they were when they arrived." In the Sahara Desert, Santiago hears from the alchemist the difference between *passing* through a place and *being* in a place. Taking its cue from Ralph Waldo Emerson, *The Alchemist* encourages its hero to find the journey's end in every step of the road. Santiago's treasure is just the starting point.

From Tangier to the oasis —Santiago's route through the desert, illustration by Rodica Prato.

But you are in the desert. So immerse yourself in it. The desert will give you an understanding of the world; in fact, anything on the face of the earth will do that.

GAO XINGJIAN

Soul Mountain
(LÍNGSHĀN) (1990)

In a novel based on the author's own travels, a quest for the fabled Lingshan or Soul Mountain becomes an epic journey through unofficial modern China, and one man's intimate search for self, memory, freedom, and peace.

Gao Xingjian, a fiction writer, critic, playwright, director, and artist, became the first Chinese writer to win the Nobel Prize in Literature in 2000.

Gao's experimental plays were banned during a renewed drive against Western modernism and "spiritual pollution." This coincided with his being diagnosed with lung cancer —from which his father had died. The existentialist reprieve resulted in *Soul Mountain*.

All his work has been banned in mainland China (most was published in Chinese in Taiwan) since 1989, when he condemned the Tiananmen Square massacre and applied for political asylum in France.

This semi-autobiographical novel grew from Xingjian's travels in the 1980s through the ancient forest highlands of Sichuan province in southwest China. A resident of Beijing, for five months he tracked the Yangtze River from its source, journeying east from Sichuan's giant panda reserve to the China Sea, covering 9,300 miles (15,000 kilometers) across eight provinces and seven nature reserves. Ostensibly researching woodcutters' lives and folk songs, "I was looking for a place of refuge," Gao said in an interview. "It was also a spiritual and cultural quest, to find the origin of Chinese culture—the source that had not yet been polluted by politics."

It opens in a litter-filled bus station where the middle-aged, unmarried narrator has been guided by a stranger on a train, who drew a map on an empty cigarette pack of how to reach the "virgin wilderness" of Soul Mountain. The epic journey takes him from riverside towns with "black rooftops overlapping like fish scales" to a coastal "network of waterways," via Daoist retreats and bustling cities with their "surging tide of bicycles." There are also mystical landscapes, such as a hallucinatory near-death experience on a glacier with "huge mineral veins, inky green like jade."

In the novel's plotless soliloquy—termed by the author a "flow of language" rather than stream of consciousness—the pronouns change as facets of the protagonist take the place of characters. "I" is a writer and critic "wrongly diagnosed with lung cancer" who travels in the real world seeking an "authentic life," while "You" makes a more mystical journey of the imagination. "She" is born of "You" and later spawns "He," entailing bickering dialogue between the protagonist's male and female selves. The polyphonic technique is used to create heightened self-scrutiny as the novelist reflects on the human craving for society ("The fiction he writes is because he can't bear the loneliness.") while recognizing the power struggles inherent in any relationship with others.

Alongside erotic encounters, mystical reveries, musings on the writer's role, and meetings with forest rangers and Daoist monk-medics, there are childhood reminiscences and testimony from people who denounced one another during the Cultural Revolution. There is an ineffable sense of what

has been lost in both culture (ancient Yangtze River culture predates Han civilization) and nature. A botanist says man is "capable of manufacturing almost anything, from rumors to test-tube babies, and yet he destroys two to three species every day. This is the absurdity of man."

The Edge of Reality— painted in ink by the author Gao Xingjian himself.

"This isn't a novel," the narrator argues with himself. "You've slapped together travel notes, moralistic ramblings, feelings, [. . .] copied out some folk songs, added some legendlike nonsense of your own invention, and are calling it fiction!" Yet gazettes and records, romances and *belles lettres*, street talk and morality tales "are all acknowledged as fiction" in the two-thousand-year-old Chinese tradition of the novel. The result is an omnivorous compendium that effervesces with vivid description, incident, humor, and the humdrum minutiae of travel—from sublime street food ("sesame-coated shallot pancakes, straight off the stove and piping-hot") to bathetic bouts of boredom and food poisoning.

If *Soul Mountain's* meaning remains elusive, God appears at the end as a small green frog with an unblinking eye. The novel is an affirmation of the individual self against the "blind mass" of the collective that would crush it. As Gao has said: "It's under the mask of fiction that you can tell the truth."

VIKRAM SETH

A SUITABLE BOY (1993)

Mrs. Rupa Mehra embarks on her "Annual Trans-India Rail Pilgrimage" across the northern and eastern states India to find a suitable boy for her daughter, Lata, to marry.

Vikram Seth is an Indian writer and poet. He has lived in India, London, California, and China. In addition to novels, poetry, and nonfiction, Seth has also translated Chinese poetry.

When it was published, *A Suitable Boy* was called the longest novel in the English language. At 1,349 pages (about 600,000 words), the manuscript had to be packed in a whiskey crate when sent to publishers in the United Kingdom.

Seth has been working on a sequel, *A Suitable Girl*, for more than a decade. Though he is often quiet about his writing habits, Seth has revealed that the novel will be set in the present day.

A Suitable Boy is an enormous saga of a novel encompassing Indianness like no other. Indian society, with its labyrinth of relationships and contradictions, is narrated in a linear manner through four interconnected families and along the railroad lines.

It opens with Mrs. Rupa Mehra embarking on what her children call her "Annual Trans-India Rail Pilgrimage." It is a trip she takes every year, accompanied by "three suitcases, filled with most of what she owned in the world," to visit her friends and relatives in north Indian cities. This time though, it is with a purpose and in panic: she must find a suitable husband for her daughter, Lata. The story is the closest Indian cousin of a love story—of arranged marriages, modern affairs, courtship, and emotional pragmatism. "You too will marry a boy I choose," she instructs, and she sends feelers to friends and family looking for potential suitors.

The novel is largely set in Brahmpur, a fictional city (based on Patna) in a fictional eastern state, which serves as a microcosm for India. Apart from the Mehras, an upper-middle-class, well-educated family, there are the prominent families they have married into: the cosmopolitan Chatterjis, the politician Kapoors, and the aristocratic Khans. This delicate network of connections is threatened when Lata falls in love with Kabir who, much to Mrs. Rupa Mehra's horror, is Muslim—and thus most unsuitable.

She flees to Calcutta, where she panics when she discovers her daughter-in-law's brother Amit's infatuation with Lata. Among Amit's faults—he is a poet who doesn't use his Oxford law degree—is that she doesn't want to be related twice over with the Chatterjis, who she thinks are all quite insane.

Indeed, the qualities for a suitable son-in-law are problematically specific: he must be from the same caste, fair to offset Lata's complexion, and not too rich that he would demand a dowry. She plans a search that will take her through Kanpur, Lucknow, and Banaras, but before she can complete her journey, she meets Haresh Khanna. Satisfied that he fulfills the criteria, she summons Lata to Kanpur for their first meeting.

Governed by the river and the railroads, *A Suitable Boy* chugs along slowly, meandering through the idyllic life of the early fifties, entertaining

The secret of life is to accept. Accept happiness, accept sorrow; accept success, accept failure; accept fame, accept disgrace; accept doubt, even accept the impression of certainty.

along the way. It has the equability of Victorian novels, unconcerned with the complexities of mind or life—but is nonetheless an intricate portrait of a newly independent India.

Though each of the central families are rooted in place, at least one member from each goes on a trip of their own. The feckless Maan Kapoor —who tumbles from grace after falling in love with a prominent singer-courtesan—is sent to a rural constituency to learn Urdu. The aristocratic Nawab Sahib of Baitar takes a trip down memory lane in his efforts to protect feudal privileges and save his estate from the Zamindari Abolition Bill (which sought to confer ownership rights from big landowners to tenant farmers). Dipankar Chatterji, an economist in perpetual spiritual crisis, finds clarity through his apparently aimless wandering around the Pul Mela: "[It] has helped me to realize that the Spiritual Source of India is not the Zero or Unity or Duality or even the Trinity, but Infinity itself."

Through crisscrossing journeys, Seth constructs a portrait of mid-century India, of caste politics, community dynamics, religious tension, and the chasm between rich and poor, urban and rural. Amit, working on a long novel, compares his work to a banyan tree. His description applies to *A Suitable Boy* itself: "it sprouts, and grows, and spreads, and drops down branches that become trunks or intertwine with other branches."

Seth's novel is a romance at the intersection of history and politics, rich in its descriptions of social mannerisms and dynamics. He shows us India in minute detail:

> The platform was as crowded as ever with passengers and their friends and families and servants, hawkers, railroad staff, coolies, vagrants, and beggars. Babies wailed and whistles blew. Stray dogs slunk about with punished eyes, monkeys bared aggressive teeth. There was a pervasive railroad platform stench. It was a hot day and the fans were not working in the bogeys.

Previous: Crossing the subcontinent east to west— a poster for the railroad company.

Apologists of the Empire consider the railroads—which were constructed by the British to control India—as one of Britain's greatest gifts (along with democracy) to the Indian subcontinent. And so it is befitting that trains and democracy are both central themes of Seth's novel, in which he takes his

readers through the year leading up to the first general election in 1952. It is a time when India is at the cusp of adulthood, trying to chart its own path. A vast sea of characters—democrats, socialists, big landowners, farmers, Hindus, Muslims, lower caste communities, and others—feel strongly about their country and the journey it will take from here. For research, Seth read newspapers, records of legislative proceedings, maps, and interviews, and immersed himself in music and film from the time. All kinds of details show up in the novel: silverfish dart across tables in the library of the Khans' old *haveli*, the Chatterji sisters drape chiffon saris over tiny blouses baring their midriffs and scandalizing the world outside Calcutta, politicians debate a law to transfer ownership of land from landlords to tenants, a vicious dog called Cuddles bites whoever he can. Seth takes his readers through jazz bars, old colonial clubs, a cricket match, legislative assemblies, shoe factories, brothels, and vast fields.

With nearly one hundred characters—almost two thirds of whom have subplots of their own—*A Suitable Boy* is an intricate display of the overlapping journeys of lives.

Getting ready for the express train—hawkers stand by with food for the next train at Calcutta station.

SHUSAKU ENDO

DEEP RIVER (FUKAI KAWA) (1993)

A Japanese tour of holy Buddhist sites in India is interrupted by the assassination of Indira Gandhi as each member of the group takes stock of their lives.

Shusaku Endo (1923–1996) was born in Tokyo. When he left for France to study Catholic literature in 1950, Endo became the first Japanese student to study abroad after World War II.

Endo is often called the "Japanese Graham Greene" for his Catholicism and spirituality, and for his writing style. It has been reported that Endo would re-read Greene's novel The End of the Affair before beginning any new writing of his own.

When Endo died in 1996, a copy of *Deep River* was one of only two books placed inside his coffin, the other being his novel *Silence* (1966).

The spine of *Deep River* is a Japanese tour to famous Buddhist sites in India. Isobe is a lonely widower mourning the passing of his wife, Keiko, from cancer. Shortly before dying, Keiko tells Isobe: "I . . . I know for sure . . . I'll be reborn somewhere in this world. Look for me . . . find me . . . promise . . . promise."

Initially sceptical, after her death he learns more about reincarnation and begins to believe. It's this faith—perhaps a symptom of deep grief—that motivates him to sign up for a tour that will ultimately lead him to the Ganges: the river of life, the river of death. "'Darling!' Once again he called out toward the river. 'Where have you gone?' The river took in his cry and silently flowed away."

He is joined on his journey by a ragtag ensemble, each carrying baggage they hope to divest along the banks of the holy river. Kiguchi fought in Burma during World War II and is haunted by guilt and ghosts; Numada, who grew up in Manchuria, Japan's occupied territories in China, survived a health scare but feels deep shame over his mistreatment of people and animals throughout his life; Mitsuko, who by coincidence nursed Isobe's wife, is searching for Ōtsu, an earnest spiritual man she tormented as a student and who has become a catholic priest in India. They are led by Enami, their tour guide, who loves India and hates his clients who cannot see the beauty he can:

> Frankly, he despised the Japanese tourists he had to shuttle around. [. . .] The deeply grateful old men and women who made the rounds of the Buddhist relics; the college women who relished the hippie-like homeless. [. . .] They always took the same souvenirs back to Japan with them. [. . .] Enami stood in the doorways of stores and watched contemptuously as the Japanese roved from showcase to showcase.

The group is completed by the Sanjos, a young couple inexplicably taking their honeymoon with the tour. This couple's selfish vacuity provides much of the novel's comic relief. The husband has spent a fortune on a new camera and despite having no experience or apparent artistic skills believes he can

win a Pulitzer if he just gets "the right shot." The right shot seems to involve ignoring local taboos:

A group of Japanese tourists photograph bathers in the holy River Ganges, Varanasi.

> "You do remember that Mr. Enami said that photographing funeral pyres along the Ganges is strictly prohibited? Last night I saw them beat a Sikh man until he was bloody. Don't you think it'd be better if you left your camera behind today?"
>
> "Robert Capra says a photographer who doesn't risk danger can never shoot a masterpiece."

Endo was a master of the juxtaposition, mirroring stories, situations, perspectives, to create a tapestry of life. This is a book of multiple journeys. Each member of the ensemble is at a different stage in the journey of life, some approaching death, some recently given a reprieve, some closer to the start than the end and blissfully ignorant of the road they are on. Multiple journeys: one destination. Mitsuko encapsulates the novel's ethos in the final pages: "I have learned, though, that there is a river of humanity. Though I still don't know what lies at the end of that flowing river."

Deep River is a global novel, outward looking, universal, embracing a multitude of faiths, of cultures, of outlooks. Despite the darkness it touches, it is a warm, nourishing novel—death and comedy have long been comfortable traveling companions—that reminds us all of that philosophical maxim: keep in mind how you go.

W.G. SEBALD

THE RINGS OF SATURN
(DIE RINGE DES SATURN) (1995)

The third of Sebald's literary works to be published, The Rings of Saturn *is an exploration of memory and movement, following an anonymous narrator as he wanders the coastal paths of the east of England in quiet contemplation.*

W.G. Sebald (1944–2001) was a German writer, poet, and academic. After studying German and English Literature in Germany and Switzerland, Sebald emigrated to the United Kingdom where he taught at the University of East Anglia from 1970 until his death in 2001.

The Rings of Saturn was first translated into English by Michael Hulse in 1998; it was the second of Sebald's works to be released for an English-speaking audience.

Originally published in German as *Die Ringe des Saturn* by Eichborn Verlag in 1995, it included the subtitle "Eine englische Wallfahrt" or "An English Pilgrimage."

Part travel writing, part memoir, part fiction, *The Rings of Saturn* offers a captivating account of one man's physical and emotional journey along the remote coastal paths of Suffolk. The unnamed narrator of Sebald's work is entranced by this stretch of coastline, a fascination made palpable through the rich descriptions of his walking tour of the region and the continuous sense of nostalgia that this evokes in him. The interconnection between place, movement, and time forms the basis of Sebald's work; he foregrounds these subjects, guiding readers through a landscape that unveils not only its own memories, but also those of a far more personal nature.

The Rings of Saturn begins with his narrator, now trapped within the confines of a cubicle in a Norwich hospital, as he reminisces about an excursion he made the previous summer. The desire to explore that same landscape drives the narrator to embark on his recollection of the journey, taking the reader along with him as he drifts through Suffolk's sleepy seaside geography and begins to build a picture of his own identity through a sequence of remembered scenes and meditations.

Sebald describes a journey that is at once both physical and imagined, with each new place provoking deeper introspection: "I felt as if I were in a deserted theater, and I should not be surprised if a curtain had suddenly risen [. . .] and I had beheld [. . .] the Dutch fleet [. . .] open fire on the English ships."

He contemplates loss and erasure through the narrator's movements: declining coastal villages, the awkward navigation of Somerleyton's hedged maze, and the wandering of Dunwich's deserted beaches where he laments the loss of All Saints' Church. Sebald introduces a variety of characters from the narrator's travels as well as a number of historical figures, such as the seventeenth-century polymath Sir Thomas Browne, whose esoteric work *Musæum Clausum* acts as a template for Sebald's text, allowing the author to seamlessly shift in and out of topics, times, and places.

Sebald opens each chapter with a poetic account of the specific places in which the narrator pauses on his journey, before moving into drifting ruminations on other sites and times. This permits Sebald's protagonist to meander his way not only through the physical landscape of Suffolk, but also through a series of interwoven historical topics, ranging from silkworm cultivation and sunken villages, to

imperial power and ancient Chinese emperors. Sebald's narrator finds malleability of landscape while out walking the Suffolk coast, allowing him to imagine himself elsewhere and move between past and present places and events:

The empty and deserted landscape of Suffolk—Dunwich Heath is an area of coastal lowland heath just south of the village of Dunwich.

> The region is so empty and deserted that, if one were abandoned there, one could scarcely say whether one was on the North Sea coast or perhaps by the Caspian Sea or the Gulf of Lian-tung.

The journey along the coastal paths described by Sebald is as much about history and personal discovery as it is about the Suffolk landscape itself.

The Rings of Saturn presents readers with a complex narrative that folds in and out of times, places, and experiences. An awareness of the passing of time and the impermanence of the landscape is central to Sebald's journey and is mirrored in the changes he describes as daylight wanes and the coast transitions into night. He describes how "as darkness closed in from the horizon like a noose being tightened," the "swirling and ever denser obscurement, landmarks that a short while ago still stood out clearly, but with each passing moment the space around became more constricted."

While the narrator's decision to wander derives from a desire to free himself of restlessness, the journey that Sebald depicts is ultimately one of self-reflection, personal trauma, and loss. Indeed, the original subtitle, "An English Pilgrimage," suggests that Sebald is hoping for some kind of awakening to take place, spiritual or otherwise, and yet the landscape he traverses is described as "nothing but gray water, mudflats, and emptiness." In many ways, the narrator of the book echoes Sebald's own biography: a man dislocated from his homeland and its complicated history. It is perhaps through this reading of *The Rings of Saturn* that we can best understand the journey described as one integral to the author's own struggle with the past and the memories it refuses to bury: "I knew then as little as I know now whether walking in this solitary way was more of a pleasure or a pain."

ALESSANDRO BARICCO

SILK (SETA) (1996)

Set against the backdrop of the silkworm epidemic of 1845 onward, Baricco's novel follows a French silk merchant's trips to Japan. Fascinated by the culture and the women, he returns several times.

Alessandro Baricco (1958–) is an Italian storyteller, public intellectual, educator, and co-founder of the Holden writing school and bookstore in Turin.

He is a passionate advocate of the importance of good stories, and a critic of the division between "high" and popular culture.

His bestseller *Silk* (Seta) was translated into English by Guido Waldman (1997) and Ann Goldstein (2006). The novel was adapted into the 2007 film of the same name directed by François Girard, starring Keira Knightley and Michael Pitt. The screenplay was written by François Girard and Michael Golding.

The year of publication of *Seta* (1996), Lake Baikal, the oldest, deepest lake in the world, was declared a UNESCO World Heritage site, and Kathryn Gustafson's visionary garden "Les Jardins de l'Imaginaire" (Gardens of the Imagination, declared a "notable garden of France" by the French government), opened in Terrasson-Lavilledieu, France. In *Silk*, this lake, this city, and a fictional park are highly symbolic of the protagonist's negotiation between home and distant land through the construction of an Orientalized space in-between. The protagonist's own life remains as unfathomable to him as Lake Baikal (which he sees eight times yet cannot describe once).

Silk recounts thirty-two-year-old Hervé Joncour's four strenuous trips alone across Europe and Asia by train, horse, foot, and boat, to illicitly procure silkworm eggs for the textile industry of his city, Lavilledieu, which has been affected by a worm pandemic. Between 1861 and 1865 he visits "the other side of the world"—Japan at the end of the isolationist Edo period (1603–1867). Joncour becomes fascinated by the nameless young lover of a powerful leader, Hara Kei, whose eyes, like Joncour's, "did not have an Oriental shape." His infatuation—which echoes "Japonisme," France's own infatuation with Japanese culture as a consequence of burgeoning trade relations—affects his unhappy marriage, though does not put an end to it.

Joncour is expelled from Japan due to a civil war sparked by an American military intervention. To contain his nostalgia, he creates a Japanese-inspired park in Lavilledieu, and travels through Europe with his wife Hélène of the "beautiful voice," ironically silent until her unexpected final words transform the whole story.

Joncour cannot see others or himself. He is in Japan during some of its most transformational years, yet he literally travels blindfolded. "How is the end of the world?" his mentor-employer Baldabiou asks him upon return. "Invisible" he replies. Women are to him precious and immaterial as silk, the touch of which, according to Baldabiou, feels "like holding between the fingers nothingness." His own life "felt like rain before his eyes, a quiet spectacle"—or like the water that flows over his body like oil in a bathing ritual performed by veiled women.

Joncour shares endurance and resourcefulness with the heroes of traditional travel narratives, and narcissism with the nineteenth-century Orientalist tradition. Flaubert's *Salammbô* (1862), an icon of the genre, is repeatedly mentioned in *Silk*. The exotic "other" (Japan, woman) is just a tool to re-affirm the male protagonist's fragile ego. It is significant that *Silk* ends in two scenes of self-centeredness: an invitation to masturbation while fantasizing about the Japanese woman and a view of Joncour looking at his lake's surface, a clear allusion to Narcissus, the Greek hunter who fell in love with his reflection on a lake.

Lavilledieu's citizens think that Joncour "had returned from Japan changed, perhaps ill." Robert Rushing's interesting psychoanalytical approach to *Silk* explains how, upon return, the unbreachable distance Joncour experienced "between" himself and Japan becomes a distance "within" himself. It is revealing that, in the emblematic scene in which Joncour looks at a lake, he is not looking at himself but at the surface. Like Narcissus, he is isolated; unlike Narcissus, he never develops a sense of himself.

An infatuation with all things Japanese—*Women Looking at Japanese Objects*, oil by James Tissot, ca. 1869.

Is he masculine or vaguely feminine as the narrator describes him; a military man or a garden designer; a happy husband or an unhappy lover; a foreigner in Japan or "il giapponese" in Lavilledieu; a misanthropic loner or a benefactor? Regardless of his travel experiences, Japan, women, his own life, remain incomprehensible to him. However, something new and extremely important happens to Joncour upon return. He, the silent man who can only write "Hélas!" (Alas!) on his wife's grave, begins to tell stories of his travels. "Listening to him, the people of Lavilledieu learned about the world, and the children discovered what marvel was," concludes the narrator.

Silk reflects Baricco's pursuit of accessible storytelling of high quality. His bookstore in Turin displayed a sentence by Nora Joyce, James's wife: "Why don't you write books people can read?" Indeed, one of *Silk*'s merits is its Cervantine capacity to attract a diverse audience. Consequently, it can be read as a superficial exotic romance or as a profound fable about disorientation, lack of communication, and the power of storytelling—perhaps more so than other travel stories, given the hypnotic seductiveness of its pristine poetic style.

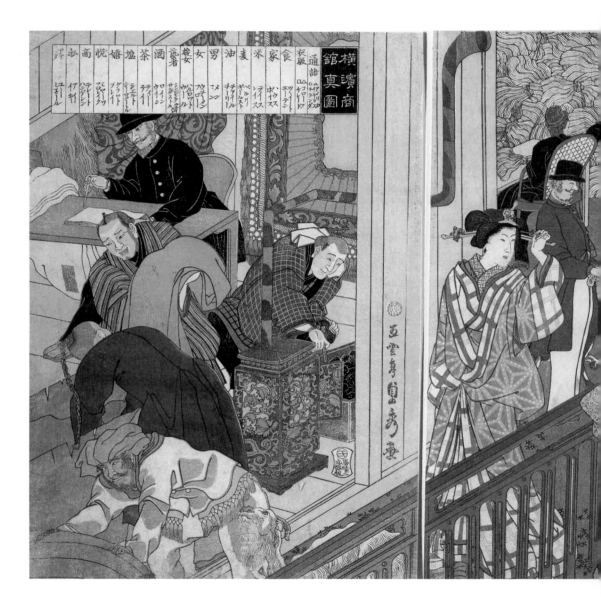

Trading House of a Yokohama Merchant, woodblock print by Utagawa (Gountei) Sadahide, 1861. Sadahide often drew foreigners shopping after Japan ended its self-imposed isolation in 1854.

ROBERTO BOLAÑO
THE SAVAGE DETECTIVES (LOS DETECTIVES SALVAJES) (1998)

A wild, idiosyncratic search to reconstitute the story of the visceral realists, a group of radical poets that tore through Mexico City in the middle of the 70s before being disbanded in murky circumstances .

Roberto Bolaño, the Chilean *enfant terrible* of Spanish language literature, became an international literary sensation in the mid-2000s —something that unfortunately for him he never got to experience, having died at fifty in 2003 of liver failure.

Arturo Belano, one of the two main figures in *The Savage Detectives*, was modeled on Roberto Bolaño himself.

As a young impoverished poet, Bolaño would interrupt the public readings of other writers in Mexico City by shouting out his poems.

The Savage Detectives, the novel that propelled Roberto Bolaño to literary prominence in both the Spanish (while he was still alive) and English-speaking (after his untimely death) worlds, is a tale of multiple journeys, both physical and metaphorical.

The novel opens in diary form: in 1975, seventeen-year-old Juan García Madero, an aspiring poet and law student in Mexico City, falls in with two firebrands, Arturo Belano and Ulises Lima, who have founded a new poetry movement—the visceral realists. García Madero quits law school to devote himself to the poetic existence, and takes us on a rambling journey through the Bohemian world of Mexico City, from cafés and bars where the poets spend hours discussing literature to bookshops from which they steal their reading material and houses and apartments where they make love to beautiful women.

This moving through the city is thus also a journey of initiation: to sex, as García Madero's initial fumblings lead to a positive explosion of promiscuity; and to the life of a poet, which in Bolaño's world is dark, provocative, radical, wonderful. By the time we get to December 30, where the diary ends, García Madero has definitively abandoned his old, conventional petit bourgeois life, and is jumping into a car with Lima, Belano, and Lupe, a young prostitute, to escape from the ire of Lupe's pimp, the terrifying Alberto.

The second and longest section of the book is a succession of monologues by a dizzying range of characters, spanning the period from 1976 to 1996, and ranging across three different continents. Together they create a prismatic retelling of the journeys undertaken by Arturo Belano and Ulises Lima over this twenty-year period, after the point where García Madero's diary breaks off. The story emerges in fragments, glimpses caught of our two main characters: Lima crops up in Paris, Belano in Barcelona, then Lima is back in Mexico. . . . And throughout, the story is pervaded with a question surrounding the whereabouts of a long-forgotten poet, Cesárea Tinajero, who founded the original visceral realist movement in the 1920s, and who Lima and Belano seem to have set off to find when they jump into the car with García Madero at the end of 1975. And it seems that this search led to

something terrible, something that has haunted Lima and Belano for the rest of their lives.

The third and final section of the book is a fast-paced, hard-boiled road trip from Mexico City to the small towns that dot the Sonoran Desert. We pick up García Madero's diary where we left off, and discover that the trio set off in Cesárea Tinajero's footsteps, with the violent Alberto hot on their tracks. The outcome is that Belano and Lima eventually return to civilization profoundly changed by the experience, and leaving García Madero behind.

There are many journeys to follow here: geographical ones, such as Ulises Lima and Arturo Belano's separate peregrinations across continents, or the road trip at the end of the book. But essentially, *The Savage Detectives* is about poetry as a journey, a way of life. The most autobiographical of Bolaño's novels, this book is an homage to his wild, passionate youth, when Bolaño tossed everything to devote himself to poetry (founding a group called the infrarealists—the real-life visceral realists), and to a life of stealing books, doing drugs, reading and writing constantly and furiously, talking about reading and writing constantly and furiously, making love, dreaming, and fighting for a better world—a life of intensity and meaning. In this book, the life of the poet is a journey that takes

Saguaro cacti growing in the Sonoran Desert—the hottest desert in North America —which straddles both the United States and Mexico.

Life left us all where we were meant to be or where it was convenient to leave us and then forgot us, which is as it should be.

them to the very heart of the city and all over the world, and ultimately to the very edge of death—and reading it offers us the privilege of taking this wild, breathless journey ourselves.

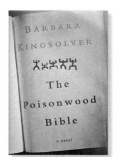

BARBARA KINGSOLVER

THE POISONWOOD BIBLE (1998)

An evangelical Baptist from Georgia relocates his wife and four daughters to the Belgian Congo in 1959.

Barbara Kingsolver was born in 1955 in Maryland and was raised mostly in rural Kentucky. She has lived, worked, and studied across five continents.

Kingsolver has said that *The Poisonwood Bible* haunted her for a decade before she found the courage to write it; notes resided in a filing cabinet where it was labeled "DAB"—the Damned Africa Book.

The author lived for two years in a Congolese village as a child but wasn't able to enter the Congo or Zaire while writing the novel, so, as she writes in her introduction, she "relied on memory, travel in other parts of Africa, and many people's accounts of the natural, cultural, and social history."

The Price family arrive in the Congo fresh from Bethlehem, Georgia, "bearing Betty Crocker cake mixes" into the jungle. Zealous missionary father Nathan Price, a man who "wears his faith like the bronze breastplate of God's foot soldiers," sets out to convert whoever he can get his hands on; his four daughters look on with differing levels of bemusement, disdain, and respect. But *The Poisonwood Bible* is not told in Nathan's voice and it is not his story; Barbara Kingsolver shifts between the perspectives of his wife, Orleanna, and daughters Rachel, Leah, Adah, and Ruth May, as they get to grips with the Congo and it gets to grips with them—or as Rachel, prone to malapropisms, puts it: "you can't just sashay into the jungle aiming to change it all over to the Christian style, without expecting the jungle to change you right back."

Kingsolver's America is a world of pinking shears and hand mirrors, one the Price women try to carry with them to the Congo but which their father—"Our Father," Adah calls him, privately and with loathing—tells them portentously is superfluous to requirements where they are going: "Consider the lilies of the field, which have no need of a hand mirror or aspirin tablets." Kingsolver's Congo "breathed behind the curtain of forest, preparing to roll over us like a river," full of endless rains, "vipers on the doorstep, and drums in the forest," biblical plagues of illness and pestilence, and more death than the Prices have ever seen before, including that of their youngest child.

Each of the Prices undertakes their own journey, the death of Ruth May igniting a spark that sends them to vastly different places—back to America, to South Africa, or deeper into the life of the Congo—and to vastly different understandings of the world. Kingsolver writes in dialogue with the postcolonial literature of the past; the "heart of darkness" she references—and yes, she does use that term—is saved for Orleanna, who uses it to describe her nightmare marriage to a damaged, controlling monster of a husband: "I was lodged in the heart of darkness, so thoroughly bent to the shape of marriage I could hardly see any other way to stand." Kingsolver's Congo is beloved and beautiful, hated and deadly, "barefoot bride of men who took her jewels and promised the Kingdom," a "cradle of rewarded evils and murdered goodness."

The journeys undertaken in *The Poisonwood Bible* are titanic, whether

they are across the chasm of grief to a small, quiet life far from an Africa "where one of my children remains in the dank red earth," or on the tidal waves of the devastation wrought on the people of the Congo through the 1960s and 70s. They are thrown into stark relief by the fixed nature of the Prices' eldest daughter, Rachel, who against all the odds and everything thrown at her, manages to end the book largely as she began it.

An early postcard of Kikwit on the Kwilu River in southeastern Congo, credited to Mr. Benson, published by Marque Gevaert.

Set against the struggle for Congolese independence, as Patrice Lumumba comes briefly to power before Mobutu begins his reign of terror and corruption, *The Poisonwood Bible* is at its most powerful as it shows Leah, who throws in her lot with

As long as I kept moving, my grief streamed out behind me like a swimmer's long hair in water

the Congolese, struggling to come to terms with her increasingly despised whiteness. And Kingsolver's aim, in portraying the blindness and lack of humanity of a man who thinks he is bringing enlightenment to the jungle, is perhaps best encapsulated by Nathan Price's sermons, in which he solemnly informs his perplexed congregation that "Tata Jesus is Bängala!" *Bängala*, which in Kikongo means "most precious" but also "most insufferable and also poisonwood." Yet again, he fails to understand the smallest thing about this land and its people.

2000–PRESENT

4 CONTEMPORARY CROSSINGS

For many, modern travel is not about tourism, but about migration, escape, displacement, and finding a new life. Belonging and identity become themes of the new century.

Part of the *Paseo de la humanidad* (Passage of Humanity) mural on the U.S.–Mexico border fence at Nogales, Sonora. This section depicts a U.S. border patrol officer holding a baton and chasing several migrants.

CÉSAR AIRA

AN EPISODE IN THE LIFE OF A LANDSCAPE PAINTER (UN EPISODIO EN LA VIDA DEL PINTOR VIAJERO) (2000)

The fictionalized account of landscape painter Johann Moritz Rugendas's abruptly abbreviated journey across the pampas of Argentina.

Aira lived in Pringles, Argentina, until he was eighteen, feeding himself books from the municipal library. Aira says, "In that era, at the end of the 50s and the beginning of the 60s, the industry of the bestseller, of cheap and popular entertainment, didn't exist yet, so everything I read was good."

Aira reports that though he writes very little, he writes every day and, since the year has many days, by the end of it he will have 300–400 pages. In his case: three or four books.

Aira has also translated and edited books from France, England, Italy, Brazil, Spain, Mexico, and Venezuela.

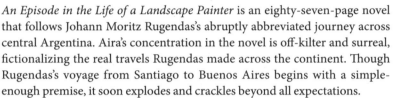

An Episode in the Life of a Landscape Painter is an eighty-seven-page novel that follows Johann Moritz Rugendas's abruptly abbreviated journey across central Argentina. Aira's concentration in the novel is off-kilter and surreal, fictionalizing the real travels Rugendas made across the continent. Though Rugendas's voyage from Santiago to Buenos Aires begins with a simple-enough premise, it soon explodes and crackles beyond all expectations.

Spirit-suffocating hardship reverberates throughout the Rugendas family and strikes hardest upon Johann Moritz Rugendas. He grew famous from the publication of *A Picturesque Voyage through Brazil*, a text based on his travels in Rio de Janeiro, Minas Gerais, Matos Grosso, Espiritu Santo, and Bahia. Like his great-great-grandfather, who was also a painter and who introduced his grandson to the trade, Rugendas is a man of "methodical deliberation." He approaches painting as the precise arrangement of layered elements that enable the viewer to intuitively grasp "climate, history, customs, economy, race, fauna, flora, rainfall, prevailing winds"—a technique that turns richer in the lush landscapes of the tropics. Of Rugendas, Aira writes, "His industrious journeying took him from Mexico, Chile, Peru, Brazil again, and Argentina, and resulted in hundreds, indeed thousands of paintings."

An Episode in the Life of a Landscape Painter fictionalizes Rugendas's first trip to Argentina, in 1822, when he traveled across the Andes from Chile. The journey is planned to take advantage of warm summer weather to cross the passes of the Cordillera, stopping to paint whenever an interesting subject presents itself. As anticipated, the method leads to great production, but the route is brutal:

> Near the watershed, at an altitude of two thousand meters, amid peaks disappearing into the clouds, rather than a way of getting from point A to point B, the path seemed to have become quite simply a way of departing from all points at once. Jagged lines, impossible angles, trees growing downward from ceilings of rock, sheer slopes plunging into mantles of snow under a scorching sun.

An Episode in the Life of a Landscape Painter is a hybrid creature, stitched together by luxurious ways of looking. Defying genre, Aira pulls the reader in by committing to an intense level of specificity, detailing everything from the minutiae of the massive, gorgeous landscapes, to the grisly particulars of bodily harm.

While riding his horse near the ranges of El Monigote and Agua Hedionda, a lightning bolt strikes Rugendas on the head: "The sensation of having electrified blood was horrible but very brief." As both man and horse are shaking off the paralyzing flow of electricity through their bodies, a second, more powerful and devastating bolt hits them. "Horse and rider were thrown about twenty meters, glowing and crackling like a cold bonfire." Amazingly, they survive, and the horse gets up and starts running. Unfortunately, for Rugendas, his foot is caught in the stirrup. The next morning, Rugendas's friend finds him as a bloody bundle, still hooked to the calmly grazing horse; still breathing: "[Rugendas] would never have imagined that his nervous system could produce so much pain."

... someone would, no doubt, attempt to repeat their journey, sooner or later. This thought made them feel they should be at once very careful and very daring: careful not to make a mistake that would render the repetition impossible; daring, so that the journey would be worth repeating, like an adventure.

Instead of journeying to Buenos Aires, they turn back toward Santiago, the nearest place where Rugendas can receive proper medical treatment. The accident puts Rugendas into a semi-invalid and perpetually medicated state; he suffers frequent migraines and paralyzing nervous attacks, but nonetheless he insists on dedicating hours of each day to still painting the landscapes that surround him. A dividing moment between a life with a well-functioning body and a painful, distorted one, Rugendas's feverish focus increases after his accident. The accident actually leaves him with an altered vision and an elevated purpose; his output increases. An incomplete catalogue of Rugendas's work, including oil painting, watercolors, and drawings, numbers over three thousand works.

An Episode in the Life of a Landscape Painter conveys the rich indulgences, the patience, and the compression of an Aira novel. Aira writes with the sound understanding that the journey as intended is a fine way to begin, but far more interesting are the unimagined and life-bending departures that happen along the way.

Left: The Countryside around Lima by the landscape painter Johann Moritz Rugendas in 1843.

TIM WINTON

Dirt Music (2001)

A deliciously slow-paced story about love, memory, and freedom, set in the massive, mesmerizing landscapes of Western Australia.

Tim Winton, author of twenty-nine books, was born near Perth in 1960, has lived in France, Italy, Greece, and Spain, and now lives back in Western Australia.

Dirt Music won several awards after it was published in 2002 and Winton donated $25,000 of his prize money to a successful campaign to save Ningaloo Reef from developers.

Signs of Life, a play by Tim Winton, continues the story of Lu Fox and Georgie Jutland from *Dirt Music*.

In *Dirt Music*, ex-musician Luther Fox, a loner, book-lover, and illegal fisherman, lives in White Point, an invented composite coastal town a few hours' drive north of Perth. The town's brutal buried histories rise gradually to the surface through the novel's leisurely unearthing.

Georgie Jutland is rootless, restless, and maverick; a forty-year-old former nurse, when the novel opens, she is lost and purposeless. She comes from a privileged background ("just another princess from the lady-mill") and lives with rich, licensed fisherman Jim Buckridge but is plotting her own challenging course through the world. White Point's luminous dunes and "get-fucked Fish Deco vibe" appeal to her, but she is impatient with people nostalgically clinging to the past, "staying on in houses or towns out of some perverted homage." By contrast, Lu Fox lingers in his family's farmhouse, up a dirt drive beside rotting melon paddocks, unable to shake off the memories that haunt him. The two of them take an unplanned drive to Perth, where a night in a hotel together changes both their lives.

When aggrieved locals kill Lu's dog and destroy his truck, he hitches north to find an island wilderness Georgie has described. Lu's trip is the novel's most vividly evoked journey, full of idiosyncratic people and dramatic places. There is a vivid, cinematic quality in Winton's descriptions of the Pilbara, the scorched, red region in the north of Western Australia. In the gorges, Lu feels "like he's driving through a movie. A western. Mesas, buttes. Cliffs, gulches." The slopes of the Ophthalmia Range are defined by contrasting colors: orange peaks against blue sky, purple gully shadows, screes like dried blood, shocking green gum trees, and white cockatoos.

Along the route, Lu visits the ghost town of Wittenoom, where his father mined lethal asbestos. Broome, the last real town on the journey, seems a parody of itself to Georgie, who is following Lu northward with Jim: "so many palm trees, so many brand new old-timey corrugated-iron storefronts." The place she had felt was "the tropical dream town" was becoming "a suburban outpost with a hokey pearl-diving theme."

Winton often conjures the hugeness of Australia. Lu's destination is as far from Perth as London is from Moscow; he passes road signs where towns

The iconic outback —Hammersley Range, Karijini National Park, Western Australia.

"have three- or four-digit distances" and tries to imagine "the impossible amplitude of the continent." The novel also explores the limitless spaces of human grief and redemption. Georgie mocks Lu for liking the writer Joseph Conrad. Lu's ultimate mapless journey to "the heartless heart of nature" parallels Conrad's voyage up the Congo in *Heart of Darkness*, but Winton's protagonists find peace as well as horror.

The island "wilderness within a wilderness," where the characters eventually converge, lies in fictional Coronation Gulf ("a long gut of milky-blue water, edged by beaches and belts of mangroves"). The setting—red rock rising from rain forest with looping echoes of birdsong—is an "iconic Australian landscape." The narrative lingers here as Lu reconnects with nature and music and learns to pay "attention to now." He fashions a makeshift stringed instrument and

Everything looks big and Technicolor ... This land looks dreamed, willed, potent

plays until he wonders "if he's the singer or the sung," stirring sounds and emotions that the novel's title suggests are rooted in the soil of the land. Like Lu's playing, *Dirt Music* is both exuberant and wistful. It recreates the shifting patterns of the natural world and gropes toward the wild places beyond language, grief, and memory.

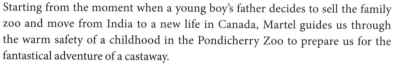

A METAPHORIC VOYAGE ON THE PACIFIC OCEAN FROM PONDICHERRY, INDIA, TO CANADA

YANN MARTEL

LIFE OF PI (2001)

The extraordinary story of a castaway on the high seas is a tale of the unexpected, of complex ideas and multiple pleasures.

Life of Pi won the Booker prize in 2002; it has sold more than 10 million copies worldwide and has been translated into fifty-five languages in fifty territories.

Martel, who is French Canadian, had his novel rejected by five London publishers before it was picked up by Knopf Canada. *Life of Pi*'s first publication was in Martel's home country in 2001.

The novel has been adapted both for the screen in 2012 —directed by Ang Lee— and for the stage. Lolita Chakrabarti's theatrical adaptation opened in London's West End in 2021 and won five Olivier awards in 2022.

Starting from the moment when a young boy's father decides to sell the family zoo and move from India to a new life in Canada, Martel guides us through the warm safety of a childhood in the Pondicherry Zoo to prepare us for the fantastical adventure of a castaway.

Such is the depth of his zoological knowledge that you might readily believe the author's father also ran a zoo, and that the young Martel had indeed spent his time with the animals while his brother played cricket. From the outset, Pi humanizes the creatures by comparing the running of a zoo to running a hotel. These animals have personalities, like the characters in Orwell's *Animal Farm*: each one has meaning and purpose. The Bengal tiger is christened Richard Parker following a bureaucratic bungle. The orangutan is known as Orange Juice. The sloth is like an "upside down yogi in deep meditation." The camel has a "senile lecherous look."

Yet early on Martel intimates that this will be more than a beast fable, but rather a story of metaphysical color with subplots of different journeys: of coming of age, of political upheaval, of human overcrowding and vanishing habitats, of disappearing old village ways, of conflicting faiths, of man versus beast, of capturing animals and caging wildlife for display. It is a saga of a world turned upside down, a civilization entrapped with everything wild it has sought to cage, confronted on the mortal stage of a small life raft.

Pi's sole companions are animals: a hyena, an orangutan, a zebra, a Bengal tiger—and, as Pi observes, God. Pi's journey carries a spiritual dimension with each creature made equal by its shared peril. By now we have moved into the realm of the adventure story. Pi must confront the practicalities of survival on board, and the cruel viciousness of his equally desperate shipmates. Finding drinking water involves a hazardous search beneath a tarpaulin, around a 450-pound seasick Bengal tiger, to find provisions. The water is in a can. How to open it?

The imagery evokes shipwrecked sailors crawling out of the sea—then the geopolitically bizarre, as Pi finds rations, made in Bergen, Norway—wheat, animal fat, and glucose. An Indian boy, stranded in the Pacific, on his way to Canada, eating food made in a Norway factory. Salvation is a cookie. "Pity about

We sailed from Madras across the Bay of Bengal, down through the Straits of Malacca around Singapore and up to Manila . . . on our fourth day out, midway to Midway, we sank.

the fat but given the exceptional circumstances the vegetarian part of me would simply pinch its nose and bear it."

The animals, reduced to their wild natures, are instinctive predators with no such qualms about animal fats. They are manifest Victorian sailors adrift who would like to eat the cabin boy. They are integral to the story for a purpose. And so, we come to a duel, an almost fundamental combat between man and beast, brain and brawn, a contest of survival against the odds, against the elements themselves. Pi must prove himself.

Pi is us, all of us, humankind being tested. Beyond the thrilling, frightening narrative, Martel's narrative purpose is to test conventions, to give arguments life. The zoo animals are released, the wild meets the civilized, the watched become the watchers, the savage meet the sagacious. On a level deck the question hangs: who is the most predatory of creatures?

Alone in the company of an adult Bengal tiger . . . Richard Parker looks over the edge of the lifeboat in Ang Lee's 2012 film version starring Suraj Sharma and Gérard Depardieu.

JOSEPH O'CONNOR

STAR OF THE SEA (2002)

The perilous transatlantic sea journey escaping from the potato famine in Connemara, Ireland to New York in 1847.

Joseph O'Connor was born in Dublin and now lives between New York, London, and Dublin. In 2012 he was awarded an Irish PEN Award for outstanding contribution to Irish Literature.

Star of the Sea is the eighth and best known of Joseph O'Connor's novels, which have earned him the Irish Pen award for outstanding contribution to Irish literature. It sold 800,000 copies in its first year of publication. A sequel, *Redemption Falls*, set after the civil war, was published in 2007.

The title is steeped in Catholic tradition: in Latin, *Stella Maris* (which translates as "star of the sea") denotes the Virgin Mary, who protects all seafarers.

Star of the Sea is drama on a grand Victorian scale, spanning continents and the best part of a century. O'Connor reduces his overarching tale of those caught up in the Irish potato famine into believable, manageable, bite-sized chunks. The novel is made up of letters, of secret loves, of fragments: a jigsaw he pieces together carefully so at no point does it lurch into ponderousness. It is an Irish *Grapes of Wrath*, though not the Midwest, but the mid-Atlantic.

We are on board the *Star of the Sea* of the title. Famine has brought an unlikely mix of people together: Lord and Lady Kingscourt, forced to abandon their bankrupt estate, have to share their flight to the New World with many of their own evicted tenants, now destitute and still starving. While they are serenaded with a harp, and drink wine at the captain's table, downstairs in steerage it is still gruel. The past is about to catch up with them. A future in America beckons.

Also traveling first class with the Kingscourt family are the narrator and would-be author Grantley Dixon. Master Lockwood keeps a log to report on events for his company owners. Also at the dinner are a maharaja, a mail agent, a surgeon, and a man of the cloth—the set up might almost be an Agatha Christie murder weekend. And down among the passengers in steerage is at least one with vengeance on his mind.

Star of the Sea could be read as a murder mystery where there are many motivations. Or as a rich history of the Irish famine that has forced an unlikely cast of people to make the perilous journey to New York in stormy mid-November. Or as a catalogue of individual stories told across twenty-six days, like an oceanic *Canterbury Tales*. The novel has something of all of these things, but it also has its own stirring uniqueness.

Before any other words are on the page we have met our monster. Pius Mulvey is one of the twenty-first-century's great antiheroes. His left foot drags, he is in a tattered military overcoat, his arms are very long. His destitution is more manifest, but perhaps no less real, than the others on board. He stalks the ship, and as he moves along the galleys and guardrails checking cargo and crew, the journeys of those on board begin to emerge.

We still tell each other that we are lucky to be alive, when our being alive has almost nothing to do with luck, but with geography, pigmentation, and international exchange rates.

O'Connor draws us into the novel, to be spectators at the ringside of a fracture in history. We witness not only the ship's voyage onward, but also the journeys back into Ireland to explain how these people came to set sail in the first place. O'Connor's subtitle is "A Farewell to Old Ireland," and his text is punctuated by quotes from the time that pitch us into the heart of rural life. His prose is elegant and skilled; few can match the O'Connor dictionary. The different strands to his story emerge out of a fog of perceptions. Like the sailors on board, we get a sense of a presence before we actually see it; we get a sense of one story, when there are more. We do not get one hero, heroine, or villain but a choice of five or six.

O'Connor constructs stories within stories, including some small, delicious literary asides that creep in. There is mention of bumping into Charles Dickens, and the real story behind *Oliver Twist*; of the unmasking of Ellis Bell (Emily Brontë's pseudonym; the first edition of *Wuthering Heights* was indeed published in that year and Brontë's Yorkshire moors are here replaced by Connemara, or even the Atlantic itself); of an eloquent literary agent and printer in Thomas Newby, who did indeed publish Brontë.

Paying for their passage —emigrants at the shipping office at Cork heading for America at the height of the potato famine. Wood engraving, 1851.

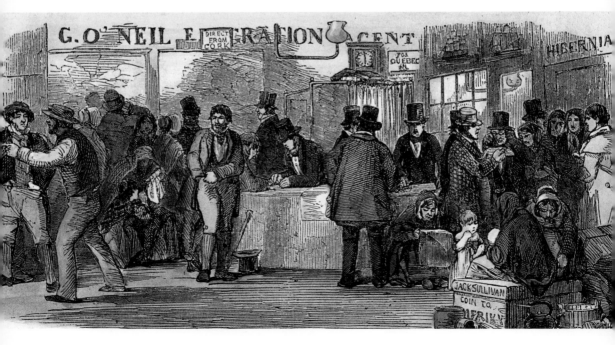

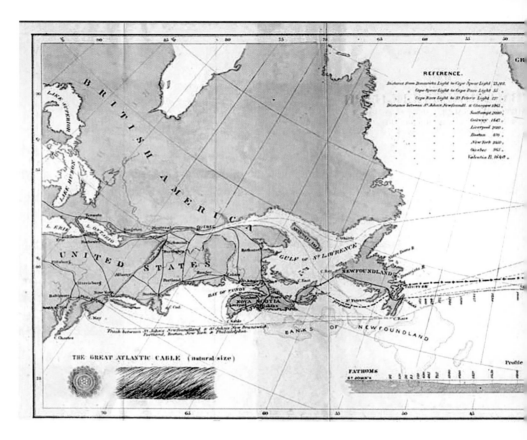

To add an extra layer of drama, this ship of their salvation is itself "absurdly out of its element, a creaking, leaking, incompetent concoction of oak and pitch and nails and faith bobbing on a wilderness of black water." There are so many holes, widgets, and new weldings needed to patch it up over the years that it whistles and sings when the wind blows in the right direction.

Within a few paragraphs, O'Connor sets up his stall. His ship, his *Star*, is of the same ilk and literary provenance as Melville's *Pequod* in *Moby-Dick*, his voyage as important as Conrad's up the Congo in *Heart of Darkness*—a thought underlined by the Victorian Gothic conceit of opening each chapter with an encouraging explanation of its own, in which we learn, "The Leave Taking," "The Victim," "The Cause" . . .

His scene setting is guilefully cinematic, moving from the overview, the log, a peek below stairs, an argument at the top table, letters from across the Atlantic, and an old newspaper opinion piece where the author goes wonderfully, scandalously and libellously over the top in defaming his targets. But beneath all this there is a mission. There is rhyme and reason among these characters where seemingly the rest of the world has been abandoned:

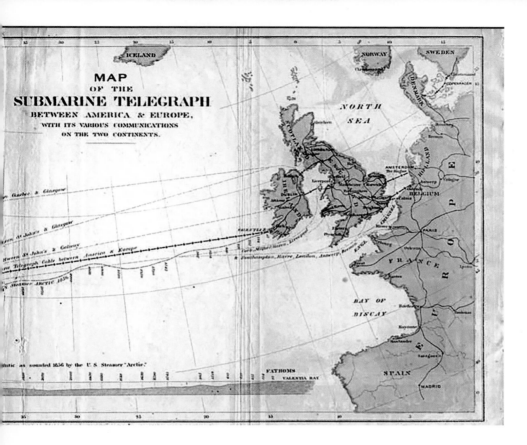

The reasons why things are the way they are could be ferociously complicated, Mulvey knew, but in this corner of the empire they worked themselves out into cadences of mathematical inevitability.

Star of the Sea is more than a polemic against the English in Ireland; other well-worked subtleties interweave and taunt established covenants. The occasional use of Gaelic is a reminder of the heritage that the characters leave behind, and a sign that neither side of the farming divide could really talk to each other. Most of the English could not speak Gaelic or be bothered to learn it at all.

O'Connor reveals something of his own methods when describing the love that Mulvey suddenly finds, on hearing the music coming out of the local inns: "as though once there had only been one great song from which the song makers kept drawing, a hidden holy well." The oceanic wrath and power is matched, even surpassed, by the emotional turmoil of everyone onboard, caught in a purgatory between eras and civilizations.

The first maps of the Atlantic —like this one from 1858—were drawn up to mark the laying of telegraph cables. The routes were followed by the ships heading for New York with their cargoes of new settlers.

AUÐUR AVA ÓLAFSDÓTTIR
BUTTERFLIES IN NOVEMBER
(RIGNING Í NÓVEMBER) (2004)

A late summer vacation turns into an inner journey of discovery when a woman loses everything in one day—her home, her husband, and her past— and sets off on a voyage in the company of a four-year-old child.

Born in Reykjavik in 1958, award-winning novelist, playwright, and poet Auður Ava Ólafsdóttir studied at the Sorbonne in Paris before becoming a professor of art history.

Auður struggled to find a publisher for *Butterflies in November*. Eventually, it was Salka Publishing who gave her a chance. *The novel was translated into English by Brian FitzGibbon in 2013.*

In Iceland, November is the beginning of the darkest time of the year: while there are about eight hours of daylight early in November, there are only about five hours of daylight toward the end of the month.

"There is a lottery prize here, money and a journey. I see a circular road, and I also see another ring that will fit on a finger, later. You'll never be the same again." The unnamed female narrator of *Butterflies in November* hears this prediction from a fortune teller whom she was not even meant to see in the first place—it was her best friend Auður who made the appointment but could not keep it and sent her instead. And, as predicted, the narrator sets off into the increasing darkness of the Icelandic winter after her husband discloses that he wants a divorce because his secretary is pregnant with his child. It is not that the narrator flees from this situation; rather, the journey is meant to help her explore her "most intimate and uncharted territories in a quest for fresh feelings."

While she had planned to spend this time alone, she finds herself in the company of Auður's four-year-old son Tumi, "a hearing-impaired child with a speech impediment." Auður is expecting twins, and complications force her to stay in the hospital for the remaining three months of her pregnancy. When the narrator agrees to look after Tumi, the responsibility fills her with doubt. "I wasn't made to be a mother," she says. "I haven't the faintest clue about children."

Although she would preferably go to a faraway place with tropical forests and coral reefs, she stays local and travels the Ring Road highway around Iceland because she has won not just one, but two lottery prizes: a vast sum of money, and a mobile bungalow that is dropped off for her on the other side of the island. Yet, "nothing is as it should be" on this road trip. It is unseasonably warm for November, and instead of snow there are butterflies in the air and constant rain, which, at times, obscures the landscape. Mudslides could interrupt the journey at any moment, and what sounds impressive—Iceland's National Highway 1—is often no more than a dirt track, broken up by single-lane bridges.

Hoping that "things might automatically start to solve themselves" by the sheer fact of being on the road, the narrator's outward journey into darkness is also an inward one; it is a woman's search for herself, as if the darkness around her in the stark landscape of black sand, black lava fields, and black

ocean mirrors her own lack of orientation after her husband has left her. And yet, it is in this darkness that she finds a feeling of security, as she states when a stranger leads her into a lava field one night to show her what utter darkness really looks like.

Route 1, often called the Ring Road, Skeiðarársandur, Skaftafell National Park. In the distance is Vatnajökull, literally "the glacier of lakes."

It is not by way of reflection that the narrator discovers new sides to herself, but through the many peculiar and seemingly mundane encounters that mark her journey, such as when she runs over a sheep and returns the cadaver to the farmer; or when she stays in a boarding house where the hosts grow cucumbers with thermal water and inscribe them with personal messages for their customers.

For the most part, however, it is Tumi who challenges her, as she has to learn new strategies of communication to cater to the child's needs. All her professional accomplishment and linguistic skill as a translator—she's fluent in eleven languages—can't help her in understanding the boy, although she gradually, and with Tumi's help, adds sign language to her repertoire. Throughout the course of their journey, she learns to pay close attention to the wishes and feelings that he conveys without words, and the tender bond between them strengthens: we get the impression that the narrator may know a little more about children than she makes us believe.

At first, the fortune teller's words, "you'll be standing with the light in your arms," do not make much sense, but when the narrator, toward the end, discloses, "I am beginning to be someone else, beginning to be me," they ring true: by traveling through the Icelandic winter darkness, she has found her way back to herself.

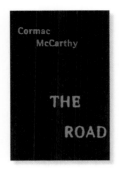

CORMAC MCCARTHY

THE ROAD (2006)

*This unflinching journey into an end-of-days scenario has at its heart
the illuminating love between father and son, which lightens their ever-
darkening world.*

Cormac McCarthy was born in 1933 in the United States and was one of his country's most revered writers. *The Road*, his tenth novel, was first published by Alfred A. Knopf in 2006. Its character of the young boy and his unfolding journey has seen the book compared to Mark Twain's *Huckleberry Finn*.

Praised as a masterpiece, *The Road* was awarded the James Tait Black Memorial Prize for Fiction in 2006 and the Pulitzer Prize for Fiction in 2007. It has been translated into countless editions and a film was released in 2009. That same year, the manual typewriter McCarthy used for fifty years was auctioned for more than a quarter of a million dollars!

The Road may well tell of the most harrowing journey in all fiction. Although the novel has little real plot, its compelling emotional journey is a culmination of centuries of apocalyptic fiction. After an unnamed catastrophe, presumably nuclear, an equally anonymous father and son journey across the "cauterized terrain" of an America that has been "looted, ransacked, ravaged." In their odyssey south along an interstate highway toward the coast they become emblematic of all humankind, especially since names, dates, ages, and locations are never identified. These reference points are no longer valid or significant. Indeed, this is the only world that the boy has ever known because he was born just after a "long shear of light and then a series of low concussions" rocked the world.

The pair scavenge through "middens of anonymous trash" for food and clothing, in an end-of-world scenario where most other humans have become cannibals, subverting all morality. Women have become their chattels, children their food. Pitted against such monsters the pair become "pilgrims in a fable." Yet, while this religious dimension casts the father as a shepherd to his son, it is nevertheless the child who comes to embody any slight potential for a future.

His father's care is bestowed "like some ancient anointing" and it is through this benediction that it is the child, not the father, who consistently connects with his wider humanity and shows empathy. He is the one who looks behind the most, who assumes the role of moral compass in the face of overwhelming odds threatening to erode his innocence. While they both "carry the fire," like primordial man tending the flame of hope and love, they yet exhibit a fundamental difference: the father's desire is for them to survive as individuals, the son's to reconnect with "the good guys" and survive as a species. While the father's creed for survival sees himself and his son as "each the other's world entire," the son embraces a more universal love.

And always there is the road giving them a focus to their journey. However, while a road in most other novels ends in a comforting destination, a homecoming, or a sanctuary, this is a road more likely to become a trap rather than a path. A fate that would strip them of their humanity and turn

them into something more akin to "apes fishing with sticks in an anthill." What maintains their humanity however is the abiding love father and son feel for each other, an unfaltering truth in a world "of things ceasing to be."

Wasteland: the man and the boy struggle to survive on the journey south in the 2009 film version, directed by John Hillcoat.

Although their physical world is obscured, their spiritual world is illuminated by this love so that by the end the father sees his son "glowing . . . like a tabernacle." It is this love, a word never actually articulated in the text, which illuminates an otherwise gray and pitiless world. And, indeed, it is love that opens and closes the book. It begins with the father waking and immediately reaching for his son; it closes with a woman, a stranger, holding the boy in a loving embrace. And, lest it be overlooked, the father's opening dream also centers around a great truth: in his nightmare it is his child who "led him by the hand." Surely we are meant to recall that Christian benediction? That a little child shall lead them.

In a *Wall Street Journal* interview in 2009, McCarthy acknowledged that his "four-year-old son practically co-wrote the book," which is dedicated to him. And surely this is why the simple, yet touching, dialogue has such an authentic ring. Why its sparse vocabulary, which mirrors the pared down landscape, is almost unbearable. Its stuttering sentences are beaten out like heartbeats until we reach the book's concluding word: "mystery." Perhaps this is the author's final opinion on where life's journey takes us all?

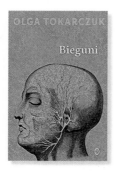

OLGA TOKARCZUK

FLIGHTS (BIEGUNI) (2007)

Two works, one "official," one of fiction, are the lodestars of this entrancingly nonlinear book, as wayward and quixotic as all truly meaningful voyages are, which thinks about the meaning and experience of travel in the twenty-first century.

Olga Tokarczuk was born in Sulechow, Poland, in 1962. After training as a psychologist at the University of Warsaw she practiced as a therapist. She published her first book of poetry in 1989.

The original title, *Bieguni*, references a nomadic sect that appears in the book, who believe that to escape evil, one must remain constantly on the move.

Flights won the Nike Award, Poland's foremost literary prize, in 2008. Its English translation won the Man Booker International Prize in 2018, and Tokarczuk also won the Nobel Prize for Literature in 2018.

"There are things that happen of their own accord, journeys that begin and end in dreams. And there are travelers who simply answer the chaotic call of their own unease." Olga Tokarczuk's *Flights* is a book for which the word cornucopia might almost have been invented. A novel, a memoir, an anti-travelogue, a compendium of curious novelties, it is also a work of anthropology, history, and philosophy, as the unnamed narrator at its center, a Polish author persistently on the move, journeys across the globe, accessing all of the accoutrements of modern travel at her disposal: airports, railroad stations, hotel rooms—and incorporates them into what is essentially a meditation on the living and the dead across time and space. Her characters and the vignettes that illustrate them might be fictional, and the incidents relatively commonplace, such as the Polish man searching for his family who have disappeared while on vacation in Croatia; or notorious and factual, like the story of the peculiar afterlife of the heart of the composer Chopin. (Following his death in Paris in 1849, it was smuggled back to Poland via the underskirts of his sister and since 1945 has resided in a crypt in Warsaw.)

The narrator of *Flights*, porous and receptive to all around her, is snippy about the usefulness of rather quotidian travel literature as an authentic guide to places and people: "The truth is terrible: describing is destroying," she complains. She herself relies on only two such guides "because they were written with real passion, and a genuine desire to portray the world. The first was written in Poland in the early eighteenth century." Following a lengthy description of the provenance of this book and its contents, the narrator lists the second in one brief, declamatory line: "The other is Melville's *Moby-Dick*."

Tokarczuk's narrator travels so often that her actual home begins to become indistinguishable from a hotel; her bed with sheets that "could be a better quality, white and well-starched linen. Instead they're the color of faded bark." This particular hotel has a "really terrific" library—"in fact," the narrator comments mischievously, "I may even end up staying here longer just because of those books." It's a salient point that Tokarczuk herself did not obtain a passport and leave Poland until 1990, at the age of twenty-eight, travel having been limited under decades of Soviet control. (New travelers,

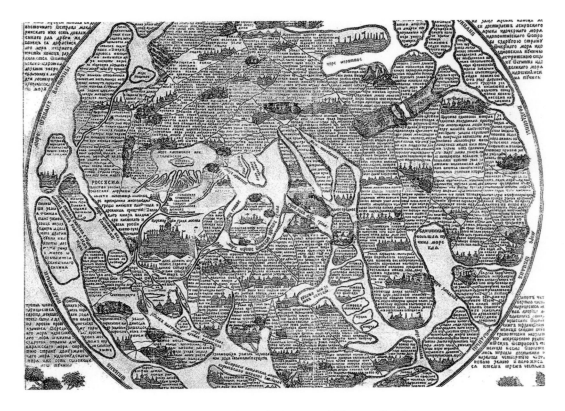

An original illustration by Olga Tokarczuk, featured in all editions of the book.

initially hesitant, often feel the need to make up for lost time.) The novel's title also gives the strong impression that humans travel because they are either seeking or running away from something—memory, perhaps, often the most resilient of pursuers. In the mini-essay "Purging the Map," Tokarczuk writes:

> If something hurts me, I erase it from my mental map. Places where I stumbled, fell, where I was struck down, cut to the quick, where things were painful—such places are simply not there any longer. This means I've got rid of several big cities and one whole province. Maybe someday I'll eliminate a country.

The other element of a dogged desire to be constantly on the move is mortality—the fear of it, and the delusion that to be endlessly mobile is to somehow escape it. "Blessed is he who leaves"—the essence of this quotation permeates throughout *Flights*. The monotony of transit lounges from Prague to Montreal, the discovery of the Achilles tendon in 1542, flight attendants "beautiful as angels": all have their randomly precise place in Tokarczuk's celestial, unearthly transmissions.

DACIA MARAINI

TRAIN TO BUDAPEST
(IL TRENO DELL'ULTIMA NOTTE) (2008)

In 1956, a young Italian journalist sets out on a journey that will take her across a divided Europe, investigating life in the communist states of Europe and attempting to discover what has become of a childhood playmate.

Dacia Maraini, born in 1936, is an Italian novelist, playwright, poet, and columnist who writes, in her own words, "from a woman's point of view."

Committed to social and political reform, she has been active in campaigns for women's rights, for the legalization of abortion, for stricter laws on domestic violence, as well as for a crackdown on corruption and organized crime.

Maraini's prolific literary output includes over 20 novels and several volumes of travel writing.

Amara, a young Florentine journalist whose name translates as "bitter," is dispatched in 1956 to report on life on the other side of the Iron Curtain. The editor's commission asks her to investigate "what remains of the suffering in the Second World War? What about memories of the Shoah?"

The English title may suggest a gentle trip to the city on the Danube, but the original title, which translates as "The Train on the Last Night," carries an echo of a primal "night journey" into the roots of consciousness of evil. Amara's task as an investigative journalist combines with a personal mission to find out what has become of Emanuele Orenstein, an Austrian Jewish boy to whom she had been close when they were children in Tuscany. While bound by a friendship they were too young to call love, they had already decided to stay together all their lives, but this idyll ended in 1939 when Emanuele's parents, buoyed by a belief that family loyalty to Austria over generations would shield them from governmental anti-Semitism, decided to return to Vienna. For a time the two children corresponded, but the messages from Emanuele suddenly stopped, although Amara did come into possession of a cache of letters written by him from Lodz but never sent.

The problems of interrogation by a succession of border guards on the journey from Florence are alleviated by meeting Hans Wilkowsky, a young fellow traveler with a command of languages. Amara's first destination is Auschwitz, where Emanuele may have been sent, and the harrowing account of conditions there are given added intensity by Maraini's own experiences of starvation and fear as a seven year old in a Japanese concentration camp. Her father, a distinguished Orientalist, was working in Japan when the country entered the war on the side of the Axis powers. Ordered to take an oath of loyalty to Mussolini, he refused, making the family enemy aliens.

A fruitless search in the Auschwitz archives is followed by renewed contact with Hans, whose offer of help in the quest for Emanuele is accepted only after Amara insists that the relationship be platonic. The party is completed by Horvath, an elderly Hungarian librarian whom they meet in Vienna but who had been with the German army at the siege of Stalingrad. The novel becomes a combination of travelogue, historical novel, and even

grim and unforgiving picaresque tale as the three travel by train from country to country, encountering the daily frustrations of bureaucracy and recording the experiences of people who had lived through the tragedies of twentieth-century Europe. Amara's own quest seems to have reached its conclusion when she comes face to face with a mysterious Peter Orenstein, who claims to be Emanuele but whose seeming age, bitterness of character, and refusal to recognize Amara leave her troubled and bemused.

Hungarian refugees on their way to the Netherlands in November 1956, seeking to escape the Russian crackdown after the failure of the Hungarian Uprising.

In their search for further documentation, the three move to Budapest; their arrival coincides with the outbreak of the anti-Soviet uprising. The mental and physical chaos of those days, the tentative hopes that turn to despair as Soviet tanks crush the rebellion, are described in vivid detail. Amara remains driven by an inner compulsion, which will not permit her to return home without again meeting the man who may be Emanuele. The final, passionate chapters recount in tormented detail Peter's or Emanuele's destruction as a man after being experimented on by Nazi doctors.

Joseph Conrad had been Amara's moral guide on her journey into recent European history, and once back home, meditating on her own failure, she picks up *Heart of Darkness* to read Marlow's recollection of Kurtz's last words: "I seemed to hear the whispered cry, 'The horror! The horror!'" The cities she had visited are sites of the clash between civilization and barbarism, while the book itself is born of Dacia Maraini's own experiences and observations of similar struggles.

JANG EUN-JIN

NO ONE WRITES BACK
(AMUDO PYEONJIHAJI ANTA) (2009)

A man and his dog travel from motel to motel in nameless, faceless Korean cities, writing letters as they go.

Jang Eun-Jin was born in South Korea in 1976 and has won several awards, including the prestigious Munhakdongne Award, which *No One Writes Back* won in 2009.

Her debut, a collection of short stories titled *Kitchen Laboratory*, was also highly decorated, winning the Chonnam Ilbo New Short Story Award in 2002 and the Joongang Ilbo New Writers Contest in 2004. The book was republished as a novel in 2008.

Jang describes writing as "being locked inside a small, dark, cold room by (her)self."

Jang Eun-Jin's *No One Writes Back* (translated by Jung Yewon) combines "classic" road-trip elements with the homogeneous and often repetitive aspects of Korean cities, culminating in a most Korean ending—a return to home. *No One Writes Back* comes from a line of Korean road-trip literature, including the classic *Hong Gildong*, one of the first works written in the Korean alphabet, when Chinese was still the language of Korean literature. But while *Hong Gildong* is a tale of adventure, *No One Writes Back* is a travel tale of the commonplace. The story begins three years into a journey, as it winds down, and takes place in unidentified locations. Jihun, the narrator, is not searching for sights or for adventure. He sums up himself and his journey:

> I'm a traveler who goes from motel to motel; [. . .] this journey wasn't meant as a means to gain something. [. . .] Still, there's probably a bit of something I hope to have gained [. . .] something like quiet stability.

The passive Jihun is led around Korea by his dog, Wajo, from motel to motel. As he travels, he meets people who he identifies as only numbers and to each of whom he writes and mails a hand-written letter. Jihun also writes a series of open, heartfelt letters to members of his family. His journey is "a journey of letters," and the nondescript nature of his travel is a reasonable representation of the similarity that cramped geography and hurried national modernization has sometimes brought to Korean cities. When a location is idiosyncratic, as in the hotel *The Moon and Sixpence* (named for the novel by W. Somerset Maugham) or a tragic *gosiwon* (study apartment), a major change is necessarily underway.

Jihun meets a vagabond novelist who travels the subways, selling her first novel. Referred to as "751," the novelist pairs with Jihun in a prickly, semi-comical relationship developing across various hotels and through various calamities, including separation, the reappearance of an old flame, and actual flames.

Daily, Jihun calls a friend back home, enquiring if anyone has written back. No one has, and Jihun continues to travel, noting that a response would

What I've learned on my journey is that the fewer destinations you have, the better. When there's no goal, there's no expectation, and when there's no expectation, there's no disappointment. Freedom is being able to go off when you feel like it.

have occasioned a move back home. Jihun's "road trip" is an extended attempt at return. To Koreans—who do not call their country "Korea" but rather "our land" (*uri nara*) and similarly do not invite you to "their" house but to "our house" (*uri jip*)—the idea of a home is central to identity. Hometowns and returning are so embedded in Korean culture that on major holidays (such as Chuseok, a harvest festival) Korean freeways jam with the traffic of urbanites returning "home." When meeting someone new, one of the first few questions Koreans ask is about their hometown. Hometowns are thought to be a part of one's character, and most Korean road-trip fiction revolves around the idea of home. This theme is found in other Korean road-trip literature, including Choe In-ho's *Deep Blue Night* and Kim Insuk's *The Long Road*.

No One Writes Back can be clever; in one scene Jihun puts a guide-dog vest on Wajo, dark glasses on himself, and feigns blindness. In fact, Wajo is blind and this is just the best way to navigate the subway system. *No One Writes Back* drops surprises of this nature until two final bombshells that tie the narrative up, explain Jihun's road trip, and give it a meaning not apparent in its bleak geography and architecture. As with *Hong Gildong*, Jihun's road trip brings him home, with a last fillip that gives home a new meaning.

KIM THÚY

RU (2009)

A testament to the extraordinary sacrifices of the Vietnamese "boat people,"
this is an enduring journey from a palatial residence in Saigon to a flea-
ridden Malaysian refugee camp, and onward to a new home in Quebec.

On a starless November night in 1978, crowds of Vietnamese people, including Kim Thúy, huddled aboard a storm-battered boat bound for Malaysia. Crouched in darkness, the refugees became numb to the smell of urine, sweat, and fear that engulfed them. Night and day became indistinguishable. Thúy was ten years old when the Vietnam War ended with the fall of her hometown Saigon—old enough to recall the deathly silence that besieged the once-lively capital, and the transformation of red gao blossoms into bomb craters. Following the communist takeover of Saigon in 1975, a million so-called "boat people" like Thúy took to the oceans, braving the threat of not only starvation but also rape and murder at the hands of pirates.

Simulating the motion of that vicious sea journey, Kim Thúy's debut novel comprises one hundred and forty poetic prose fragments that leap backward and forward through time. Passages are linked by recurring phrases, which build momentum as a poetry collection does. Translated from French, *Ru*—the word means "lullaby" in Vietnamese; in French it can mean a small stream or a flow of blood, tears, or money—is inspired by Thúy's personal voyage to safety. Readers witness the immense hardships faced by the narrator Nguyen An Tinh, who, like Thúy, journeys from Vietnam to Canada, struggles to integrate into Quebec society, returns to Vietnam as a lawyer, and experiences motherhood. While *Ru* travels through these events in relentless motion, it also crystallizes Nguyen's moments of pause, capturing the process of psychic survival across borders. For example, the narrator pinpoints the paradox that, although her family was rendered stateless by force, she remains "glad to move":

> [I]t gives me a chance to lighten my belongings, to leave objects behind so that my memory can become truly selective, can remember only images that stay luminous behind my closed eyelids . . .

Both gratitude and pain are woven into Nguyen's periods in exile—a contradiction that resounds later, in the private war waging inside her autistic son: "thanks to him, every spark of joy has become a blessing." Thúy's work

Born in Vietnam in 1968, Kim Thúy fled the country with her family after the fall of Saigon in 1975. By 1979, they had settled in Quebec.

First published in 2009 by Quebec's Libre Expression, *Ru* won the 2010 Governor General's Literary Award for French-language fiction.

As Thúy highlights during an interview with Penguin Canada, "this book is not [just] about me [. . .] if [it] was only about me, it would have lasted maybe three pages!

Thúy built her multilingual identity into her work; "ru" having translatable meanings in both French and Vietnamese.

I moved forward in the trace of their footsteps as in a waking dream where the scent of a newly blown poppy is no longer a perfume but a blossoming: where the deep red of a maple leaf in autumn is no longer a color but a grace; where a country is no longer a place but a lullaby.

of autofiction roams through wide circles and viewpoints; from her cousin Sao Mai, to the flamboyant "Uncle Two" (referred to by birth rank as is Vietnamese custom), to the prostitutes she encounters at a restaurant when she returns to Saigon. Behind the girls' "dreamy" skin, scarred by humiliation, "they carried all the invisible weight of Vietnam's history, like the [rice picker] women with hunched backs." At the start of Nguyen's journey, Vietnam's history appears oppressive; it has "stripped our names of their meaning." As divisions physically and emotionally tear up her home, Nguyen dreams of freedom in the West.

The journey's aspirational end in Canada feels like rebirth, marked by unfamiliar sensations and sounds. Upon arrival in Granby, "heaven on earth," the narrator is shocked by her snowy surroundings. The abundance and generosity of her new-found home are also dazzling in contrast to her dehumanizing existence in the Malaysian refugee camp.

But despite finally achieving her American dream and securing safety for her children, Nguyen remains buffeted by the loss of her homeland. A Vietnamese waiter in Canada awakens her to the depth of her sacrifice:

> I no longer had the right to declare I was Vietnamese because I no longer had their fragility, their uncertainty, their fears. And he was right to remind me.

In *Ru*, Thùy inserts into her history the forgotten heroines and traumatized children of American G.I.s who make up the "hidden side of the war"—the thread that binds the pages of Vietnam's past and present. The novel ends on the image of the phoenix and the hope for remembrance and renewal: even if each new generation is a little further from that original sacrifice, a little more removed from the country that was once home.

YURI HERRERA

Signs Preceding the End of the World (señales que precederán al fin del mundo) (2009)

An extraordinary novel that tackles themes of migration, translation, cultural hybridity, and the shifting borderlands between the living and the dead.

Yuri Herrera (Actopan, Mexico, 1970) is a political scientist, editor, and writer. He teaches at Tulane University in New Orleans.

His first novel *Trabajos del Reino* (*Kingdom Cons*, translated by Lisa Dillman) won prizes in both Mexico and Spain, was a huge critical success, and turned him into one of Latin America's most important contemporary writers

Signs Preceding the End of the World inspired a six-minute film by Josh Begley, "Best of Luck with the Wall," which comprises satellite images running all 19,054 miles of the U.S.–Mexico border.

Makina, the young heroine of Yuri Herrera's novel *Signs Preceding the End of the World*, is a switchboard operator in a part of Mexico that cell phone coverage has yet to reach. She is a liminal creature, a go-between, a messenger, "malleable, erasable, permeable," moving easily between Spanish, English, and the indigenous language of her hometown. Despite being a teenager, Makina is street smart, knows how to hustle, and has no trouble handling herself in a macho world of armed predators.

Her journey begins in an old silver mining community where the ground is dangerously unstable. The novel begins with a giant sinkhole swallowing even the screams of passers-by. "I'm dead," thinks Makina, but manages to scramble out of the way. She has been tasked with bringing home her brother, who left for the United States to claim a plot of land belonging to their estranged father. She leaves behind her mother, her little sister, and a devoted boyfriend who she only "shucked" because she felt like it and who she has been keeping safely at arm's length.

Having agreed to run an errand for a local crime lord in exchange for help crossing the border, she heads first to the "Big Chilango"—Mexico City—and from there takes an interminable bus through "villages emptied of men," until she reaches "the end of the land." She crosses the Río Grande in a rubber raft, but when a wave knocks her into the water "suddenly the world turned cold and green, filled with invisible water monsters." She is dragged, spluttering, onto the riverbank, and from there makes her way over the mountains to the city—though not before a run-in with an armed rancher, who leaves her with a bullet wound in her side.

North of the border is part consumerist nightmare, part ghostly netherworld: "a nebulous territory between what is dying out and what is not yet born." Her brother had warned her, in a letter home, that "It's really lonely here, but there's lots of stuff." Makina notices all the "signs prohibiting things" and how miserable everyone looks. She encounters many things for the first time: snow, an African American person, supermarket self-checkout machines. Armed only with an address, she heads off to look for "the promised land." But the land, as Makina rightly suspected, never existed.

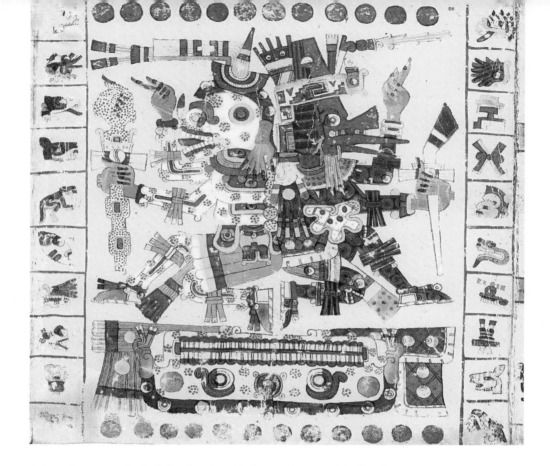

When she eventually finds her brother, she learns that a wealthy family took advantage of his undocumented status, promising to pay him handsomely to assume their son's identity and take his place in the U.S. army. Returned from active service abroad, he is a specter of what Makina remembers, and at first she doesn't recognize him.

Makina's journey is as much mythological as it is physical. As she travels north across a state border, she also makes a parallel journey through the Aztec underworld of Mictlán (remember that the novel opens with Makina uttering the words "I'm dead"). The nine chapters correspond to the nine levels of the Aztec underworld through which the dead must pass before they can rest. Their challenges include fording a river (Chapter 2: "Water Crossing") and traversing a place where beasts rip out their hearts (Chapter 7: "The Place Where People's Hearts Are Eaten"). The elusive, ambiguous final chapter makes readers return to the book's title, *Signs Preceding the End of the World*, and ask, whose world?

Written in extraordinarily concise and inventive language, *Signs* showcases Herrera's ability to weave a pre-Hispanic cosmovision around urgent contemporary concerns, including undocumented migration, racial profiling, language, and cultural hybridity.

Traversing the Underworld—the Central Mexican gods Mictlantecuhtli (left), lord of the Underworld, and Quetzalcoatl (right), god of life and lord of the West, depicted in the *Codex Borgia*, one of the few surviving pre-Columbian sacred texts.

WOLFGANG HERRNDORF

WHY WE TOOK THE CAR
(TSCHICK) (2010)

Two fifteen-year-old boys "borrow" an old Lada and leave their homes in Berlin for the road trip of a lifetime.

Born in Hamburg in 1965, Wolfgang Herrndorf initially trained as a painter and worked as a comic artist and illustrator before turning to writing because he was running out of money.

Shortly before *Why We Took the Car* was published, Herrndorf was diagnosed with glioblastoma, an aggressive form of brain cancer. He charted his struggle with the disease in a blog, *Arbeit und Struktur*. He took his own life on August 26, 2013.

The reclusive, Berlin-bound Herrndorf never actually traveled to East Germany; he researched the novel using Google Maps, which perhaps contributed to the dreamy, surreal nature of the landscapes he describes.

Adolescence is seldom much fun for anyone, but fifteen-year-old Mike Klingenberg is having a particularly hard time of it: formerly referred to by his classmates as "Psycho" because he once read out a slightly too honest essay about his alcoholic mother and soon-to-be-bankrupt father, he has now been deemed too boring to even deserve a nickname, let alone be invited to the birthday party of his secret love interest, the beautiful Tatiana Cosic.

To make things worse, it's the beginning of summer vacation, his mother is off at the "Beauty Farm" (rehab) and his father is away for two weeks on a "work trip" with his buxom "assistant." So when a fellow friendless loser from his class, the penniless new Russian boy Andrej Tschichatschow—a.k.a. Tschick—turns up on his doorstep with a stolen Lada and suggests they invite themselves to Tatiana's party, Mike figures he has nothing to lose.

Having dropped in on Tatiana and made Mike's feelings for her clear, the exhilarated boys set off on a road trip that will see them plowing through cornfields, crossing a rickety River Kwai–style wooden bridge, creating fake mustaches with bits of duct tape to make themselves look older, dodging policemen, sifting through a trash heap to find a hose with which to siphon gas out of other cars, and much more.

Why We Took the Car gets its strength from Mike's naive-yet-profound perspective on the world, the gaze of a teenager who understands very little about what he is seeing and yet, for that precise reason, sees it with a clarity that often eludes adults.

Through Mike's eyes, the early twenty-first-century hinterland of eastern Germany to the southeast of Berlin—an area associated with post-reunification deprivation, emptiness, and dissatisfaction—becomes a confusing yet fascinating place, full of surreal landscapes. He describes driving through a strange, swampy terrain when "the world ended":

> You had to have seen it: The landscape just stopped [. . .] the ground had been steeply cut away, dropping at least thirty or forty meters down. And below was a moonscape. The ground was whitish gray and pockmarked with craters so big entire buildings could have fit in them.

The one percent who weren't bad—Mike and Tschick in *Goodbye Berlin*, the 2016 film version.

Mike's innocence turns this landscape of open cast mines, huge agro-industrial monocultures, forests full of litter, and unexpected but beautiful mountains ("They were really tall, with jagged bare tops. We had no idea what mountain range it could be. There was no sign. Definitely not the Alps. Were we still in Germany? Tschick swore there were no mountains in East Germany.") into a place of wonder.

But above all, equally wonderful are the encounters Mike and Tschick have on their hurtling adventure: they include, among many others, Horst Fricke, the war veteran who takes potshots at them, then invites them into his house for a soda and an earful of his life story; Isa, a wild, stinking girl they meet on the trash heap who, having been pushed into a lake and scrubbed clean, gives Mike his first ever kiss; and an obese social worker who cheerfully drives the boys away from the police and over to the local hospital after they crash the Lada. In this wonderful coming-of-age story, the most important discovery turns out to be this:

> Ever since I was a little boy my father had told me that the world was a bad place. The world is bad and people are bad. [. . .] My parents drilled that into me, my teachers drilled that into me, even TV drilled that into me. [. . .] And maybe it was true, maybe ninety-nine percent of people were bad. But the strange thing was that on this trip, Tschick and I had run into almost only people from the one percent who weren't bad. [. . .] Maybe they should tell you about things like that in school too, just so you're not totally surprised by it.

RAHUL BHATTACHARYA

THE SLY COMPANY OF PEOPLE WHO CARE (2011)

A young Indian cricket journalist leaves his job and his home in Mumbai to spend a year in Guyana, South America.

Rahul Bhattacharya studied mathematics in college and in 2005 published his first book, *Pundits from Pakistan: On Tour with India 2003–04*, a widely acclaimed account of the first major sporting encounter between the two countries in fifteen years.

In 2011 Bhattacharya's first novel *The Sly Company of People Who Care*, set in Guyana, was published to internationally rave reviews. It won the 2011 Hindu Literary Prize and the 2012 Ondaatje Prize.

Hailed as the natural successor to Trinidadian writer and Nobel Literature Laureate V.S. Naipaul, Rahul Bhattacharya's *The Sly Company of People Who Care* is a richly textured novel about a young Indian cricket journalist who leaves his job and his home in Mumbai to spend a year in the South American country of Guyana (literally "land of waters") to "find magic." It contains, in the age of easy anodyne travel, the spirit of real adventure, as well as being an homage to writer-explorers who have gone before—from Sir Walter Raleigh and Evelyn Waugh to Naipaul himself, whose novel *In a Free State* Bhattacharya's narrator reads at a crucial point in his Caribbean odyssey.

Arriving in Guyana's capital, Georgetown, the narrator sets out his intention—to be a "slow, ramblin' stranger," traveling wherever by whatever means possible, immersing himself in local culture and language. His love of Guyanese and the patois Creolese is evident from the first page, as he delights in this country of cool, muddy waters, and its lip-smacking varied cuisine.

He has a lively, generous curiosity about "the sly company of people who care" and their tricky, multilayered past involving Spanish, Dutch, French, and British colonization as well as the colonizers' shameful legacy of importing Africans to work as slaves from the mid-1600s, and the large influx of East Indian immigration from the early nineteenth century. This history makes for an astonishingly diverse country and Bhattacharya's protagonist takes to it with relish, joining a "porknock" (diamond mining expedition), reveling in the damp and decay of Georgetown's colorful old colonial houses, and the deep impenetrability of Guyana's rain forest. Early on, on a trip to a settlement in proximity to one of the country's coastal sugarcane plantations, near a waterfall resembling that of Niagara, the narrator observes:

> The day started early and the time was all ours. It rained often, in thrilling bursts, rain running down shingles in elastic bumps, the entire settlement, the shacks, the mango tree, pixelating in sheets of water. [. . .] We collected smooth stones from the creek and stroked them and placed them on our foreheads while lying on the airstrip. We laughed at the little scuttling planes when they couldn't land in clouds.

Bhattacharya's narrator becomes restless as the novel moves on: the original motivation of his journey had been to "renew" himself but he is somehow dissatisfied: "I'd started as a watcher and a listener, that was my role. [. . .] How sorry to think that here where Africans, Indians, Portuguese, and Chinese had arrived and turned themselves into one thing or another [. . .] I had allowed myself to remain myself."

The last, and perhaps most significant part of the novel concerns a passionate, teasing love affair between the narrator and a younger Guyanese woman whom he names Jaan (Urdu for "beloved" as he explains to her), who travels with him to Trinidad and then Venezuela, a trip that is sensual, surprising, and fated: "In those half-hallucinations we stayed, ten minutes, thirty, an hour, I couldn't tell." On arrival in Venezuela "we kissed without reserve in the manner of the newly coupled in a new land."

With a companion he sees things differently, in a blur of meaning and foreboding: "Villages were perched on rocky outcrops. The heat was metallic and the sea shone with metallic hostility. At resorts people swam. The color of heat was the color of water." Their uneasy idyll ends abruptly, a reminder that not all in this mineral-rich, impoverished country is paradise: the sour sweaty taste of corruption and betrayal linger, as much as the beauty.

Dilapidated colonial buildings in downtown Georgetown, Guyana.

TOMMY WIERINGA

These Are the Names
(DIT ZIJN DE NAMEN)(2012)

Refugees walk across the steppe while a border town police chief searches for his roots in a prize-winning novel that is moving and mythic.

Born in 1967, Tommy Wieringa is a Dutch author who began his writing career as a journalist covering travel. In 2013, *These Are the Names* was awarded the Libris Prize.

The refugees in *These Are the Names* come from different places, from Turkmenistan to Ethiopia. They cross the Eastern European steppe, a huge area of forests, and grasslands, stretching from Ukraine to the Urals.

The novel's inspiration was a newspaper article about a group of refugees who had arrived in a town after months of wandering around the Ukrainian steppe, carrying a dead body wrapped in rags.

The tenth novel by Dutch writer Tommy Wieringa, *These Are the Names* won the prestigious Libris Prize (the "Dutch Booker") in 2013. It is the story of two journeys: Pontus Beg, an aging police commissioner, is looking for meaning and identity in his lonely life while a group of increasingly desperate refugees, fleeing poverty and repression, trek across the huge plains of Eastern Europe in search of safety. Until the two quests finally converge, the chapters alternate, with subtle parallels between them as both sets of characters painfully travel toward the distant hope of redemption. Sam Garrett has translated the novel with skill and nuance, evoking both biblical parallels and squalid modernity.

The story starts in the fictional Eastern European border town of Michailopol. Pontus Beg watches the lightning over the steppe while the rain-soaked refugees lie somewhere on it, waiting for dawn "like the first humans on earth." The opening chapter's title "The Thing Itself" quotes Shakespeare's King Lear describing a beggar and introduces a sense of timeless, elemental human battles: a naked man in the pitiless storm.

Migration is a topical theme, but also an ancient one with centuries of symbolic resonances. The refugees' flight mirrors the exodus from Egypt to the Promised Land. Traffickers are compared to mythological gatekeepers. Wieringa piles up images of "animals that travel in swarms," of nomads, drifters, hitchhikers, vagrants, and transients, of restless people "blown hither and thither." On the way, shaped and scarred by the journey, the refugees lose their way and their possessions, pasts, names, identities, beliefs, and, often, their lives. "The dreams with which each of them had left home had gradually wilted and died off," Wieringa writes. The survivors will eventually stumble into Beg's town, crying, starving, and carrying a severed head.

Like Hardy's Egdon Heath or Emily Brontë's moors, the steppe is a symbolic presence as much as a geographical place. This "interminable" landscape is often metaphorical; the migrants pass through "the thicket of horrors," recalling Dante's midlife "dark wood." The landmarks that matter are moral ones: stealing shoes, losing and gaining faith, condoning murder, struggling toward physical and spiritual salvation.

> The landscape before them was precisely the same as the one behind; the one on the right differed in no way from the one on the left. The only lines to guide them on the steppe were the sky above their heads and the ground beneath their feet.

Human settlements are more concretely evoked: an empty village with its "blaze gone cold," the overblown, eclectic houses of the newly rich where "the domes of Samarkand perched atop Ionian pillars" or the out-of-town bazaar full of "caustic cleansers and broiled meat." Decaying Michailopol suffers from corrosive post-Soviet corruption: it is impossible to escape the interwoven system of "kickbacks, bribes, extortion, and larceny."

But the novel also has more hopeful moments, hinting at the possible pleasures of companionship and faith along the human journey. One brief, beautiful moment of unsentimental compassion in the bleak, violent journey across the steppe is compared to "the way you light one candle with another." From Beg's childless housekeeper, praying for a baby among plastic flowers and gold icons, to a prostitute punning on the last supper ("Take this body, it's how I earn my bread"), the story is packed with conflicting images of religion.

A remembered fragment from a Yiddish love song his mother used to sing leads Beg to look for his lost Jewish heritage and become part of another ancient journey. "We are braided rope, individual threads woven to form a single cord," an old rabbi tells him, and "our memory goes back four thousand years." When Beg first sees the *mikveh*, the synagogue's ritual pool, with late afternoon sun falling through high windows onto its blue pillars and gold tiles, he feels an urge: "To shed his old soul, that tattered, worn thing, and receive a new one in its stead. Who wouldn't want that?" At the novel's heart are a search for faith in all its forms and the unquenchable, age-old desire to start again.

Following: The interminable steppe—*Vladimirka Highway* by Isaak Levitan, 1892—the main trade route to and from Moscow since the middle ages.

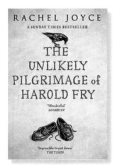

RACHEL JOYCE

THE UNLIKELY PILGRIMAGE OF HAROLD FRY (2012)

When self-effacing, ordinary Harold Fry sets out unexpectedly to walk the length of Britain and visit a dying friend, he learns a lot about himself and others along the way.

Born in 1962, Rachel Joyce is a British author. She trained at RADA and spent over 20 years as an actor. Her writing career began in radio drama. She has written major radio adaptations of all the Brontë novels.

Joyce originally wrote *The Unlikely Pilgrimage of Harold Fry* as a play. It was dedicated to her father who was terminally ill, and broadcast on BBC Radio 4. The play was expanded into a novel which has become the first book in the completed series.

In a companion novel, *The Love Song of Miss Queenie Hennessy* (2015), Joyce writes the parallel story of the dying Queenie.

Retired sales rep Harold Fry is stuck in an uneventful, stagnant, suburban life. With his wife Maureen, he lives in the small market town of Kingsbridge in Devon on an estuary near the south coast of England. He gets a letter from his former colleague, Queenie Hennessy, who writes that she is dying in a nursing home in Berwick-upon-Tweed.

Berwick is a town at the most northerly tip of England, on the east coast of Northumberland, just three miles from the Scottish border. It's hundreds of miles away from Harold, but—after a chance encounter on his way to mail a reply—he impetuously decides to walk there. He believes that if he, unfit and ill-prepared, does the most "unlikely" thing and walks the length of England, Queenie will somehow survive her terminal cancer.

> The sea lay behind; before him stretched rolling hills and the blue outline of Dartmoor. And beyond that? The Blackdown Hills, the Mendips, the Malverns, the Pennines, the Yorkshire Dales, the Cheviots, and Berwick-upon-Tweed.

The rough mental map of England's hills that Harold starts out with becomes a series of personal revelations as he takes time to consider his closest relationships and finds. His growing sense of the green English countryside is matched by deep and often troubled reflections on his own life.

The walk lasts eighty-seven days and covers six hundred and twenty-seven miles; Harold occasionally gets lost, especially toward the end. He is not dressed to walk, has little money, and no map or cell phone, but is given a compass that helps guide him northward. Setting off with a sense of beginning again, walking becomes an act of faith, a "pilgrimage"; when he explains his plan to fellow hotel guests at breakfast after his first night away, one of them sings John Bunyan's hymn about being a pilgrim: "He who would valiant be . . ."

The novel's title and epigraph from Bunyan's allegorical *Pilgrim's Progress* suggest that Harold's journey is not just a physical one from Kingsbridge to Berwick. It is also a spiritual quest, parallel to the journey Bunyan's Pilgrim

The world was made up of people putting one
foot in front of the other; and a life might appear
ordinary simply because the person living it had
been doing so for a long time

makes: an everyman character traveling through life, from his earthly home
in the "City of Destruction" to the "Celestial City" or heaven. Like Pilgrim,
Harold is an everyman whose encounters along the way with various people
—kind, selfish, vain, or visionary—are crucial elements of his journey.

The psychological dimensions of Harold's journey reach beyond its
physical scope. Arriving in South Brent, a large village where he spends
his second night (just twelve miles from home), Harold feels "the triumph
of someone returning to civilization after a long voyage." Harold's personal
landmarks are memories, emotional discoveries, and the characters he meets,
many of whom Joyce based on real people she has observed.

The settings are also real; unlike those of Bunyan's Pilgrim, the landscapes
Harold passes are not purely allegorical. There are towns and villages
("Bedworth. Nuneaton. Twycross. Ashby de la Zouche. [. . .] Alfreton. Clay
Cross"). And there are landmarks, where he buys postcards and souvenirs,
like Buckfast Abbey, Exeter Cathedral, the Roman Baths. Later, "the
silhouette of the crooked spire of Chesterfield announced the start of the
Peak District." Harold follows roads rather than using the beautiful footpaths
that run through the English countryside. "I'm sticking to the roads," he
explains to someone he meets, "because I have driven all my adult life. It's
what I know."

As he moves onward, Harold sleeps on the street to save money and sends
home his credit card, relying instead on other people's generosity and feeling
"at one with the land beneath his feet." He collects a small band of followers,
who eventually go on ahead. Harold finally arrives in the same (now very
battered) pair of boat shoes in which he set out. He has learned to accept
and celebrate the kindness and the strangeness of other people; he "could no
longer pass a stranger without acknowledging the truth that everyone was the
same, and also unique; and that this was the dilemma of being human."

ARIKAWA HIRO

THE TRAVELING CAT CHRONICLES (TABI NEKO REPŌTO) (2012)

A journey across Japan is also one into the unspoken memories of its characters as well as into the annals of Japanese literary history.

"I am a cat. As yet, I have no name." In 1905, the opening lines of Natsume Sōseki's (1867–1916) *I Am a Cat* announced an arrival that would enact profound change. At a time when writers and critics in Japan were seeking a standardized written language through which to convey a neutral and "truthful" voice for a new modern literature, Sōseki's creation of a story told from the perspective of an unwelcome housecat revealed a rebellious side to this acclaimed author. *Cat*'s distinctive voice has since become emblematic of the sense of alienation in Japan that accompanied the processes of rapid modernization.

The simplicity of the translated English title also conceals the comic complexity of the original: Japanese contains multiple versions of the first-person pronoun "I" that each indicate a speaker's status in relation to the listener, and Sōseki's narrator introduces himself as *wagahai*, an archaic form that elevates him to the highest degree. Sōseki's famed lines are therefore replete with comic potential and self-parody, in the incongruity between this feline imposter and the haughty manner in which he speaks.

Arikawa Hiro's 2012 novel, *The Traveling Cat Chronicles*, which travels to the English reader thanks to Philip Gabriel's lucid translation, opens with the same two sentences in homage to Sōseki's "famous cat." But whereas Sōseki's narrator is ill at ease in his surroundings and unattractive looks, Arikawa's stray cat exudes street-smarts and confidence. More importantly, he gets a name: Nana, the Japanese word for "seven," after his distinctive, hook-shaped tail. The man who bestows this name is Satoru, an earnest cat-lover in his thirties who at first is to Nana no more than a convenient provider of food. But after Nana is hit by a car and breaks his leg, he allows Satoru to take him in. Five years pass in one sentence, whereupon Satoru announces a need to find Nana somewhere else to stay. Thus begins a road trip by an unlikely duo in a silver van on which Satoru revisits old friends under the pretext of rehoming his beloved cat, yet always finds a reason not to.

Travel weaves through this novel in myriad ways. Nana describes himself as "the world's greatest traveling cat," and through his eyes we catch glimpses of Japan's urban and rural landscapes including the "overwhelming" spectacle

As is common in Japanese publishing tradition, this novel was first serialized in twenty-five weekly installments in a literary journal between October 2011 and April 2012. It shares this feature, too, with Sōseki's *I Am a Cat*.

Arikawa is best known in Japan as a writer of "light novels," an illustrated genre of literature aimed at young adult readers.

The Traveling Cat Chronicles was published first as a standard novel but was remade into a picture book in 2014. A film adaptation was released in 2018.

> Since we had embarked on our journey, I'd seen the town where you spent your childhood. And a farming village. And the sea. I wondered what new scenes we would see together before this journey was over.

of Mount Fuji. But this is not only Nana's story, it is also a journey toward the "compelling reason" that demands Satoru to give up the cat he adores. The narrative builds in poignancy as in each chapter the next childhood friend summons a memory that adds another gentle layer to Satoru's portrait like a watercolor. Witnessed from Nana's cat's-eye-view, these stories hover in unspoken pacts and awkward silences that reveal each of these characters to be strays in their own right: a husband who hopes that adopting Nana might help him to reconnect with his estranged wife; a child of divorce who refuses to be pitied; and at the heart, Satoru, the orphan who has lost his parents in more ways than one.

Sōseki's classic has been adapted and parodied multiple times. Arikawa's rendition is arguably one of the must human. Unlike Sōseki's narrator who is never granted a past, the journey between Nana and Satoru gives rise to memories that validate their places in one another's lives. That legacy is enhanced by the marks that their journey leave on those they call upon.

Through the explicit call-back that opens the novel, Arikawa also ensures for her narrator a place within Japan's literary history. Indeed, as Satoru's visit to one long-lost friend threatens to return a buried love triangle to the surface, the scene recalls another of Sōseki's classic works, *Kokoro* (1914), where the characters are also joined through a shared experience of loss in the past that continues to haunt their present.

To Nana's mind, "a stray cat's skill lies in building up a complex web of connections in order to survive on the streets." The skill of Arikawa's novel lies in building up a complex web of connections both between the characters inside her novel and the literary echoes that lie beyond its pages. To read this book is not simply to take a road trip with a cat, but to be led into one of the central tropes of modern Japanese literature.

CHIMAMANDA NGOZI ADICHIE

AMERICANAH (2013)

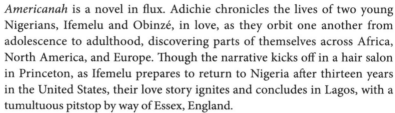

Two young Nigerians in love who travel to the West for opportunities but are confronted with a number of obstacles and romantic, racial, and economic challenges.

Adichie is an Igbo-Nigerian writer who left Nigeria to study at Drexel University in Philadelphia before completing a masters at Yale and becoming a Princeton fellow. She now lives between America and Nigeria.

Americanah won the U.S. National Book Critics Circle Award, beating Donna Tartt's *The Goldfinch*. Her first novel, *Purple Hibiscus*, was longlisted for the Booker Prize; her second, *Half of a Yellow Sun*, won the Orange Prize for Fiction.

Americanah is a novel in flux. Adichie chronicles the lives of two young Nigerians, Ifemelu and Obinzé, in love, as they orbit one another from adolescence to adulthood, discovering parts of themselves across Africa, North America, and Europe. Though the narrative kicks off in a hair salon in Princeton, as Ifemelu prepares to return to Nigeria after thirteen years in the United States, their love story ignites and concludes in Lagos, with a tumultuous pitstop by way of Essex, England.

The journeys alone are not remarkable, following those made by many immigrants drawn to the West by tales of abundance. But they trace historic movements of colonialism and slave trade in their paths, events that still ripple within the societies they ravaged despite being often forgotten in discussions of borders today.

Between the start of their romance and their reunion, Ifemelu travels to Philadelphia pursuing further education, starts a race blog, and becomes a Princeton fellow; Obinzé tackles working life in an unforgiving London before being deported and starting a family back home. Their contrast spans the full spectrum of the immigrant experience. Their odysseys see them confronting their own expectations for their futures in direct opposition to a harsher reality: who they become and how they are perceived in foreign spaces with regards to race, class, gender, even nationality and tribe.

For Ifemelu, traveling to the United States is a revelation that expands her vocabulary on identity with newly gained nuance. At a party she states: "I became Black when I came to America," alluding to the blindspot uncovered by palpable interracial tensions in the United States, as opposed to intraracial prejudices present somewhere like Nigeria. In the "Land of the Free," she's not only African but also Black. This identity simultaneously bonds her to and separates her from a complex African American history, seen as both privilege and disadvantage, depending on who you ask.

Adichie weaves this tension into Ifemelu's hair: while she confidently donned box braids in her youth, Ifemelu's introduction into "professional" white America forces her to realize her default style is no longer welcome. She succumbs to pressures to chemically relax her hair. But unable to recognize

herself, and suffering from literal damage, she chops it all off iconoclastically and reverts back to a natural Afro, to both Black and White dismay. Unlearning the policing enforced on hair like hers is a journey in itself, and a reflection of her wider struggle to assimilate, resist, and reach a state of balance. In more ways than one, only by stepping outside of her world and feeling tugged in conflicting directions, does she learn what she truly wants.

Victor Ehikhamenor's 2014 cover for the Nigerian edition.

Obinzé's plan to join Ifemelu in the hallowed America and begin his "real life" is terminated abruptly by xenophobic immigration policies. Still disenchanted with hometown prospects, he instead journeys to Britain on a temporary visa and spends subsequent years living a lonely, undocumented life, amid anti-immigrant rhetoric and paralyzing fear of discovery. Eventually the worst happens, and he is deported minutes before his green-card wedding.

Displacement colors Obinzé's vision, worsening when his and Ifemelu's paths splinter from one another's, fueling his search for refuge anywhere he can find it. It is only toward the end of the novel that he realizes the certainty he had left his homeland looking for was already his to claim. It is in this way that *Americanah* is a story as much about false starts as the journeys completed.

WU MING-YI
THE STOLEN BICYCLE
(DĀNCHĒ SHĪQIÈ JÌ) (2015)

A son travels across Taiwan to track down a missing bicycle in the hope that it might lead him to his father.

Wu Ming-Yi, born in Taiwan in 1970, is a butterfly scholar, environmental activist, painter, photographer, and award-winning novelist. He is one of Taiwan's most influential writers.

The Stolen Bicycle won the Taiwan Literature Award. The English translation by Darryl Sterk was longlisted for the International Booker Prize.

The novel stemmed from a memory of an antique bicycle left outside a forest "as if its owner had walked into the wood over a half century before. [. . .] And so I found myself on a new path, which eventually led to *The Stolen Bicycle*."

A bicycle is more often the means for a journey than the purpose of one. But bicycles, literally "iron horses" in Taiwanese, are the objects sought within the stories in Wu Ming-Yi's intricate and sprawling fifth novel. Bicycles have their own lifetimes—different owners, by theft or by gift, with parts gone astray—and around them, in Ming-Yi's book, the stories of wartime, the "Silverwheel Squad," and the journeys of soldiers deep into the jungles of Myanmar with elephants, coalesce.

"Iron horses have influenced the date of our entire family," the narrator's mother goes so far as to say, and Ch'eng the narrator's story begins with the return of the bicycle that disappeared with his father decades ago: "Twenty years ago, when my father first went missing, it occurred to us that if we could find his bicycle, we might find him. Only then did we discover that his bicycle was gone, too—that Pa and his iron steed had left together."

Intuiting the important kinship between a bicycle and its owner, Ming-Yi unfolds from here "a quest for a bicycle that ends up involving the history of an epoch," in his own words: the bicycle not only as an object of personal revelation, but as a key card to Taiwan's scarred and polyphonic past.

Much of the book is set in Taipei, Taiwan's capital, both in its present and past iterations. Ch'eng's story starts in a place preoccupied with attempts to retrieve time: an antique dealer's shop, whose owner, Apu, introduces Ch'eng to the lucky bicycle he recognizes to be his father's.

Underlining the patience and attrition expected by a quest in search of a lost object, the journey that follows is enabled by a series of carefully cultivated friendships, leading Ch'eng to photographer Abbas (whose ex-girlfriend looked after the bicycle) and his hometown in the Nan-t'ou area, among the Tsou tribal community; to Sabina (the current owner of the bicycle) and her enigmatic emails, set in the mountains near Bâi-khe ("Eyebrow River"), detailing Taiwan's history as a center for butterfly handicrafts; to Abbas's stories of his time spent in a village called Sec-kao in southwestern Taiwan, and the bicycle loaned to him there; and to the cassette of Abbas's father, speaking about his experiences as a member of the Japanese army's bike-mounted unit, the Silverwheels, in the jungles of Myanmar.

Ma used to say that I had "iron teeth"—that I was arrogant to think I could defy Heaven and decide my own destiny. But the instant I touched that serial number, I felt—in a moment of vulnerability— that some higher power must have arranged its return.

As this might indicate, the journey to trace the bicycle's history is meandering rather than linear, and densely interwoven with the stories of other bicycles, as well as biographies and meditations on language, twisting between the Taiwanese, Japanese, and Mandarin identities of places and things:

> In the world I grew up in, the word a person used for "bicycle" told you a lot about them. *Jiten-sha* ("self-turn vehicle") indicated a person who had received a Japanese education. *Thih-bé* ("iron horse") meant he was a native-speaker of Taiwanese, as did *Khóng-bîng-tshia* ("Kung-ming vehicle"), named for an ancient Chinese inventor.

Ch'eng wonders, "Could all the walking in my imagination be tiring me out?" Yet the effect, rather than an onward march, is of a tightly controlled collage, amplified by the interruptions within the narrative by "Bike Notes," featuring facts about Taiwan's bicycle industry and delicate drawings of the different antique models. Like a bike fashioned from stray parts, Ming-Yi's book is assembled from the scraps of history: "Behold, I ride before you on an antique bicycle built up with body parts stripped from meat bikes or bought from collections," he writes in the postscript, eliding his role as writer with the collector as well as the bicyclist. The question this comes to stage is less about bicycles and their owners, and more fundamentally about the forces that determine life's course: "Life was not formless like smoke, but had a pattern and a posture," Ch'eng observes near the end of the novel, suggesting a fateful shape for the events of several generations. Yet earlier, Ming-Yi made the distinction linguistic:

> The word for "fate" in Mandarin is composed of two characters, *ming* and *yün*, each of which is independently meaningful. Ming means the life we are each allotted—our destiny—while yün means luck—the ups and downs of life, the twists and turns of fortune. [. . .] But in my mother's native tongue of Taiwanese, it's the other way around: *ūn-mia*, putting luck in front of life.

It is via such dexterous movement between far-reaching ideas and intimate observation that the personal journey in *The Stolen Bicycle* comes to delve deep into a country's collective memory: it's a quest for understanding and for completeness, as much as it is also a paean to the humble but trustworthy two-wheeled vehicle: "As I ride like that on the bicycle, everything in the distance draws near and everything near recedes."

COLSON WHITEHEAD

THE UNDERGROUND RAILROAD (2016)

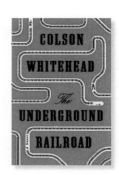

Cora, a young Black woman, flees her enslaved condition via the Underground Railroad. During her journey, she encounters various forms of racism, as she travels from the South to the North seeking freedom.

In antebellum America, prior to the Emancipation Proclamation of 1863, the Underground Railroad was a historical network of abolitionists. If discovered, Blacks and Whites faced execution for using safe houses and secret passageways to journey fugitive slaves to freedom. In his award-winning novel, Colson Whitehead's reimagines the railroad as an actual train network underneath the Southern soil.

As Whitehead's protagonist Cora travels from state to state, racial horrors permeate every aspect of North American culture. Searching for a safer refuge, like the fugitive slave narratives that served as inspiration for *The Underground Railroad*, Cora journeys farther and farther across the country. *The Narrative of the Life of Frederick Douglass, An American Slave* by Frederick Douglass and *Incidents in the Life of a Slave Girl* by Harriet Jacobs offered Whitehead foundational research for building Cora's character and the conflicts she faces.

When Caesar—another slave seeking freedom, extends an invitation to Cora—she initially refuses. However, after considering the horrors she's witnessed and experienced at the hands of slave owners and overseers, she changes her mind. Using the Underground Railroad, they flee from Georgia. For Caesar and Cora, the Underground Railroad is a literal transport to freedom; the juxtaposition of historical realism and science-fiction becomes a metaphor for Black progress.

After Cora escapes Georgia, she stops in South Carolina. To evade future capture by her owners, the station agent provides her with a new name. The new name is symbolic with a new identity, in turn providing new opportunities for Cora to reinvent herself as a free Black person. But she soon discovers that South Carolina's belief in "colored progress" is a macabre façade, and Cora flees, once again on the Underground Railroad.

Like the real-life fugitive slave Harriet Jacobs, Cora hides in a house attic. Since North Carolina has outlawed the presence of Black residents, once discovered, Cora is recaptured and taken farther west. Slave catchers Ridgeway and Boseman, and a Black boy named Homer frustrate Cora's journey toward a new life.

Colson Whitehead was born in New York City in 1969. After graduating from Harvard University in 1991, Whitehead began drafting his first novels whilst working at an alternative newsweekly publisher in New York.

The Underground Railroad, a New York Times bestseller, won both the National Book Award and Pulitzer Prize and took sixteen years for Colson Whitehead to complete.

Academy Award winner, Barry Jenkins, adapted The Underground Railroad as a television series for Amazon studios in 2021.

MAP

showing the lines of the
UNDERGROUND RAILROAD
IN
Chester and the Neighboring
Counties of Pennsylvania
*Based on R. C. Smedley's History of
the Road in these Counties*

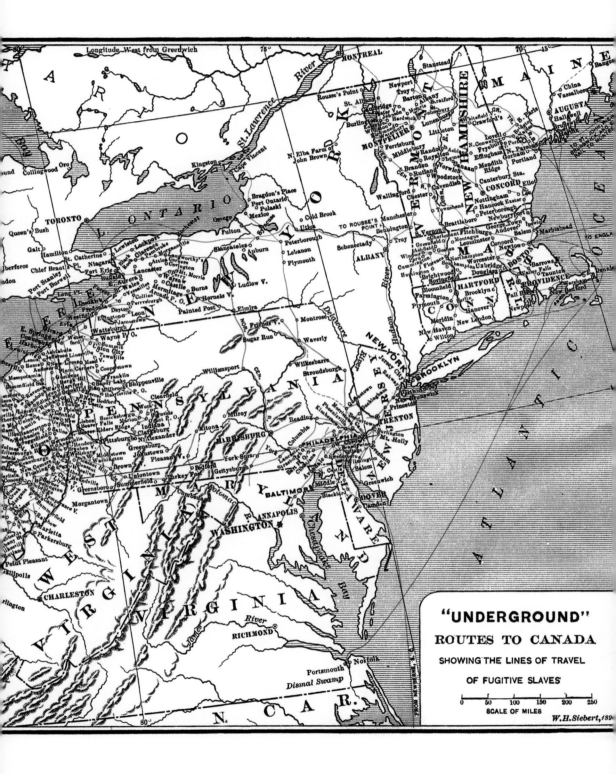

"UNDERGROUND"

ROUTES TO CANADA

SHOWING THE LINES OF TRAVEL

OF FUGITIVE SLAVES

SCALE OF MILES

W. H. Siebert, 189–

American newspapers also economically benefit from the institution of slavery. Whitehead addresses this history by featuring slave advertisements in five different sections of the book. Each fugitive slave ad states the reward amount, age, personality trait, physical description, and first name of the slave. Through the slave ads, including the one featuring Cora, Whitehead balances the conflicting interest of a slave's quest for freedom with the slave economy of the South.

Whitehead's narrative structure provides insight to the night riders, slave patrollers, and slave catchers—such as Ridgeway—who hunt runaway slaves for profit. In Ridgeway's vigilant pursuit of Mabel and Cora, the reader learns that he is motivated by way more than money. Pursuing the mother and the daughter has become personal. Their ability to elude Ridgeway's capture tests his skills as a hunter of Black bodies. His sense of racial superiority both emotionally and physically drives him through America's tumultuous terrain.

Elijah Lander, a political orator, embodies Frederick Douglass. After Cora escapes the violent clutches of Ridgeway in Indiana, Lander publicly expresses the consequences of slavery's stain on America:

> The White race believes with all its heart that it is their right to take the land. To kill Indians. Make war. Enslave their brothers. This nation shouldn't exist, if there is any justice in the world, for its foundations are murder, theft, and cruelty.

Once Lander finishes speaking, the tragic consequences of freedom of speech for African Americans becomes painfully evident. Distracted by the chaos his words cause, Cora is captured again by Ridgeway and Homer. As Cora uses the Underground Railroad to escape her hunters once again, the metaphor of Black progress is continued by Whitehead. Many fugitive slaves have sought status as free Black people. However, Caesar and Mabel's fate in a free world ends tragically. As she pumps her arms, moving quickly into a tunnel, she must forge her own path. Driving a pickax into rock, she progresses forward toward the Black freedom that has escaped her. Here, again, the juxtaposition of historical realism and science-fiction make a physical escape through rock possible for Cora.

In the twenty-first century, *The Underground Railroad* offers readers an alternative view of American freedom. Whitehead contends that journeying forward in this allegorical tale is symbolic of Black progress. By running away, Cora confronts White indifference to the generational costs of slavery. With Cora, Whitehead presents a reimagining of freedom from the perspective of those who are deserved of humanity. *The Underground Railroad* demonstrates how America's economic might has been gained at the expense of African Americans' freedom.

MOHSIN HAMID

EXIT WEST (2017)

A Booker-shortlisted novel about migration, the refugee struggle, and two people in love.

In a world familiar with the refugee crisis that is glaringly visible across our screens, many narratives about migrant journeys focus on the physical journey itself—harrowing tales of people escaping homes that repress or endanger them, smuggled out via cargo ships or trundling across borders. But instead of focusing on its characters' physical transport from one city to the next, *Exit West* does away with this fetishization. Hamid tells us the emotional journey of people who no longer belong in their home, and perhaps will never belong elsewhere either.

Saeed and Nadia meet as young urbanites in an unnamed city "swollen with refugees" but "not yet openly at war"—a city that is possibly Lahore, possibly Karachi but definitely one on the verge of something violent. Despite their differences, Saeed and Nadia fall in love and start a mundane sort-of romance of smoking joints together and eating burgers, living their lives quietly as the city starts to change around them into violence and aggression. When radical militants take over the city, Saeed's father convinces Nadia that the two young people need to leave for somewhere better and safer.

In this city that has no name, in a country that has no name, doorways have started to appear, suddenly, quietly, as they have the world over. In Tokyo, a door that has always been kept locked is now "somehow open, a portal of complete blackness, as though no light were on inside, almost as though no light could penetrate inside." In Sydney, a sleeping woman's closet doorway is dark, "darker than night, a rectangle of complete darkness—the heart of darkness." These doors lead to other parts of the world. They are portals, literal thresholds joining places thousands of miles apart: in Hamid's novel, the membrane between where you are and where you want to be becomes suddenly porous and accessible.

The migrant's journey is no longer about the act of moving, or the experiences along the way, but about who you were and who you can become. The act of transportation from one place to another is telescoped into a simple step through a door. The real journey becomes one of personal growth, awareness, and identity; once the physical aspect of transit is removed, the experience we are left with resonates widely.

Hamid is a Pakistani writer who lives in Lahore, and whose writing has been translated into forty languages.

Hamid was previously shortlisted for the Booker Prize in 2007 for *The Reluctant Fundamentalist*. *Exit West* won the *L.A. Times* Book Prize in 2018.

By the end of 2017, a record 68.5 million people had been forcibly displaced from their home countries, the vast majority due to conflict.

Does removing the danger of a refugee's journey remove its emotional or spiritual weight? Hamid tells us that this is not the case. Saeed and Nadia, in their search for a new home, inevitably give up any sense of belonging that they may have had in their native city. They also give up rights, recognition, and the ability to be citizens, because no country will recognize them as such. The journey may have promised freedom as its destination, but it is not freedom to live completely at ease but rather a rebirth:

> It was said in those days that the passage was both like dying and like being born, and indeed Nadia experienced a kind of extinguishing as she entered the blackness and a gasping struggle as she fought to exit it, and she felt cold and bruised and damp as she lay on the floor of the room at the other side, trembling and too spent at first to stand, and she thought, while she strained to fill her lungs, that this dampness must be her own sweat.

Hamid does not sanitize the physical toll of a journey to seek asylum, but rather shows us that this toll is as much a result of emotional displacement as it is the literal reality of hiding in the back of a truck or huddling on a small boat across deadly seas.

Saeed and Nadia find an agent who whispers to them like "a poet or a psychopath," and guides them to a door. Pushing through this portal one afternoon, they find themselves in what is often the first port for refugees into Europe: Mykonos, Greece. From there, they eventually make their way via another door to London, and finally, to the west coast of the United States.

All over the world people were slipping away from where they had been, from once fertile plains cracking with dryness, from seaside villages gasping beneath tidal surges, from overcrowded cities and murderous battlefields, and slipping away from other people too.

It is easy to imagine *Exit West* as a portal fantasy, an idealistic dream of worlds coming together, of wish fulfillment and a hero's journey. And while at points it may be all of those things, Hamid makes it clear that all migration is fantasy. What is a refugee's dream, after all, than to step into a better world?

But *Exit West* does not gloss over the hardships that come with this. Stepping through the magical portal, Saeed and Nadia still need to survive a city that is not willing to simply accept them or integrate them. In Mykonos they live in a refugee tent settlement with others who have wandered through doors from all sorts of poorer places; in London they squat in a large house with other refugees; and eventually, in County Marin, California, they find their way to a new makeshift settlement of migrants. No matter where they go, they are always part of "the other." And like many relationships that cannot bear the weight of a huge upheaval, they, too, begin to see cracks where there had been none noticeable before.

Exit West reminds us that no matter what the imagined world across the threshold may be, the emotional toll on a refugee is never outweighed by what they find at the other end. To leave behind everything and everyone they have ever known is to leave behind parts of their hearts and souls; they must force themselves on an emotional journey that has no predictable destination, while knowing "that is the way of things, for when we migrate, we murder from our lives those we leave behind."

In the modern world, borders can feel porous, given how much quick access we have to other places, other spaces, even other times. The Internet, our phones, our computers, all our electronic screens act like little portals to the curated lives of others. In some ways the magical doorways of *Exit West* already exist, but this digital integration is often at odds with the frequently cruel, xenophobic new world faced by many refugees. The apocalypse, writes Hamid, appeared to have arrived, and "yet it was not apocalyptic." Saeed and Nadia's physical journey takes them all over the world and eventually back home, but their real destination is not a place—it's an internal sense of belonging in a world that has irrevocably changed.

AZAREEN VAN DER VLIET OLOOMI
CALL ME ZEBRA (2018)

A bereaved and outspoken daughter pursues a reverse-exile tour of her family's anguish from New York City, to Barcelona, to Girona, to Albanyà, retracing the steps of her family's dislocation.

Van der Vliet Oloomi has spent portions of her life in Europe, Iran, and other parts of the Arab world. She eventually resettled in the United States, presently residing in South Bend, Indiana, and refers to herself as an "immigrant who happens to be an American citizen."

The core of *Call Me Zebra* is rooted in Van der Vliet Oloomi's 2010 Fulbright fellowship in Barcelona to research Catalan writer Quim Monzó. During that time she delved into the works of authors who fled Catalonia during the Spanish Civil War.

Zebra is an anarchist, atheist, and autodidact. She is also an exile, carried in utero from her parents' home city of Tehran, her parents driven out by a long line of tyrannical conquerors, "each of whom briefly took pleasure in the rubble of dynasties past." Saddam Hussein was the despot who ultimately displaced her father and mother, sending them "numb, astonished, bewildered" across the Turkish border.

The bulk of the novel features grown-up Zebra carrying out a reverse-exile of her family's anguish, beginning in her temporary landing place of New York City and passing through Barcelona, Girona, and Albanyà, retracing the steps of her family's dislocation and finding kinship among those who had also survived under the threat of erasure. Zebra's father passed them through Barcelona, for example, because he said they were brethren under the sign of death. Zebra says:

> More than anything else in the world, I felt the need to record the uselessness of my family's suffering in my notebook. . . . That obligation to share our story, to sound it out as an alarm, had been assigned to me by my dead father, and was so exhaustive that it competed with every other rudimentary need: food, sleep, the company of others.

Call Me Zebra deftly threads the journey through with theory made enticing. It's an international road novel that is stuffed with irresistible ideas, symbiotically using philosophy to clarify and amplify the human story. "The literature produced by exiles [is designed to] objectify and lend dignity to a condition designed to deny dignity," Zebra says, citing the postcolonial theorist Edward Said. "By transcribing the literature of such writers we will be restoring dignity not only to literature, but also to ourselves."

As she travels, Zebra takes the sagas of both exile and literature on her shoulders. She believes in a "giant literary womb" in which every text is a mutant and a doppelgänger; all books are "connected to one another via nearly invisible superhighways of language." Literature has evolved through a process of "borrowing, repetition, plagiarism." Once Zebra starts down this

path of finding everything to be connected, she doesn't stop until everything is included.

Albanyà, one of several ink and digital drawings produced by Murphy Chang for the first American edition.

As Zebra rightly identifies, "a book is a counselor, a multitude of counselors," but a force that mediates can also be one that separates. One night unable to sleep, she wanders her room, with her bird walking by her heels. She thinks of the words of Albert Camus:

> Everything is strange to me, everything without a single person who belongs to me, with no place to heal this wound. I am not from here—not from anywhere else either. And the world has become merely an unknown landscape where my heart can lean on nothing.

Rather than finding herself represented at each stop on her journey, Zebra is reminded of the manner in which—in a physical sense—exiles are erased. Alienated from her worldly experience, Zebra digs deeper into the inherited ideas of her father's idols. "I redirected my attention to [Walter] Benjamin," Zebra says, "a man unafraid of holding a candle to the night in order to measure the immensity of the darkness that surrounds us."

Zebra is one of the smartest narrators who will ever take you on a journey and she's smart enough to finally know that she cannot reliably chart meaning in a senseless world. "We can only conquer life a little at a time," Zebra reflects. "There will always be a remainder out of reach."

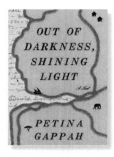

PETINA GAPPAH

OUT OF DARKNESS, SHINING LIGHT (2019)

Nine years before the Scramble for Africa, David Livingstone's African companions prepare and carry his body across fifteen hundred miles, so that his remains may be returned to England.

Petina Gappah is a Zimbabwean lawyer and writer. *Out of Darkness, Shining Light*, her third book, was inspired by Livingstone's companions and Faulkner's *As I Lay Dying*.

The novel took twenty years to write. During the process, Gappah lived for some time in Zanzibar, learned Swahili, and did research at the David Livingstone Memorial Trust.

On May 1, 1873, David Livingstone, the Scottish physician and missionary, died in Chief Chitambo's village in Ilala, present-day Zambia. A well-known explorer, Livingstone spent his final days away from his family, searching for the source of the Nile. He was not alone. As David Livingstone became a near-mythical figure in British history, history remembered his name, his trials, and his discoveries. The same cannot be said for Livingstone's African companions, those who served him and delivered his remains many months after his death.

Petina Gappah confronts this erasure, reimagining history as an epic tale of resilience and betrayal, love, and loss. While the novel is narrated by Halima (the Doctor's cook) and Jacob Wainwright (a manumitted slave-turned-missionary), the story opens with the collective voice of Livingstone's companions, an oracle of a prologue:

> This is how we carried out of Africa the poor broken body of Bwana Daudi, the Doctor, David Livingstone, so that he could be borne across the sea and buried in his own land. For over one thousand and five hundred miles, from the interior to the western coast, we marched with his body.

They are sixty-nine in all, including expedition leaders; educated missionaries, and manumitted slaves. History speaks of Susi and Chuma, Livingstone's first companions, who would come to be recognized as Livingstone's "most faithful servants."

What binds Livingstone's companions to the task of delivering his remains may seem abstract and tangled. But their ties are as undeniable and complex as colonialization itself. Even before his death, Halima emphasizes the inanity of the Doctor's search and asks why he does not return to his children. She does not understand how the source of the Nile can consume the lives of men.

With Halima's urging, and much debate, the leaders of the party decide to carry the Doctor's body to the coast. How? Halima suggests they salt and dry the corpse. They erect a tent for the task. They delegate. They work together,

in spite of their differences. After burying the Doctor's heart in Chitambo's village, they carry his preserved remains and begin the journey to Bagamoyo.

From Chitambo's and Muanamuzungu's villages, past the Lualaba river to Chawende and Kumbakumba, death shadows the party and their losses compound. They bury lovers and rivals in the wilderness alongside numerous unnamed slaves, whose bones already mark the paths of the living. In death, the only distinction between the two groups is the act of burial: the mark of a name, the living's attention to ritual and mourning. Through all this, Livingstone's companions remain tied to his body. Still, bluntly comparing their servitude to slavery is a disservice to Gappah's craft. There is freedom in their choice, even as the notion of "freedom" is questioned: how can one be set free, Halima wonders, if one has no knowledge or guidance on what it means to be free? There are unspoken commitments, too. Here are individuals who did not choose one another but will fight and celebrate, bury and mourn one another.

Eventually, the perpetuity of loss wears down the living. Pushed to their limits, members of the expedition begin to give up hope of relief. In a rare moment when Jacob Wainwright agrees with the group, he writes: "It is the Doctor's corpse that calls death into our midst."

Out of Darkness, Shining Light reveals some of what has been eclipsed in history's definition of a hero. If Livingstone's death is the skeleton around which the novel is framed, the heart lies in the human connections within this unlikely group: their grief alongside small triumphs, the stories they tell together, what is lost in their inevitable severing.

An engraving featured in the May 16, 1874 edition of *Harper's Weekly*. The original caption reads "Jacob Wainwright and the body of Dr. Livingstone —from a photograph taken at Aden."

VALERIA LUISELLI

LOST CHILDREN ARCHIVE (2019)

Ghosts from the past and present people the landscape of a road trip through the southern United States in this modernist epic for the twenty-first century.

The daughter of a Mexican diplomat, Valeria Luiselli grew up bilingual; in fact, deciding which language in which to write is a crucial moment at the beginning of each project. *Lost Children Archive* is the first novel she has written in English.

Luiselli's novel grew out of her experience volunteering as a court interpreter for migrant children threatened with deportation; she documented this experience in the book of essays *Tell Me How It Ends*.

Lost Children Archive opens on an all-American scene: a car advances "in the slow lava of traffic toward the city limits," husband behind the wheel, wife in the front passenger seat turning back to look at their two children, a sleeping "boy and girl, foreheads pearled with sweat, cheeks red and streaked white with dry spit." But this car is not just leaving the city for a weekend in the country. And this apparently perfect nuclear family is more complicated than it seems: the girl, five, is the woman's daughter, not the man's, while the boy, ten, is the man's son and not the woman's—and their darker skins and brown eyes betray origins beyond corn-fed WASPishness.

As the mother, who narrates the first section of the book, explains, the car is leaving their home in cosmopolitan, cerebral New York—the world of a Susan Sontag, whose journals and notebooks she leafs through on their trip—for Arizona: the American southwest, a universe of bleak motels, diners, Westerns, Cormac McCarthy (their trip is rhythmed by an audiobook of *The Road*), unending highways, an Elvis-themed motel with a guitar-shaped pool. . . .

The journey is overshadowed by the breakdown of the mother and father's marriage. The father has decided to move to Arizona in order to record the sounds of the Apaches, and he spends the long days of driving entertaining his children with tales of Geronimo, the last warrior to make a stand against the "white-eyes"; the mother, meanwhile, is tagging along with vague plans to make a sound documentary about the lost migrant children who perish on their perilous journey from Latin and Central America to the United States, just as U.S. immigration policy is getting ever harsher. As they drive through the landscapes of countless American movies, they carry with them the repressed tales of past genocide and present cruelty—and, tragically, the twin consciousnesses of these twin horrors seem too hard to reconcile, as father and mother are driven further apart by their respective obsessions.

In this complex, meandering, variegated text, Luiselli combines essayistic musings—this trip mirrors one her real family took in the summer of 2014, as the child refugee crisis was erupting along the southern U.S. border— with multiple references to other texts, archival lists, photographs, maps, and a novel-within-a-novel, the *Elegies for Lost Children* by Ella Camposanto

(a fictitious author who is, in fact, none other than Luiselli herself). This latter text describes the journey of seven children from an unnamed Latin American country as they ride the infamous La Bestia train on their way to smuggle themselves into the United States.

Then, in the second section of the book, the ten-year-old boy takes over the narration. He describes how he and his sister, feeling ignored by their bickering parents, slip out of their motel room one night in the hope that, by becoming lost children themselves, their parents might pay more attention to them. This turn of events is a terrifying cold shower that cleverly highlights one of Luiselli's central questions: how can we tell the stories of these voiceless children who die in the desert? Perhaps putting two middle-class kids of New York intellectuals into the same position as migrant, trafficked Latino children will do the trick. . . . The story culminates in a powerful, twenty-page-long single sentence that brings together the narratives of the lost children and the boy and girl, who meet in the middle of the desert in an abandoned train carriage in Echo Canyon.

This novel offers a searing, clear-eyed portrayal of the United States and the violence that has defined the country from its beginnings to the present-day—but also, in Luiselli's own words, of the "landscape of abandonment" she saw emerging before her when she set off on the road trip that inspired the novel: "I did not expect the U.S. that I saw while we crossed it—a U.S. so much more rundown and empty and beautiful and complex than what I always thought about it."

Polaroid photographs featured at the end of the book. Taken by Luiselli herself, these images document the author's own travels in the American southwest, which are reflected in the journeys of her protagonists.

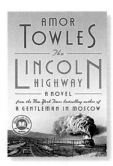

AMOR TOWLES

THE LINCOLN HIGHWAY (2021)

In this sweeping epic, a trio of teenagers—and one brilliant boy—take to the open road. It's a wild chase in mid-century America, and a timeless odyssey.

Born and raised in the Boston area, Amor Towles graduated from Yale College and Stanford University with degrees in English. After working for more than twenty years on Wall Street, Towles left his career in 2012 to return to his first love: fiction writing.

Woolly, one of the teenagers in *The Lincoln Highway*, is the nephew of Wallace Wolcott, one of the Gatsbyesque characters in Towles's first best-selling novel, *Rules of Civility*.

A Gentleman in Moscow, Towles's second novel, begins in 1922 and ends in 1954—when *The Lincoln Highway* takes place.

Like countless dreamers the world over, Emmett Watson wants to journey to California to begin a new life. After all, not much is holding him back in Nebraska. The eighteen year old has been released early from a reform school—his father has died—and the bank is repossessing the family farm. Why not hit the road in his sole possession, a 1948 powder-blue Studebaker?

Emmett is joined by his brother Billy. He's only eight, but he's brilliant. And determined. He wants to find their mother, who fled home years earlier, and so he's plotted out a route to San Francisco. All the brothers need to do is hop on the Lincoln Highway, the nation's first-ever transcontinental road, which passes through their state. There's just one problem: tagging along are two fellow teenagers who escaped from the reform school. Woolly, a gentle naïf, is simply going along for the ride, but conniving Duchess has other plans. Rather than head west with earnest Emmett and "Mr. Know-It-All" Billy, Duchess steals the car, and he and Woolly venture east (Manifest destiny be damned!) to New York City—the complete opposite end of the Lincoln Highway.

What ensues, in Amor Towles's *The Lincoln Highway*, is a sweeping and supremely entertaining adventure. The novel's titular road stretches 3,000 miles from coast to coast, but the book takes place in the Midwest and Northeast. Even without the west, the expanse makes for a grand canvas that allows Towles to explore themes of greed, revenge, loyalty, and good old-fashioned morality. Set over ten days in 1954, a generation after the Lincoln Highway was dedicated in 1913, the novel leaves readers musing on what has so often been depicted as a bygone time of optimism in America—a wholesome, postwar era whose gleaming Interstate Highway System promised a bright future down the road. Billy shares in that optimism; he's a sweet kid, a history buff who loves maps and mythic tales of heroes conquering evildoers. His innocence reminds us that there is fundamental goodness in the world. Duchess, a double-crossing character, presents a far different worldview. He sees the dark side of things, as when, in one of the book's alternating perspectives—and many comic moments—he casually describes a new fast-food restaurant chain:

From the standpoint of ambience, the good people at Howard Johnson's had decided to carry the colors of their well-known rooftop into the restaurant by dressing the booths in bright orange and the waitresses in bright blue—despite the fact that the combination of orange and blue hasn't been known to stimulate an appetite since the beginning of time.

A landmark for hungry Americans . . . the iconic orange rooftops of a roadside Howard Johnson's restaurant, from a 1950s magazine advertisement.

The open road is a tabula rasa for Towles's characters. Some are looking for second acts in greener pastures. Some hope to find love. Others, including a heroic figure named Ulysses, no less, have no destination in mind, straying far from home to forget their past. The novel hurtles readers across rural and urban landscapes, in cars and trains and subways and cabs. Fists are applied to faces, guns are drawn, and a mountain of cash is fought over. It's a wild chase story, in the well-trodden American tradition. But *The Lincoln Highway* is also an odyssey that transcends time and place. As Sally, a neighbor who pines for Emmett, observes, "Every bit of evidence would suggest that the will to be moving is as old as mankind." That leaves the eternal question: who will choose the righteous path?

FURTHER READING
ABOUT THE CONTRIBUTORS
INDEX & CREDITS

Crossroads of the World, Los Angeles by contemporary photographer David George, whose work often features nighttime landscapes. As he says, "the known becomes the unknown at night."

FURTHER READING

Although the journeys within them can feel boundless, all books are finite. The following are a few suggestions for where to go next on your literary travels.

JAMES VANCE MARSHALL
Walkabout (1959)
Two western children stranded in the Australian outback find their prejudices challenged when an Aboriginal boy on his walkabout becomes their only hope for salvation. The three embark on a journey of difference and understanding, survival and sacrifice.

ROBERT PIRSIG
Zen and the Art of Motorcycle Maintenance (1974)
A father and son set out on a seventeen-day motorcycle trip across the United States from Minnesota to Northern California. The result is a carefully introspective meditation on life and how to live it.

JACQUES POULIN
Volkswagen Blues (1984)
A road trip novel that gives way to something deeper: parallels between the protagonist's own journey in a VW bus from Eastern Quebec to San Francisco and the French exploration of North America lead to reflections on discovery, invasion, and belonging.

MAYLIS DE KERANGAL
Eastbound (2012)
On the trans-Siberian railway, tourist and conscript unite, each seeking escape before the land runs out below them at Vladivostok. A novella as thrilling and sobering as the Siberian hinterland which flies past the window, *Eastbound* features two characters fighting to choose their own destinations.

DUŠAN ŠAROTAR
Panorama (2016)
A Sebaldian reflection on people and place, *Panorama* narrates travels across Europe in immersive, tumbling prose that is reflected in Šarotar's moody photographs of shorelines, flooded plains, and swollen streams.

DAVID PARK
Traveling in a Strange Land (2018)
A haunting introspection on parenthood, love, and loss, as a father navigates a snowstorm to fetch his sick son from college. Grief, fear, and guilt are brought to the surface on the lonely drive from Belfast through the north of England.

ABOUT THE CONTRIBUTORS

ELINAM AGBO
Elinam Agbo is the 2021–2023 Kenyon Review Fellow in Prose. Her writing has appeared in *American Short Fiction, Sojourners, PEN America Best Debut Short Stories 2018,* and elsewhere. A graduate of the Helen Zell Writers' Program, she was born in Ghana and raised in the U.S. Midwest.
Out of Darkness, Shining Light (page 238)

SUZANNE CONKLIN AKBARI
Suzanne Conklin Akbari is Professor of Medieval Studies at the Institute for Advanced Study at Princeton. Her recent books include *Idols in the East; Marco Polo and the Encounter of East and West; A Sea of Languages; How We Write;* and *How We Read.* She co-curated the recent Aga Khan Museum exhibition "Hidden Stories: Books Along the Silk Roads"(2021–2022).
The Travels of Marco Polo (page 18)

MICHAEL BOURNE
Michael Bourne is the author of the novel *Blithedale Canyon* (Regal House, 2022) and a long-time contributing editor for *Poets & Writers* magazine. He lives in Vancouver, where he teaches at the British Columbia Institute of Technology.
Rabbit, Run (page 146)

LESLEY DOWNER
Lesley Downer is a journalist, author, and Japan specialist. She is the author of *On the Narrow Road to the Deep North, Geisha: The Secret History of a Vanishing World,* and four novels, *The Shogun Quartet,* set during Japan's mid-nineteenth-century civil war. She gives frequent lectures plus TV and radio appearances and is consulted on all matters to do with Japan.
Narrow Road to the Interior (page 40)

KIMBERLY FAIN

Kimberly Fain, Ph.D., J.D. teaches literature and writing as a Visiting Professor at Texas Southern University. She has authored over fifty publications —essays, articles, reviews, and three books: *Colson Whitehead: The Postracial Voice of Contemporary Literature, Black Hollywood: From Butlers to Superheroes, the Changing Role of African American Men in the Movies,* and *African American Literature Anthology: Slavery, Liberation, and Resistance.*
The Underground Railroad (page 229)

JOSEPH FARRELL

Joseph Farrell is Professor Emeritus of Italian at the University of Strathclyde, Glasgow. He has translated film scripts, novels, and plays, has been a theater reviewer and author of several works including: *Sicily: A Cultural History,* a biography of *Dario Fo and Franca Rame,* as well as the biographical study *Robert Louis Stevenson in Samoa.*
Train to Budapest (page 200)

ALISON FINCH

Alison Finch is a specialist in post–1800 French literature and is Honorary Professor Emerita in French Literature at Cambridge University. She has published several books and articles on nineteenth- and twentieth-century authors, including, *Women's Writing in Nineteenth-Century France* (2000) and *French Literature: A Cultural History* (2010). In recognition of her contributions to the study of French literature and culture, Professor Finch was named an *Officier* in the *Ordre des Palmes Académiques.*
Charterhouse of Parma (page 55)

ALISON FLOOD

Alison Flood is the comment and culture editor at the *New Scientist.* She also reviews thrillers monthly for the *Observer,* and is the former books reporter at the *Guardian.* She has judged literary prizes including the Costa first novel award and the British Book Awards.
The Poisonwood Bible (page 178)

W.B. GOODERHAM

W.B. Gooderham is the author of *Dedicated To: The Forgotten Friendships, Hidden Stories, and Lost Loves found in Second-Hand Books.* He has written for the *Guardian,* the *Observer, Time Out,* and *Wasafiri* and has had fiction published by Comma Press, Fairlight Books and Tank Magazine.
Lolita (page 134)

ROSEMARY GORING

Rosemary Goring is a columnist and reviewer with the *Herald,* where she was literary editor for many years. Her books include the novels *After Flodden* and *Dacre's War,* plus *Scotland: The Autobiography, Scotland: Her Story,* and *Homecoming: The Scottish Years of Mary, Queen of Scots.*
Doctor Zhivago, (page 144) *Life & Times of Michael K.* (page 152)

ROBERT HANKS

Robert Hanks is a freelance journalist and broadcaster based in Cambridge, U.K. He contributes to, among other things, *Apollo* magazine and *Sight and Sound;* for BBC radio he has written and presented programs about the relationship between writing and pubs and the place of dogs in human lives.
A Sentimental Journey Through France and Italy, (page 46) *Around the World in 80 Days* (page 68)

ROBERT HOLDEN

Australia-based lecturer, curator, and historian, and the author of over thirty books, Robert Holden has received awards from the Literature Board of the Australia Council, held a Mitchell Library Fellowship, and has spoken at numerous conferences in Australia and at the Universities of Oxford and Cambridge. He also contributed to *Literary Wonderlands* (2016) and *Literary Landscapes* (2018) and has just finished writing his fortieth book—a biography of Ruby Lindsay.
Voss (page 142), *The Road* (page 196)

JON HUGHES

Jon Hughes is Reader (associate professor) in German and Cultural Studies at Royal Holloway, University of London. He has published extensively on the work of Joseph Roth, the subject of his first book, and on many aspects of modern German and Austrian literature, history, and culture. His most recent book is *Max Schmeling and the Making of a National Hero in Twentieth-Century Germany* (2017).
Flight Without End (page 106)

MAYA JAGGI

Maya Jaggi is an award-winning writer, cultural journalist, critic, and artistic director whose writing appears in the *Guardian, FT, New York Review of Books,* and elsewhere. She is Critic at Large for Words

Without Borders, and a former staff journalist on the *Guardian,* where she was a leading arts profile writer and fiction critic. Her collection *How to Read the World: Profiles of Writers on Five Continents* is forthcoming. All Gao Xingjian quotations are from her 2008 *Guardian* interview.
Soul Mountain (page 162)

SAUDAMINI JAIN
Jain is a journalist covering books and culture based in New Delhi. She has reported on feature stories across India, Israel, Palestinian territories, and New York, and won the Ramnath Goenka Award for Excellence in Journalism (Feature Writing, 2013).
A Suitable Boy (page 164)

ELLEN JONES
Ellen Jones is a translator, editor, and writer based in Mexico City. Her book *Literature in Motion: Translating Multilingualism Across the Americas* was published in 2022. Her recent and forthcoming translations from Spanish include Iván de la Nuez's *Cubanthropy* (2023), Ave Barrera's *The Forgery* (2022), and Bruno Lloret's *Nancy* (2020).
Don Quixote (page 30), *Signs Preceding the End of the World* (page 208)

SAM JORDISON
Sam Jordison is the co-director of the independent publisher Galley Beggar Press, a journalist and literary critic, and the author of several works of nonfiction, including *Crap Towns Returns: Back by Unpopular Demand* (2013), *Enemies of the People* (2017), and *The 10 Worst of Everything: The Big Book of Bad* (2018).
The Canterbury Tales (page 24)

NATTY KASAMBALA
Kasambala is a culture writer, broadcaster, and director, as well as music editor-at-large at *Dazed* magazine. She has also contributed to and worked with the likes of *Vogue, i-D, The Face, Evening Standard,* BBC, and the *Guardian.*
Americanah (page 224)

DECLAN KIBERD
Declan Kiberd is an Irish writer and scholar. He is the author of *Ulysses and Us: The Art of Everyday Living* (2009), has introduced the Penguin Modern Classics edition of *Ulysses,* and also published an Annotated Student's Edition. He has published many books on Irish culture and social and political issues.
Ulysses (page 102)

REYES LÁZARO
Reyes Lázaro teaches Spanish language and Iberian literatures and cultures at Smith College, in Massachusetts, where she also directs the Translation Studies Concentration. Her most recent courses and research focus on racial formation in Iberia with respect to Africa and Blackness, and on reading *Don Quixote* through the lens of translation. She is currently working on a collection of short-stories.
Silk (page 172)

EMILY LETHBRIDGE
Emily Lethbridge is Associate Research Professor at the Árni Magnússon Institute of Icelandic Studies in Reykjavík and the University of Iceland. Her research explores aspects of the relationship between place and narrative in Iceland from medieval to modern times, with a special focus on place-names. She has also developed digital resources such as the Icelandic Saga Map.
The Great Weaver from Kashmir (page 108)

KATIE DA CUNHA LEWIN
Katie da Cunha Lewin is a Lecturer in twentieth- and twenty-first-century literature at Coventry University. She is the co-editor of *Don DeLillo: Contemporary Critical Perspectives* published by Bloomsbury, 2018. Her essays and reviews have been published widely. She is currently working on a nonfiction book about writing rooms.
The Call of the Wild (page 94), *The Voyage* (page 99), *The Sheltering Sky* (page 125)

NICHOLAS LEZARD
Nicholas Lezard is an English writer and critic who has written for the *Guardian,* the *Daily Telegraph,* the *Spectator,* and many other publications; he writes the weekly column "Down and Out" for the *New Statesman,* and has published three books: *The Nolympics, Bitter Experience Has Taught Me,* and *It Gets Worse.*
The Unfortunate Traveller (page 28), *Robinson Crusoe* (43)

IAIN MALONEY
Dr. Iain Maloney is the author of seven books of fiction, nonfiction, and poetry He is also an editor, journalist, and teacher. He lives in Japan where he writes as "The Only Gaijin in the Village."
Deep River (page 168)

ROBERT MCCRUM

Robert McCrum is an associate editor of the *Observer*. He was born and educated in Cambridge and is now based in London, U.K. For nearly twenty years he was editor-in-chief of the publishers Faber & Faber. He is the co-author of *The Story of English (1986)*, and has written six novels. He was the literary editor of the *Observer* from 1996 to 2008, and has been a regular contributor to the *Guardian* since 1990
The Pilgrim's Progress (page 35), *As I Lay Dying* (page 111), *On the Road* (page 138)

JARRED MCGINNIS

Jarred McGinnis was chosen as one of the *Guardian's* ten best emerging writers. His debut novel *The Coward* was selected for BBC 2's *Between the Covers* and listed for the Barbellion Prize. He was the creative director for "Moby-Dick Unabridged" at the Southbank Centre. He also has a Ph.D. in Artificial Intelligence, but mostly he inspires the able-bodied by using public transport and taking his daughters to the playground.
Moby-Dick; or, the Whale (page 63)

ROGER MCKNIGHT

Roger Mcknight is a professor emeritus of Scandinavian Studies at Gustavus Adolphus College in Minnesota. He has graduate degrees from universities in Illinois and Minnesota. Roger has written extensively about Scandinavian literature and Swedish-American culture. *Hopeful Monsters,* his own collection of short stories about present-day Minnesota, appeared in 2019.
The Emigrants (page 127)

JOHN MCMURTRIE

John McMurtrie is an editor for McSweeney's Publishing. His writing has appeared in *The New York Times,* the *Los Angeles Times, Literary Hub,* and the literary journal *Zyzzyva.* From 2008 to 2019, he was the books editor of the *San Francisco Chronicle.* A native of Boston, he lives in the San Francisco Bay Area.
Introduction (page 10), *The Lincoln Highway* (page 242)

NATHAN MCNAMARA

Nathan Scott McNamara's work has been published at the *Atlantic, The Washington Post,* the *Village Voice,* the *Poetry Foundation,* the *Los Angeles Review of Books,* and more. He grew up in Spencer, NY, spent stretches of his life in the Hudson Valley and Baltimore, and now

lives in Providence, RI.
An Episode in the Life of a Landscape Painter (page 182), *Call Me Zebra* (page 236)

KATE MCNAUGHTON

Kate McNaughton is an author, translator, and filmmaker. Born and raised in Paris by British parents, and currently living in Berlin, Kate is fascinated with the role of place in literature. Her debut novel *How I Lose You* (2018) was published in the U.K. and in France.
Heart of Darkness (page 86), *The Savage Detectives* (page 176), *Why We Took the Car* (page 210), *Lost Children Archive* (page 240)

SARAH MESLE

Sarah Mesle is a professor of writing at the University of Southern California. She is Senior Editor at Large at the Los Angeles Review of Books, where she also regularly writes about gender, literature, and popular culture. She edits the LARB channel *Avidly* and the New York University Press short book series, *Avidly Reads.*
Dracula (page 78)

CHARLES MONTGOMERY

Charles Montgomery teaches in the English Interpretation and Translation Division of Dongguk University in Seoul. Obviously, he is interested in Korean literature, which he reads in English. Charles has worked with LTI Korea on various projects, and received an Honorary Citizenship of Seoul for his work in Korean literature in translation
No One Writes Back (page 202)

MAHVESH MURAD

Mahvesh Murad is a writer, editor, and voice artist from Karachi, Pakistan, who is currently based out of Kuala Lumpur. She is the co-editor of the World Fantasy Award–nominated short story anthologies *The Djinn Falls in Love* and *The Outcast Hours.*
Exit West (page 233)

KATHARINE MURPHY

Katharine Murphy is an Associate Professor of Hispanic Studies and Comparative Literature at the University of Exeter. Author of *Bodies of Disorder: Gender and Degeneration in Baroja and Blasco Ibáñez* (2017) and *Re-Reading Pío Baroja and English Literature*

(2004), she has published widely on Spanish modernism, gender, and comparative literary studies. *Road to Perfection* (page 91)

MARGARET OAKES

Margaret Oakes is a Professor of English at Furman University in Greenville, South Carolina, specializing in early modern British poetry and drama. She holds a B.A. in English, a J.D. from the University of Illinois at Urbana-Champaign, and a Ph.D. in English from Stanford University. *Uncle Tom's Cabin* (page 66)

JESS PAYN

Jess Payn is a writer based in Berlin. Her writing has been published in *SPAM zine, Review31,* the *i Paper, London Magazine,* and *Still Point.* She is books editor at the *Arts Desk* and co-editor of *The Germ.* *The Stolen Bicycle* (page 226)

XENOBE PURVIS

Xenobe Purvis is a writer, critic, and literary scholar, whose writing has been published in the *TLS,* the *London Magazine,* and elsewhere. She is currently co-editing a volume of Christopher Isherwood's selected letters. *The Voyage Out* (page 96)

GEORGINA QUACH

Georgina Quach is a British-born Vietnamese journalist. She has received many accolades such as the *Guardian's* Scott Trust Bursary and the George Weidenfeld award. In her role as archivist on the An Viet Foundation steering panel, she works to preserve stories and materials from the Vietnamese refugee community in London. *Ru* (page 205)

ADAM ROBERTS

Adam Roberts is a writer and critic, author of *The Palgrave History of Science Fiction* (2006) and twenty-one science fiction novels. He recently published *H. G. Wells: A Literary Life* (2019). He lives not far from Wells's Woking, just over the Surrey border. *The Prelude* (page 60), *The Wheels of Chance* (page 76)

CHARLOTTE ROGERS

Dr. Charlotte Rogers is Associate Professor of Spanish at the University of Virginia. She specializes in twentieth- and twenty-first-century Latin America and the Caribbean. She is the author of

Jungle Fever: Exploring Madness and Medicine in Twentieth-Century Tropical Narratives and *Mourning El Dorado: Literature and Extractivism in the American Tropics.* *The Lost Steps* (page 130)

SAM SACKS

After graduating in English literature at Tufts University, Sam Sacks received his MFA in creative writing from the University of Arizona. In 2007 he cofounded the online literary journal *Open Letters Monthly.* He has written the Fiction Chronicle for the *Wall Street Journal* since 2010 and his criticism has also appeared in *Harper's,* the *London Review of Books,* the *New Republic, Commentary* and *Prospect.* *True Grit* (page 148)

MAURICIO SELLMANN OLIVERIA

Mauricio Sellmann Oliveira received a Ph.D. from the University of Manchester (U.K.) for his research on the city in Jorge Amado's urban novels. He has published many articles and chapters on Brazilian literature, film, and culture. *The Alchemist* (page 160)

ELENA SHEPPARD

Sheppard is a New York–based writer with a focus on literature and culture at large. She holds an M.F.A. in nonfiction writing at Columbia University and is working on a manuscript about her family's exile from Cuba during the Cuban Revolution. Her writing has appeared in the *New Yorker,* the *New York Times,* the *Guardian,* and *Vogue* among many other publications. *The Passion* (page 157)

SUSAN SHILLINGLAW

Susan Shillinglaw is a Professor of English Emerita at San Jose State University and SJSU President's Scholar for 2012–13. For eighteen years, she was Director of the Center for Steinbeck Studies at San Jose State University. She has been teaching and writing about Steinbeck for thirty-five years, currently editing and contributing to a book on *Travels with Charley* and completing another on Steinbeck's landscapes. *The Grapes of Wrath* (page 116)

JARED SHURIN

Jared Shurin is the editor of the *The Djinn Falls in Love, The Best of British Fantasy series, The Big Book of Cyberpunk,* and many others, including the award-winning pop culture website *Pornokitsch.* Born in

Kansas City, he currently lives in London.
Adventures of Huckleberry Finn (page 71), *Lonesome Dove* (page 154)

DREW SMITH

Drew Smith is an author and editor who curates the blog www.101greatreads.com, which focuses on twentieth-century writing. He began his journalistic career at *Argosy* short story magazine, editing William Trevor and Sean O'Faolain. He is the author of *Oyster: A Gastronomic History* (2015).
Life of Pi (page 188), *Star of the Sea* (page 190)

JOHN SUTHERLAND

John Sutherland is an English academic, columnist, and author, and is Emeritus Lord Northcliffe Professor of Modern English Literature at University College London. He is the author of many books including *How to Read a Novel: A User's Guide* and *Curiosities of Literature: A Feast for Book Lovers*. He writes regularly for *The Times*, the *Guardian* and *The New York Times* among others.
Frankenstein (page 48)

PHOEBE TAPLIN

Phoebe Taplin is a freelance journalist and writer based in the U.K. She specializes in culture and travel and has written eleven guidebooks about walking, film locations, and literary exploration in Britain and beyond. Her work has appeared in the *Guardian*, *Country Walking*, *Sunday Times Travel Magazine*, the *Moscow News*, and numerous other publications.
Three Men in a Boat (page 74), *Dirt Music* (page 186), *These Are the Names* (page 214), *The Unlikely Pilgrimage of Harold Fry* (page 218)

ALYSON TAPP

Alyson Tapp taught Russian literature at the University of Cambridge and is the author of essays on Tolstoy, Dostoevsky, the tram in Russia's literary imagination, and elegiac poetry.
Dead Souls (page 58), *Moscow to the End of the Line* (page 150)

ALAN TAYLOR

Alan Taylor has presented and written innumerable TV and radio programs and for the past decade has formed half of the "underperforming" Scottish team on Radio 4's *Round Britain Quiz*. He is the founding editor of the *Scottish Review of Books* and was a Booker Prize judge. He has written for countless newspapers and magazines from *Life and Work* to

the *New Yorker*.
The Heart of Midlothian (page 53)

CATHERINE TAYLOR

Catherine Taylor is a London-based writer, editor, and critic. She has been publisher at the *Folio Society* and is the former deputy director of English PEN. Her first book, *The Stirrings*, was published in 2023.
Journey by Moonlight (page 114), *Transit* (page 122), *Flights* (page 198), *The Sly Company of People Who Care* (page 212)

IAN THOMSON

Ian Thomson is a writer and critic, author of Primo Levi's biography, works of travel, and other nonfiction, including a study of Dante. He is currently writing a book set in the Baltic city of Tallinn during World War II.
The Odyssey (page 16)

JAMES THURGILL

James Thurgill is Associate Professor by Special Appointment at the University of Tokyo, Japan, where he teaches cultural and literary geography. James is co-author of *A Todai Philosophical Walk* (2021), co-editor of *Literary Geography: Theory and Practice* series, and a Fellow of the Royal Geographical Society.
The Rings of Saturn (page 170)

ANJA TROGER

Anja Tröger teaches Norwegian language and Scandinavian literature at the University of Edinburgh. Her research focuses on Scandinavian literature, and on the depictions of difficulties that migrants experience when they cross borders.
Butterflies in November (page 194)

VICTORIA YOUNG

Dr. Victoria Young is the Kawashima Assistant Professor in Japanese Literature and Culture at the University of Cambridge, where she teaches modern and contemporary Japanese literature and Japanese cinema. Her research interests include writing by minorities in Japan and literary translation.
The Traveling Cat Chronicles (page 221)

INDEX

Achebe, Chinua, 87–90
Adichie, Chimamanda Ngozi, 224–5
Adventures of Huckleberry Finn, (Twain), 12, 71–2
Africa, journeys across, 66, 125–6, 160, 238–9
Aira, César, 182–3
Alaska, U.S.A., 94–5
Altman, Robert, 136
Alchemist, The (Coelho), 160–1
allegorical journeys, 35–8, 45, 74, 218–20, 238
Alps, the, 60–2
American Civil War, 66, 67, 71, 121, 148–9
Americanah (Adichie), 224–5
Andalusia, Spain, 160–1
Argentina, 182–3
Arizona, U.S.A., 240–1
Arkansas, U.S.A., 148–9
Around the World in Eighty Days (Verne), 12, 68–70
As I Lay Dying (Faulkner), 111–13, 239
Asia, journeys across, 18–23, 172–3
Atlantic crossings, 96–8, 190–3
Australian outback, 141–3, 186–7,

Baca, Judith, 234
Baikal, Lake, 172
Baricco, Alessandro, 172–3
Baroja, Pío, 91–3
Basho, Matsuo, 12, 40–2
Batthyany, Gyula, 115
Bayot, Adolphe Jean-Baptiste, 67
Belgian Congo, 178–9
Benjamin, Walter, 122
Benton, Thomas Hart, 113
Berlin, Germany, 106, 210–11
Berwick-Upon-Tweed, England, 218–20
Bhattacharya, Rahul, 212–13
bicycles, 76–7, 226–8
Blake, William, 26–7, 39

boat journeys, 43, 46, 60, 99–101, 172
 refugees, 205–7, 206, 234
 riverboats, 86, 113, 128
 rowboats, 74–5
 see also sea journeys
Bolaño, Roberto, 176–7
Bowles, Paul, 125–6
Brazil, 43–5, 130, 182
Bunyan, John, 35–8
Burroughs, William, 140
Butterflies in November (Ólafsdóttir), 194–5

California, U.S.A., 116–21, 233–5
Call Me Zebra (Van der Vliet Oloomi), 236–7
Call of the Wild, The (London), 94–5
Canada, 66–7, 94–5, 188–9, 205–7
Canterbury Tales, The (Chaucer), 24–7
Cape Town, South Africa, 152–3
car journeys
 across America, 116–21, 136–41, 146–7, 240–3
 across Germany, 210–11
 across Japan, 221–3
 across Korea, 202–4
 Icelandic Ring Road, 194–5
Carpentier, Alejo, 130–1
cat characters, 188–9, 221–3
cattle drives, 154–6
Cervantes, Miguel de, 30–4
Charterhouse of Parma (Stendhal), 55–7
Chaucer, Geoffrey, 24–7
Chang, Murphy, 237
China, journeys across, 18–22, 162–3
Coelho, Paulo, 160–1
Coetzee, J.M., 152–3
Columbus, Christopher, 19
Como, Lake, 55–7
Congo, Belgian, 178–9
Congo River, 86–90
Conrad, Joseph, 12, 86–90, 201
Cranach, Lucas the elder, 29
cycling *see* bicycles
Czech Republic, Prague, 210–11

Daumier, Honoré, 31
Dead Souls (Gogol), 58–9, 150
Deep River (Endo), 168–9

Deep South, U.S.A., 66–7, 111–13
Defoe, Daniel, 43–5
Degeneration (Nordau), 92
Dirt Music (Winton), 186–7
Doctor Zhivago (Pasternak), 144–5
dog characters, 94–5, 202–4
Don Quixote (Cervantes), 30–4
Dracula (Stoker), 78–83
Dublin, Ireland, 102–3

Edinburgh, Scotland, 53–4
Egyptian pyramids, 160–1
El Dorado, 130–1
Emigrants, The (Moberg), 127–29
Endo, Shusaku, 168–9
England, 26, 38, 43–5, 74–81
 coastlines, 170–1
 journeys the length of, 218–20
Episode in the Life of a Landscape Painter, An (Aira), 182–5
Eun-Jin, Jang, 202–4
Europe
 former Soviet, 78, 200–1
 journeys across, 28–9, 60–2, 114–15, 157–9, 176–7
 journeys to, 106–10, 172–3
 Northern, 48–52
exile, 16, 28, 121, 122–4, 205–7
 reverse-journey of, 236–7
 see also migrant and refugee journeys
Exit West (Hamid), 233–5

Faulkner, William, 111–13, 238
Flight Without End (Roth), 106–7
Flights (Tokarczuk), 198–9
Florence, Italy, 114–15, 200
Forster, E.M., 98
Foster, Miles Birket, 56–7
France, 28–9, 46–7, 60–2, 107, 122–4, 172–3
Frankenstein (Shelley), 48–52
Frith, William Powell, 47

Gao Xingjian, 162–3
Gappah, Petina, 238–9
Geneva, Switzerland, 48–52
Germany, 29, 48–52, 106, 210–11
Ginsberg, Allen, 140
Gogol, Nikolai, 58–9, 150
grand tour, 46, 52
Grapes of Wrath, The (Steinbeck), 116–21
Great Weaver from Kashmir, The

(Laxness), 108–10
Greece, ancient, 16–17
Greece, Mykonos, 233–5
Guyana, 212–13

Hader, Elmer, 117
Hamid, Mohsin, 233–5
Heart of Darkness (Conrad), 12, 86–90, 201
Heart of Midlothian, The (Scott), 53–4
Herman, Josef, 123
Herrera, Yuri, 208–9
Herrndorf, Wolfgang, 210–11
Hickey, Aidan, 104–5
Hiro, Arikawa, 221–3
Hiroshige, Utagawa, 222
hitchhiking, 116, 139
Hokusai, 42
Homer, 16–17, 102, 111
homeward journeys, 16–17, 42, 106–7, 152–3, 202–4, 236–7
Hong Kong, 18–19
Hopper, Edward, 4–5, 147
horse-drawn wagons, 112–13, 128
horses, 13, 30, 31, 32–33, 40, 53–4, 113, 172, 183
Hungary, 78, 115, 200–1

Iceland, 108–10
  Ring Road, 194–5
India, 19, 70, 188–9, 212–13
  journeys across, 164–9
Indonesia, 19
Ingolstadt, Germany, 48–52
Iran, 22, 236–7
Ireland, 102–3, 190–3
Italy, 28, 46, 55–7, 60–2, 200–1
  journeys across, 46–7, 114–15
  Venice, 114–15, 157–9

Japan, 168–9, 172–5
  journeys across, 40–2, 221–3
Jerome, Jerome K., 74–5
Journey by Moonlight (Szerb), 114–15
Joyce, James, 16, 102–3
Joyce, Rachel, 218–20

Kerouac, Jack, 138–40, 146
Kingsbridge, England, 218–20
Kingsolver, Barbara, 178–9
Kingston-Upon-Thames, England, 74–5
Kublai Khan (Great Khan), 18–23

Lange, Dorothea, 117–119
Laxness, Halldór, 108–10
Levitan, Isaak, 216–17
Life of Pi (Martel), 188–9
Life & Times of Michael K. (Coetzee), 152–3
Lincoln Highway, The (Towles), 242–3
Livingstone, David, 238–9
Lolita (Nabokov), 134–7
London, England, 24, 46, 53–4, 60, 68, 74–5, 233–5
London, Jack, 94–5
Lonesome Dove (McMurtry), 154–6
Lost Children Archive (Luiselli), 240–1
Lost Steps, The (Carpenter), 130–1
Luiselli, Valeria, 240–1

Mansfield, Katherine, 99–101
Maraini, Dacia, 200–1
Marec, Victor, 107
Marseilles, France, 122–4
Martel, Yann, 188–9
Maryland, U.S.A., 146–7
McCarthy, Cormac, 196–7
McMurtry, Larry, 154–6
Melville, Herman, 63–5
Mexico, 208–9
Mexico City, 138–40, 176–7
migrant and refugee journeys
  across America, 116–21, 240–1
  across Europe, 200–1
  across the steppe, 214–17
  to America, 127–29, 190–3, 208–9, 224–5, 233–5
  fleeing World War II, 122–4
  Vietnamese, 205–7
  see also exile
Minnesota, U.S.A., 127–9
Mississippi, U.S.A., 111–13
Mississippi River, 71–3, 128
Moberg, Vilhelm, 127–9
Moby-Dick; or, The Whale (Melville), 63–5
Moscow, Russia, 144–5, 150–1, 157–9
Moscow to the End of the Line (Yerofeev), 150–1
motels
  American, 134–7, 240–1
  South Korean, 202–4
Mumbai, India, 212–13

Nabokov, Vladimir, 134–5
Narrow Road to the Interior (Basho), 12, 40–2
Nashe, Thomas, 28–9
New York, U.S.A., 125–6, 190–3, 236–7, 240–1
New Zealand, 99–101
Nigeria, 224–5
No One Writes Back (Eun-Jin), 202–4
Nolan, Sidney, 143
Nordau, Max, 92

O'Connor, Joseph, 190–3
Odyssey, The (Homer), 16–17, 102, 111
Oklahoma, U.S.A., 116–21, 148–9
Ólafsdóttir, Auður Ava, 194–5
On the Road (Kerouac), 138–41, 146
Out of Darkness, Shining Light (Gappah), 238–9
Oxford, England, 74–5

Pacific Ocean, 64, 188–9
Paris, France, 107
Passion, The (Winterson), 157–9
Pasternak, Boris, 144–5
Pennsylvania, U.S.A., 146–7
Picton, New Zealand, 99–101
pilgrimage, 24–7, 35–8, 40–2, 108, 164–7
Pilgrim's Progress, The (Bunyan), 35–9
Poisonwood Bible, The (Kingsolver), 178–9
Poland, 198–9
Polo, Marco, 18–23
Pondicherry, India, 188–9
Porláksson, Þórarinn B., 109
Portis, Charles, 148–9
Prelude, The (Wordsworth), 60–2
Prince Albert, South Africa, 152–3

Quebec, Canada, 205–7

Rabbit, Run (Updike), 146–7
Ravenna, Italy, 114–15
refugees *see* migrant and refugee journeys
Rings of Saturn, The (Sebald), 170–2
Rio Grande, 208–9
Road, The (McCarthy), 196–7

Road to Perfection (Baroja), 91–3
road trips *see* car journeys
Robinson Crusoe (Defoe), 43–5
Rome, Italy, 114–15
Roth, Joseph, 106–7
Route 66, 116–21
Ru (Thúy), 205–7
Rugendas, Johann Moritz, 182–5
Russia, 58–9, 157–9
    Siberia, 106–7, 144–5
    train journeys across, 150–1
Rustichello da Pisa, 18–23

Sadahide, Utagawa, 174–5
Sahara Desert, 125–6, 161
Savage Detectives, The (Bolaño),
    176–7
Scott, Sir Walter, 53–4
Scouller, Glen, 153
sea journeys, 16, 63–5
    castaways, 43, 188–9
    transatlantic, 96–8, 190–3
    see also boat journeys
Sebald, W.G., 170–1
Seghers, Anna, 122–4
*Sentimental Journey through
    France and Italy, A* (Sterne),
    12, 46–7, 151
Seth, Vikram, 164–7
Shelley, Mary, 48–52
Sheltering Sky, The (Bowles),
    125–6
Siberia, 106–7, 144–5
*Signs Preceding the End of the
    World* (Herrera), 208–9
Silk (Baricco), 172–5
Silk Road, 18–19
*Sly Company of People Who
    Care, The* (Bhattacharya),
    212–13
Sonora Desert, 176–7
Sōseki, Natsume, 221, 223
Soul Mountain (Gao), 162–3
South Africa, 152–3
South America, 96–8, 130–1,
    182–3, 212–13
South Korea, 202–4
Spain, 28, 30–4, 91–3, 160–1
spiritual journeys, 43, 60, 91–3,
    108–10, 150–1, 162–9, 188, 197,
    218–20
Star of the Sea (O'Connor), 190–3
Steinbeck, John, 116–21
Stendhal, 55–7
steppe, the, 214–17
Sterne, Laurence, 12, 46–7, 151

Stoker, Bram, 78–83
Stolen Bicycle, The (Wu Ming-
    Yi), 226–8
Stowe, Harriet Beecher, 66–7
Suffolk coast, England, 170–1
Suitable Boy, A (Seth), 164–7
Surrey, England, 76–7
Sussex, England, 76–7
Sweden, 127–9
Switzerland, 48–52
Szerb, Antal, 114–15

Taiwan, 226–8
Tehran, Iran, 236–7
Thames River, 74–5, 86, 96
These Are the Names (Wieringa),
    214–17
Three Men in a Boat (Jerome),
    74–5
Thúy, Kim, 205–7
Tissot, James, 173
Tokarczuk, Olga, 198–9
Tolstoy, Leo, 70
Towles, Amor, 242–3
train journeys, 68, 70
    across Europe, 106–7, 200–1
    across Russia, 150–1
    trans-India, 164–7
Train to Budapest (Maraini),
    200–1
Transit (Seghers), 122–4
Transylvania, Romania, 78–83
Traveling Cat Chronicles, The
    (Hiro), 221–3
Travels of Marco Polo, The
    (Rustichello da Pisa), 18–23
True Grit (Portis), 148–9
Twain, Mark, 12, 71–2

Ulysses (Joyce), 16, 102–5
Uncle Tom's Cabin (Stowe), 66–7
Underground Railroad, The
    (Whitehead), 229–32
Unfortunate Traveller, The
    (Nashe), 28–9
United States of America
    car journeys across, 116–21,
    134–40, 146–7, 240–3
    escaping southern, 66–7,
    229–32, 240–1,
    journeys across, 71–3, 154–6,
    196–7, 242–3
    journeys from, 178–9, 236–7
    migrant journeys to, 127–9,
    190–3, 208–9, 224–5, 233–5
Unlikely Pilgrimage of Harold

Fry, The (Joyce), 218–20
Updike, John, 146–7

Van der Vliet Oloomi, Azareen,
    236–7
Venezuela, 130–1
Venice, Italy, 114–15, 157–9
Verne, Jules, 12, 68–70
Vienna, Austria, 106
Vietnam, 205–7
Voss (White), 142–3
Voyage, The (Mansfield), 99–101
Voyage Out, The (Woolf), 96–8

walking, 40–2, 53–4, 60–2,
    102–3, 170–1, 218–20
Waterloo, Battle of, 55–7
Wellington, New Zealand,
    99–101
Wells, H.G., 76–7
West, William, 61
West Virginia, U.S.A., 146–7
Western Australia, 186–7
*Wheels of Chance, The:
    A Bicycling Idyll* (Wells), 76–7
Whitby, England, 79–83
White, Patrick, 142–3
Whitehead, Colson, 229–32
Why We Took the Car
    (Herrndorf), 210–11
Wieringa, Tommy, 214–15
Winterson, Jeanette, 157–9
Winton, Tim, 186–7
Woolf, Virginia, 96–8, 101
Wordsworth, William, 60–2
World War I, 144–5
World War II, 122–4, 129, 130,
    138, 140, 168, 200
Wu Ming-Yi, 226–8

Yangtze River, 162–3
Yerofeev, Venedikt, 150–1
Yoshitsune, 40–1
Yukon Valley, 94–5

PICTURE CREDITS

© Aidan Hickey, from the series Painting Ulysses, 2022,104–105.

Alamy Stock Photo: © Albert Knapp, 93. © Album, 126, 189; © Arctic Images, 195. © ART Collection, 11. © Artepics, 61, 147; © blickwinkel/Hartl, 177. © CPA Media Pte Ltd, 206. © David George, 244–245. © De Luan, 129. © Dimension Films—2929 Productions—Road Rebel, 197. © dpa picture alliance, 201. © Everett Collection Historical, 82–83, 84–85, 121. © Gbimages, 74. © Granger Historical Picture Archive, 50–51. © Heritage Image Partnership Ltd, 14–15, 49, 96, 118–119, 216–217. © Hi-Story, 36–37. © Homer Sykes, 133–134. © James Gifford-Mead, 218. © Jean Schweitzer, 203. © Jim West, 180–181. © Joerg Boethling, 167. © Julio Etchart, 169. © Kathy de-Witt, 186. © Keith Corrigan, 79. © KGPA Ltd, 79. © Konrad Zelazowski, 17. © Lebrecht Music & Arts, 54, 143. © Niday Picture Library, 65. © North Wind Picture Archives, 88–9, 156. © NPC Collection, 73. © Painters, 81. ©Paramount/Courtesy Everett Collection, 149. © Peter Barritt, 113. © Peter Horree, 32–33. © Photo12, 26–27, 69. © Pictorial Press Ltd, 67, 111. © PWB Images, 107. © Retro AdArchives, 97, 141, 243. © Robertharding, 213. © TCD/Prod. DB, 197, 211. © The Granger Collection, 191. © The Picture Art Collection, 47, 77, 142. © The Protected Art Archive, 71. © Tuul and Bruno Morandi, 103. © United Archives GmbH, 145.

© World History Archive, 158-159.

© Albert and Shirley Small Collections, University of Virginia, 112. © Artist Unknown, Picton Harbour, 1912, used by permission of Alexander Turnbull Library, Wellington, New Zealand, 100–101. © Alfred A. Knopf, 1960, 146. © Alfred A. Knopf, 2006, 196. © Anagrama, 1998, 176. © Art Renewal Centre, 56–57. © Avon Books, 1979, 131. © Bezige Bij, 2012, 214. © Bjartur, 2004, 194. © Bloomsbury, 1987, 157. © Bonniers Forlag, 1949, 127. © Boston Public Library Tichnor Brothers collection #88594, 136–137.

Bridgeman Images: © Christie's Images, 4–5; © Ben Uri Collection, 123.

© British Library, 25, 48, 78. © Brooklyn Museum, 222. © Bruguera Libro Amigo, 1979 131. © Division of Rare & Manuscript Collections via Wikimedia Commons, 60. © Doubleday, 2012 218. © Doubleday, 2016, 229. © EDIAPSA, 1953, 130. © Editorial Periférica, 2009, 208. © Eichborn, 1995, 170. © Eyre & Spottiswoode, 1957, 142. © Farrar, Straus & Giroux, 2011, 212. © FOLIO, 1976, 131. © Fourth Estate, 2014, 224. © Gao Xingjian via Asia Art Centre, 163.

Getty Images: © Historical/CORBIS, 239; © Imagno, 20–21; © DEA/A. DAGLI ORTI, 23; © Marka/Touring Club Italiano/Universal Images Group, 227; © Mondadori Portfolio, 98; © Picturenow, 184–185; © Sovfoto, 70; © The Sydney Morning Herald, 187.

© Giangiacomo Feltrinelli, 1957, 146. © Google Art Project via Wikimedia Commons, 31. © Gyula Batthyány, used by permission of the Kieselbach Gallery Archive, 115. © Hamish Hamilton, 2017, 233. © Harper, 1998, 178. © HarperCollins U.S., 1993, 164. © HarperPerennial Classics, 2014, 99. © Hogarth Press, 1957, 96. © Houghton Library—Harvard University—Modern Books and Manuscripts, 63. © Houghton Mifflin Harcourt, 2018, 236. © John Lehmann Limited, 1949, 125. © John Taylor for the 2012 Doubleday edition, 219. © Jonathan Cape and Harrison Smith, 1930, 111. © Knopf Canada, 2001, 188. © Knopf Publishing Group, 2019, 240. © Kodansha, 1996, 168. © Lianjing Chubanshe, 1990, 162. © Libre Expression, 2009, 205. © Literackie, 2018, 198. © Literatura Random House, 2005, 182. © Llyfrgell Genedlaethol Cymru—The National Library of Wales, 24. © macalaster.edu, 58. © Mariusz Kubik, 152. © Mary Evans Picture Library, 165. © Max Häring, "Steamboat," 2013, 87. © Munhakdongnae, 2009, 202. © Murphy Chang for the 2018 first edition published by Houghton Mifflin Harcourt, 237. © National Archives and Records Administration, 66. © National Library NZ on The Commons, 46. © National Portrait Gallery, 35, 46, 48. © New Millennium Books, 2021, 242. © Olympia Press, 1955, 134. © Paralela, 2017, 160. © Penguin, 1984, 86. © Penguin, 2009, 62. © Penguin, 2013, 116. © Penguin, 1986, 74. © Picador, 2001, 186. © Ravan Press, 1983, 152. © Rizzoli Libri, 2008, 200. © Rizzoli, 1996, 172. © Rodica Prato, 161. © Rowohlt Taschenbuch Verlag, 2010, 210. © Rye Field, 2015, 226. © Scribner, 2019, 238. © Secker & Warburg, 2002, 190. © Signet, 1957, 139. © Simon & Schuster, 1985, 154. © Texas Map Store, Alan W. Uecker, Owner True North Publishing, 155. © The Beat Museum, 139. © The Huntington Library. JLP 12, Jack London papers, The Huntington Library, San Marino, California, 95. © United States Library of Congress's Prints and Photographs division, 58. © Victor Ehikamenor, 2014, 225. © Viking Press, 1937, 117. © W.G. Sebald Estate, 170. © Weller Verlag, 1944, 122.

Published by Princeton University Press in 2024 in North America and
the United Kingdom

41 William Street
Princeton, NJ 08540, USA

99 Banbury Road
Oxford OX2 6JX UK
press.princeton.edu

Conceived and produced by
Elwin Street Productions Limited
10 Elwin Street
London, E2 7BU
elwinstreet.com

Cover illustration by Abigail Daker
Cover design by Moira Clinch

Every effort has been made to trace copyright holders and to obtain their
permission for the use of copyright material. The publisher apologizes for
any errors or omissions in the following list and would be grateful if notified
of any corrections that should be incorporated in future reprints or editions
of this book.

ISBN 978-0-691-26639-8
Library of Congress Control Number: 2024931587
British Library Cataloging-in-Publication Data is available

Printed in Dubai

10 9 8 7 6 5 4 3 2 1